SELECTED LETTERS
OF
NATHANIEL HAWTHORNE

SELECTED LETTERS ᴄᴏ OF ᴄᴏ NATHANIEL HAWTHORNE

Edited by Joel Myerson

THE OHIO STATE UNIVERSITY PRESS
Columbus

Library of Congress Cataloging-in-Publication Data

Hawthorne, Nathaniel, 1804–1864.
    [Correspondence. Selections]
    The selected letters of Nathaniel Hawthorne / edited by Joel Myerson.
        p. cm.
Includes index.
    ISBN 0-8142-0897-5 (cloth : alk. paper) -- ISBN 0-8142-5093-9 (pbk. : alk.
paper)
    1. Hawthorne, Nathaniel, 1804–1864--Correspondence. 2. Novelists, American--19th
century--Correspondence. I. Myerson, Joel. II. Title.
    PS1881 .A4 2001
    813'.3--dc21

                2001006334

Text design by Jason Stauter.
Cover design by Dan O'Dair.
Type set in Minion.
Printed by Thomson-Shore Inc.

9 8 7 6 5 4 3 2 1

For Greta

CONTENTS

INTRODUCTION

Nathaniel Hawthorne did not enjoy writing for a public. His extensive journals demonstrate his abilities as a chronicler of his personal and intellectual travels,[1] but when he wrote for the public, be they readers of his fiction or recipients of his letters, he was generally unenthusiastic, proclaiming his "utter detestation of pen and ink!"[2] He tells one friend "I have a natural abhorrence of pen and ink, and nothing short of absolute necessity ever drives me to them" (1850; 16:311). Even when it comes to the role of the artist, Hawthorne claims the "only sensible ends of literature are, first, the pleasurable toil of writing, secondly, the gratification of one's family and friends, and lastly the solid cash" (1851; 16:407). If we extend the traditional concept of "literature" beyond that of belles lettres to include personal letters, we can see how this statement holds true for nearly all of Hawthorne's writings.[3]

The seemingly oxymoronic "pleasurable toil of writing" was, for Hawthorne, a means of answering the charges that his Puritan ancestors had leveled against "an idler like myself" in "The Custom-House" section of *The Scarlet Letter:* "'What is he?' murmurs one gray shadow of my forefathers to the other. 'A writer of story-books! What kind of a business in life,—what mode of glorifying God, or being serviceable to mankind in his day and generation,—may that be? Why, the degenerate fellow might as well have been a fiddler!'"[4] Hawthorne's use of "toil" suggests physical rather than creative work, reflecting traditional dictionary definitions of "work" or "labor" that may be seen in a line of verse from Longfellow's "Nuremberg": "The nobility of labor,—the long pedigree of toil."[5] Thus both fiction and letter writing serve to demonstrate Hawthorne's work ethic. As to gratifying "one's family and friends," even a quick look at Hawthorne's letters will show how many of them are written to people comprising a small circle of acquaintances: his sisters Elizabeth and Louisa; his Bowdoin College classmates Horatio Bridge, Henry Wadsworth Longfellow, and Franklin Pierce; his wife, Sophia Amelia Peabody Hawthorne; his publishers William D. Ticknor and James T. Fields; and his friends in England, Francis Bennoch and Henry A. Bright. And the "solid cash" that rewarded his literary productions found its parallel in the personal and emotional rewards that incoming letters often brought to Hawthorne.

Hawthorne was born in 1804, and much of his early literary training was in the works of the seventeenth and eighteenth centuries. One might also assume that his letter-writing skills were honed by the practitioners of these early ages, about whom one recent critic has written: "The universal dictum, which pervades all levels of discourse about letter writing, is that letters should sound like conversation; that they are in fact simply substitutes for conversation with an absent person."[6] Or, as the anonymous author of *The Fashionable American Letter Writer* (1837) phrased it: "To *speak* to those we love or esteem, is the greatest satisfaction we are capable of knowing, and the next is, being able to converse, with them by *letter.*"[7] Fortunately, Hawthorne seems to have taken this sense of the interactive nature of letter writing from the works of the time, and possibly from the letters he received, rather than from the models they used. His letters do not read like those extended epistolary exchanges in the eighteenth-century novel, nor, fortunately, like the examples used in contemporary letter-writing books, such as this representative "Letter from a Gentleman to a Lady, disclosing his passion":

> Madam,
>   Those only who have suffered them, can tell the unhappy moments of hesitating uncertainty which attend the formation of a resolution to declare the sentiments of affection; I, who have felt their greatest and most acute torments, could not, previous to my experience, have formed the remotest idea of their severity. Every one of those qualities in you which claim my admiration increased my diffidence, by showing the great risk I run in venturing, perhaps before my affectionate assiduities have made the desired impression on your mind, to make a declaration of the ardent passion I have long since felt for you.[8]

This model was clearly not in Hawthorne's mind when he wrote to Sophia Peabody "My dear Sophie, your letters are no small portion of my spiritual food, and help to keep my soul alive, when otherwise it might languish unto death" (1839; 15:291).

Indeed, it is in the letters to Sophia that we see Hawthorne's most candid comments on the act of letter writing.[9] He considers that they may "hold communion" by means of "heartfelt words," by "holy kisses," and by "letters (dipping our pens as deep as may be into our hearts)" (1839; 1:295). After replying to one of Sophia's letters, he says "I shall sleep the more quietly, sweetest wife, for having had this talk with thee," and of her letters, he claims they are "my heart's food; and oftentimes my heart absolutely insists upon pouring itself out on paper, for thy perusal."[10] Simply inscribing "Sophia Hawthorne" in a letter prior to their marriage "thrills my heart to write it, and still more, I think, to read it in the fairy letters of your own hand" (1839; 15:348). But over the three years of their courtship, and particularly as the date of their marriage grew closer, Hawthorne felt that if his heart had "any other means at hand, it certainly would not choose to communicate by the scratchings of an iron pen" (1839; 15:321). The incorporeality of letters is a poor substitute for physical contact: "I never use words, either with the tongue or pen, when I can possibly express myself in any other way . . . words come like an earthly wall betwixt us. Then our minds are compelled to stand apart, and make signals of our meaning, instead of rushing into one another, and holding converse in an infinite and eternal language" (1840; 15:440); and that "language" is physical, not verbal:

> We have left expression—at least, such expression as can be achieved with pen and ink—far behind us. Even the spoken word has long been inadequate. Looks—pressures of the lips and hands, and the touch of bosom to bosom—these are a better language; but, bye-and-bye, our spirits will demand some more adequate expression even than these. And thus it will go on; until we shall be divested of these earthly forms, which are at once our medium of expression, and the impediments to full communion. Then we shall melt into another, and all be expressed, once and continually, without a word—without an effort. (1842; 15:606)

Finally, less than a month before their nuptials, he writes: "Sweetest wife, I cannot write to thee. The time for that species of communication is past. Hereafter, I cannot write my feelings, but only external things, business, facts, details, matters which do not relate to the heart and soul, but merely to our earthly condition" (1842; 15:630). No wonder that a recent critic has commented that for Hawthorne "letter writing is not only a redundant activity but one that dramatizes the degree to which all language degrades what it is asked to represent."[11]

It is natural for Hawthorne to question the representationality of language; after all, he did write an entire book about the manifold ways to interpret a single letter of the alphabet. And this questioning, perhaps, partially expresses his frustration with the act of letter writing: "I am the worst correspondent that ever man had" and "I have a personal interest in defending all persons who are sluggish about writing letters, because I fall into that grievous sin myself, and have suffered, I doubt not, disgrace and loss of friends thereby" (1850, 1861; 16:315, 18:370). Nevertheless, it is in his letters that Hawthorne reveals some of his most intimate thoughts and confidential opinions.

Hawthorne also used the inherent defects of language to his own purposes: he could manipulate language to encompass the numerous personae he adopted (such as son, brother, husband, father, friend, supplicant, magazine editor and contributor, political officeholder, book author, critic of others' writings). The result is an extensive series of letters that allows readers both to confirm and to dispel the common public views of Hawthorne as the dour Calvinistic author of gloomy Puritan tales and as the painfully awkward man in public.[12]

Those looking to the letters for evidence of Hawthorne's "dark" side will find it in his expressions of self-doubt: while at Bowdoin he declared that "I am heartily tired of myself," and that his family had "conceived much too high an opinion of my talents, and had probably formed expectations, which I shall never realise. I have thought much upon the subject, and have finally come to the conclusion, that I shall never make a distinguished figure in the world, and all I hope or wish is to plod along with the multitude" (1824, 1825; 15:184, 194). Or when, twenty years later, he returns to his room in Salem to resignedly state "I am again established in the old chamber where I wasted so many years of my life" (1845; 16:122). And he can be unsparing in listing his personal flaws: a "condescending affability," "the sin of exaggeration," his "utilitarianism," and having "fewer friends than most men" (1824, 1840, 1855; 15:187, 428, 434, 17:303).

There is evidence of what Hawthorne calls his "involuntary reserve," as when he wishes to be spared "the mortification of making my appearance in public at commencement" from Bowdoin (1842, 1824; 15:612, 195). Later, when he must perform in public as part of his consular duties, he sometimes does so after priming himself with false courage: "For my part, I charge myself pretty high with champagne and port before I get upon my legs"; or, when describing "the most successful of my oratorical efforts," "a very pretty speech, which was received with more cheering and applause," Hawthorne gives as the reason that "I had missed no opportunity of gulping down champagne, and so had got myself into that state of pot-valor which . . . is best adapted to bring out my heroic qualities" (1853, 1854; 17:106, 205).

But there are also numerous examples of the lighter side of Hawthorne, the man with a sense of humor and earthiness. Describing sixteen-day-old Una Hawthorne, her father comments that she has "already smiled once," but that he was "inclined to attribute it to wind, which sometimes produces a sardonic grin" (1844; 16:24). Reporting on his achievement in converting to "total abstinence" a sea captain who had "fallen into dissipated habits," Hawthorne declares that on "the strength of this good deed, I thought myself entitled to drink an extra glass or two of wine in the evening" (1855; 17:379). He was also good at aphorisms: "An office-holder's credit, like woman's chastity, suffers by being talked about, even though the defence be perfectly successful" and "like every other Abolitionist, you look at matters with an awful squint, which distorts everything within your line of vision; and it is queer, though natural, that you think everybody squints except yourselves" (1855, 1857; 17:190, 18:89). He enjoys a good drink: he would "rather have gin than champagne, as being both wholesomer and more agreeable," and he pleads "guilty to some few hankerings after brandy and water, rum and molasses" (1850, 16:340–41). And he appreciates a good cigar, at one time asking a friend to "reserve a quarter of a thousand for me. . . . I smoke occasionally; and the above mentioned quantity would be about a year's supply" (1851; 16:415).

These letters also show us a great deal about Hawthorne's views on literature. We discover that he dislikes poetry, would prefer writing juvenile literature "as being both easier and more agreeable (by way of variety) than literature for grown people" if only he could make a "reasonable profit" from it, and at one point declares "If I am to support myself by literature, it must be by what is called drudgery, but which is incomparably less irksome, as a business, than imaginative writing—by translation, concocting of school-books, newspaper-scribbling &c." (1855, 1843, 1854; 17:372, 16:1, 23). His comments on his own works are fascinating:

My book [*The Scarlet Letter*], the publisher tells me, will not be out before April. He speaks of it in tremendous terms of approbation; so does Mrs Hawthorne, to whom I read the conclusion, last night. It broke her heart and sent her to bed with a grievous headache—which I look upon as triumphant success! Judging from its effect on her and the publisher, I may calculate on what bowlers call a 'ten-strike.' Yet I do not make any such calculation. Some portions of the book are powerfully written; but my writings do not, nor ever will, appeal to the broadest class of sympathies, and therefore will not attain a very wide populari-ty. Some like them very much; others care nothing for them, and see nothing in them. There is an introduction to this book—giving a sketch of my Custom House life, with an imaginative touch here and there—which perhaps may be more widely attractive than the main narrative. The latter lacks sunshine. To tell you the truth it is (I hope Mrs. Bridge [the recipient's wife] is not present)—it is positively a h—ll-fired story, into which I found it almost impossible to throw any cheering light. (1850; 16:311–12)

The House of the Seven Gables, in my opinion, is better than the Scarlet Letter; but I should not wonder if I had refined upon the principal char-acter a little too much for popular appreciation, nor if the romance of the book should be found somewhat at odds with the humble and familiar scenery in which I invest it. But I feel that portions of it are as good as anything that I can hope to write; and the publisher speaks encouragingly of its success. (1851; 16:406)

I have received and skimmed through the Seven Gables; and I heartily pray Heaven the public may like the book a great deal better than I do—

else we make a poor business of it. But I am in the cold fit now, and should not see its merit, if it had any. (1851; 16:417)

I thank you most heartily for your kind wishes in favour of the forth-coming work [*The Marble Faun*], and sincerely join my own prayers to yours in its behalf, but without much confidence of a good result. My own opinion is, that I am not really a popular writer, and that what pop-ularity I have gained is chiefly accidental, and owing to other causes than my own kind or degree of merit. Possibly I may (or may not) deserve something better than popularity; but looking at all my pro-ductions, and especially this latter one, with a cold and critical eye, I can see that they do not make their appeal to the popular mind. It is odd enough, moreover, that my own individual taste is for quite another class of works than those which I myself am able to write. If I were to meet with such books as mine, by another writer, I don't believe I should be able to get through them. (1860; 18:229)[13]

And even well after a book was published, Hawthorne admitted misgivings. Writing about a new edition of *Mosses from an Old Manse,* he comments to his publisher, James T. Fields,

I am not quite sure that I entirely comprehend my own meaning in some of these blasted allegories; but I remember that I always had a meaning—or, at least, thought I had. I am a good deal changed since those times; and to tell you the truth, my past self is not very much to my taste, as I see myself in this book. Yet certainly there is more in it than the public generally gave me credit for, at the time it was written. But I don't think myself worthy of very much more credit than I got. (1854; 17:201)

Perhaps Hawthorne's most (in)famous comment on literature, one that is quoted in most books discussing nineteenth-century American women writers, is this: "America is now wholly given over to a d—d mob of scribbling women, and I should have no chance of success while the public taste is occupied with their trash—and should be ashamed of myself if I did succeed" (1855; 17:304). This comment may be in part, as many critics have suggested, sour grapes on Hawthorne's part, but it is also helpful in understanding his comments on indi-vidual women novelists. For example, consider this comment to Sophia:

In Grace Greenwood's last "Little Pilgrim," there is a description of her new baby !!! in response to numerous enquiries which, she says, have been received from her subscribers. I wonder she did not think it necessary to be brought to bed in public, or, at least, in presence of a committee of the subscribers. My dearest, I cannot enough thank God, that, with a higher and deeper intellect than any other woman, thou hast never— forgive me the bare idea!—never prostituted thyself to the public, as that woman has, and as a thousand others do. It does seem to me to deprive women of all delicacy; it has pretty much such an effect on them as it would to walk abroad through the streets, physically stark naked. Women are too good for authorship, and that is the reason it spoils them so. (1856; 17:456–57)

or this description, in a letter to William D. Ticknor:

I enclose a critique on a volume of poems by Mrs. [Julia Ward] Howe.... I read her play . . . but her genius does not appear to be of the dramatic order. In fact, she has no genius or talent, except for making public what she ought to keep to herself—viz. her passions, emotions, and womanly weaknesses. "Passion Flowers" were delightful; but she ought to have been soundly whipt for publishing them. (1857; 18:53)

On the other hand, he could be generous in his praise of women writers, as he was to "Fanny Fern" (Sarah Payson Willis Parton). Writing again to Ticknor, Hawthorne begins by acknowledging that in an earlier letter "I bestowed some vituperation on female authors." But of Fern's *Ruth Hall*, the story of a woman who overcomes the death of her husband and establishes herself as a best-selling author while raising her child, Hawthorne admits "I enjoyed it a good deal." To him, Fern "writes as if the devil was in her; and that is the only condition under which a woman ever writes anything worth reading. Generally, women write like emasculated men, and are only to be distinguished from male authors by greater feebleness and folly; but when they throw off the restraints of decency, and come before the public stark naked, as it were—then their books are sure to possess character and value." And he tells Ticknor, "If you meet her, I wish you would let her know how much I admire her" (1855; 17:307–8).

Throughout his life Hawthorne distanced himself from his audience. He withdrew and burned most copies of his first novel, *Fanshawe*, because he was dissatisfied with it; most of his earlier short fiction was published anonymously; and his journals present him as a private person, much more at home observing than being observed. Hawthorne did not receive a great deal of mail from outside his immediate circle of personal and professional acquaintances because he did not become well known as an author until the publication of *The Scarlet Letter* in 1850, when he was forty-six; he left for a seven-year European sojourn only two years after establishing himself in the literary world, during which period he published only one essay; after returning to America, he published only one more novel; and his return coincided with the disruptions occasioned by the Civil War. In short, he was a far less public person than was Longfellow, who maintained a highly visible profile as a public poet his entire life, or than Emerson, who maintained an extended professional correspondence dealing solely with the pursuit of his lecturing career. Also, the people to whom Hawthorne was most candid with his feelings were family and close friends who normally resided close by in Salem, Boston, Concord, Liverpool, or London. Nevertheless, the letters in this volume present an unusual opportunity to read Hawthorne in a way that presents his "inmost heart" to a public that has previously only seen glimpses of the man behind the fiction.[14]

From the over thirteen hundred letters and nearly two hundred and fifty consular letters printed in the *Centenary Edition of the Works of Nathaniel Hawthorne*, I have chosen 169 letters and eight consular letters for inclusion here. I have tried to select letters that focus on Hawthorne's relations with the major figures of his day; his exceptional relationship with Sophia; his descriptions of people and life in Salem, Boston, Concord, Britain, France, and Italy; his comments on contemporary literature; his professional career as an author; and those personal letters that best show us his thoughts and beliefs.

Editorial Policy

This selected edition of Hawthorne's letters reprints the texts from the *Centenary Edition of the Works of Nathaniel Hawthorne*. In this edition, there are four volumes of letters (edited by Thomas Woodson, James A. Rubino, L. Neal Smith, and Norman Holmes Pearson) and two volumes of consular letters (edited by Bill Ellis), all six volumes completed under the general editorship of Woodson.[15] I have generally followed the styling practices of the *Centenary Edition*, though I have indented all paragraphs the same distance and lowered all superscripts to the line. All ellipses in the *Centenary Edition*, indicating that material was missing in the source text used, are reproduced here.

Square brackets in the texts of letters indicate my interpolations. When Sophia Hawthorne read many of these letters after her husband's death, she found some passages too frank for her taste, and she removed them either by writing over Hawthorne's texts or by cutting out the offending passages (which also resulted in the loss of the text on the other side of the page). I follow the *Centenary Edition* editors in using '[*obliteration*]' to indicate where they have been unable to recover Hawthorne's text from under Sophia's overmarkings, '[*excision*]' to indicate the physical destruction of the manuscript, and '[*excision verso*]' to indicate where the passage on the other side of the main excision was also destroyed.

The *Centenary Edition* is superbly annotated, and I have kept the annotations here to a minimum, knowing that readers may return to the originals for more information. I have rewritten some notes in order to compress them and added others based on information that became available after the publication of the *Centenary Edition* volumes. Whenever I quote substantively the wording in a note in the *Centenary Edition,* I indicate this fact by placing '[*CE*]' after the text. This edition has a chronology to present the outline of Hawthorne's life for reference, and biographies to help introduce his major correspondents. The chronology is redacted from the chronologies in vols. 15 and 17 of the *Centenary Edition* and is used by permission of the publisher. For more information on people mentioned in the letters, see the notes to the *Centenary Edition* and Robert L. Gale, *A Nathaniel Hawthorne Encyclopedia* (Westport, Conn.: Greenwood, 1991).

I have, in general, attempted to create readable texts for this edition, while retaining as much of Hawthorne's original style as possible; full textual information is, of course, available in the *Centenary Edition* notes.

The *Centenary Edition of the Works of Nathaniel Hawthorne* is a monumental accomplishment, and all scholars are grateful to the work of the general editors— William Charvat, Roy Harvey Pearce, Claude M. Simpson, and, especially, Thomas Woodson—and the general textual editor Fredson Bowers for making this edition possible. I am particularly indebted to the editors of the letters and consular letter volumes—Woodson, James A. Rubino, L. Neal Smith, Norman Holmes Pearson, and Bill Ellis. Without their work, this edition—and much of the scholarship on Hawthorne over the past thirty years—would not have been possible.

For many years the great collector C. E. Frazer Clark, Jr. assisted all scholars working on Hawthorne, and I join them in thanking this generous man for making so much good work possible by his zeal and example. Clark's collection is now at the Peabody Essex Museum, Salem, and I am grateful to the museum for permission to reproduce items from its collections. The following have also granted permission to reproduce materials: the Grolier Club, New York; Northern Illinois University Press; and St. Lawrence University.

Barbara Hanrahan first approached me about doing this edition, and I am indebted to her for the opportunity.

In preparing this edition I am grateful to the University of South Carolina, and especially Robert Newman and Steve Lynn, chairs of the English department, for support. Michael McLoughlin assisted in the early stages of the project, and Chris Nesmith and Todd Richardson helped see the work through press. Ezra Greenspan and Leon Jackson made valuable suggestions about the introduction. As always, Greta's name is on this book because she puts up with me—and delightfully so.

Joel Myerson
Edisto Beach, South Carolina

1. See the editions of the *American Notebooks, English Notebooks,* and *French and Italian Notebooks* in *CE* (vols. 8, 14, 21–22, respectively), as well as *Hawthorne's Lost Notebook, 1835–1841,* ed. Barbara S. Mouffe (University Park: Pennsylvania State University Press, 1978), re-edited for *CE,* 23:123–224.

2. 1852; 16:532. Further references to the four volumes of Hawthorne's Letters in *CE* (vols. 15–18) will be cited parenthetically in the text.

3. *Hawthorne's Consular Letters* (vols. 19–20 of CE) are of a different order entirely, being letters written in his official capacity as consul to Liverpool, and generally composed and written out by his secretary.

4. *The Scarlet Letter, CE,* 1:10.

5. Longfellow, "Nuremberg" (1846), last line.

6. Rosemarie Bodenheimer, *The Real Life of Mary Ann Evans: George Eliot, Her Letters and Fiction* (Ithaca, N.Y.: Cornell University Press, 1994), 8.

7. Anonymous, *The Fashionable American Letter Writer; or, The Art of Polite Correspondence. Containing a Variety of Plain and Elegant Letters on Business, Love, Courtship, Marriage, Relationship, Friendship, &c, With Forms of Complimentary Cards. To the Whole is Prefixed, Directions for Letter Writing, and Rules for Composition* (Boston: J. Loring, 1826), iv.

8. *The Fashionable American Letter Writer,* 59.

9. Few of Sophia's letters to Nathaniel survive because he burned, in his words, "hundreds of Sophia's maiden letters" (*CE,* 15:6).

10. Both 1840, 15:459, 442. Hawthorne addresses Sophia as his "wife" in most of their courtship letters.

11. William Merrill Decker, *Epistolary Practices: Letter Writing in America before Telecommunications* (Chapel Hill: University of North Carolina Press, 1998), 47. Decker's is the only book devoted to the subject of nineteenth-century American letter writing.

12. Perhaps the classic description of Hawthorne's shyness and inarticulateness is this account of him by George William Curtis at an "esthetic tea" at Ralph Waldo Emerson's home in Concord as "a man who sat upon the edge of the circle, a little withdrawn, his head slightly thrown forward upon his breast, and his bright eyes clearly burning under his black brow." As Curtis listened to the conversation,

this person, who sat silent as a shadow, looked to me, as [Daniel] Webster might have looked, had he been a poet,—a kind of poetic Webster. He rose and walked to the window, and stood quietly there for a long time, watching the dead white landscape. No appeal was made to him, nobody looked after him, the conversation flowed steadily on as if everyone understood that his silence was to be respected. It was the same thing at table. In vain the silent man imbibed esthetic tea. Whatever fancies it inspired did not flower at his lips. But there was a light in his eye that assured me that nothing was lost. So supreme was his silence that it presently engrossed me to the exclusion of everything else.

And when Hawthorne finally left, "Emerson, with the 'slow, wise smile' that breaks over his face, like day over sky, said: 'Hawthorne rides well his horse of the night'" ("Hawthorne," in *The Homes of American Authors* [New York: G. P. Putnam, 1853], 299–300. Later on Curtis reports on an awkward non-conversation between Emerson, Hawthorne, and Henry David Thoreau [p. 302]).

13. For Sophia Hawthorne's comments on her husband's lack of faith in the quality of his writings, see note 2 to 10 October 1859, below.

14. For the "inmost heart" phrase, see the penultimate paragraph of "The Minister's Black Veil."

15. Six additional letters are printed in vol. 23.

ABBREVIATIONS

The following abbreviations are used throughout this edition:

CE: *Centenary Edition of the Works of Nathaniel Hawthorne,* ed. William L. Charvat, Thomas Woodson, et al., 23 vols. (Columbus: Ohio State University Press, 1962–1997).

NH: Nathaniel Hawthorne

SPH: Sophia Peabody Hawthorne

CHRONOLOGY

1801	2 August	Nathaniel Hathorne and Elizabeth Clarke Manning married
1802	7 March	Elizabeth Manning Hathorne born
1804	4 July	NH born in Salem
1808	Winter	Father dies at sea
	9 January	Maria Louisa Hathorne born
	April	Word of father's death arrives; family moves in with grandfather Richard Manning at Herbert Street, Salem
1809	21 September	Sophia Amelia Peabody born in Salem
1813	19 April	Grandfather Manning dies; Uncle Robert Manning assumes guardianship
	10 November	Injures foot; lame for next fourteen months
1816	Summer	Hathornes board at Manning property in Maine
1818	Late October	Hathornes move to Raymond, Maine
	Mid-December	Attends school at Stroudwater, Maine
1819	Late January	Leaves school; returns to Raymond
	5 July	Enters school in Salem
1820	By 7 March	Prepares in Salem for college
1821	Early October	Enters Bowdoin College, Brunswick, Maine

1825	**Summer**	Shows first literary works to sister Elizabeth
	September 7	Graduates from Bowdoin; returns to live with family at Herbert Street, Salem
1828	**Late October**	*Fanshawe* published anonymously at NH's expense, and soon after suppressed by him; Hathornes move into house built by Robert Manning on Dearborn Street, Salem; by now NH has added 'w' to spelling of his name
1832		Hathornes return to Herbert Street house
1836	**January**	Becomes editor of *American Magazine of Useful and Entertaining Knowledge;* moves to Hancock Street, Beacon Hill, Boston
	March	First of NH's issues of *American Magazine*
	May	Agrees to write (with sister Elizabeth) Peter Parley's *Universal History, on the Basis of Geography*
	August	Resigns editorship; returns to Salem
1837	**6 or 7 March**	*Twice-Told Tales* published
	Late July	*Peter Parley's Universal History, on the Basis of Geography* published
	11 November	NH and his sisters first visit the Peabodys; NH meets SPH on a visit shortly after
1838	**November**	Offered post of Boston Custom House inspector by George Bancroft; declines
1839	**11 January**	Accepts position of measurer in Boston Custom House; begins work 17 January

	6 March	First surviving love letter to SPH
	24 July	Proposes marriage to SPH in letter; subsequently refers to himself to her as "thy husband"
1840	August	Peabodys, including SPH, move to Boston
	November	Resigns from Custom House, effective 1 January; considers settling at Brook Farm
	3 December	*Grandfather's Chair* published
1841	Mid-January	Leaves Custom House; returns to Salem
	18 January	*Famous Old People* published
	March	*Liberty Tree* published
	12 April	Arrives at Brook Farm
	Late August	Takes vacation in Salem; decides to return to Brook Farm as a paying boarder, free from labor obligations
	29 September	Appointed a trustee of Brook Farm and director of finance; purchases two shares in the project, intended toward a house in which to live
	Late October	Leaves Brook Farm for Boston
	December	*Biographical Stories for Children* published
1842	13 January	Second edition of *Twice-Told Tales* published
	9 July	NH and SPH married at the Peabody house in Boston; they settle at the Old Manse in Concord

	17 October	Resigns from Brook Farm project; asks to withdraw his stock
1843	Early February	SPH miscarries
	March	Begins publishing monthly articles in *United States Magazine and Democratic Review*
1844	3 March	Una born
1845	20 June	*Journal of an African Cruiser* published
	6 September	Sues for the remainder of his investment in Brook Farm
	September	Samuel Ripley asks the Hawthornes to vacate the Old Manse; NH agrees to be out by 1 October; they move to a room on Herbert Street, Salem, rented from William Manning
	Early November	Salem Democrats propose NH for Custom House surveyor
1846	4 February	Bancroft recommends NH's appointment to President Polk
	7 March	Awarded $585.70 in suit against Brook Farm; none apparently collected
	23 March	Learns that Polk has nominated him for surveyor
	9 April	Sworn in at Salem Custom House
	April	SPH moves to 77 Carver Street, Boston; NH follows her in May, commuting to Salem Custom House
	ca. 5 June	*Mosses from an Old Manse* published

	22 June	Julian born
	August	Hawthornes rent a house on Chestnut Street, Salem
1847	27 September	Hawthornes rent a larger house on Mall Street, Salem; NH's mother and sisters live upstairs
1848	June–July	SPH and children in Boston with her family
	November	Becomes corresponding secretary of the Salem Lyceum, inviting lecturers
1849	7 June	Dismissed from Custom House; controversy results
	31 July	NH's mother dies
1850	16 March	*The Scarlet Letter* published
	23 May	Hawthornes arrive in Lenox, Massachusetts; live with Caroline Sturgis and William Tappan for about a week; then move into "Red Cottage"
	5 August	Attends literary picnics with Herman Melville and others
	17, 24 August	Melville (writing as "A Virginian") publishes "Hawthorne and His Mosses" in the *Literary World*
	16 November	*True Stories from History and Biography* published (reissue of *Famous Old People, Liberty Tree, Grandfather's Chair,* and *Biographical Stories*)
1851	8 March	Third edition of *Twice-Told Tales* published

	9 April	*The House of the Seven Gables* published
	20 May	Rose born
	28 July–16 August	SPH in West Newton
	8 November	*A Wonder-Book for Boys and Girls* published
	ca. 14 November	*Moby-Dick,* dedicated to NH by Melville, published
	Mid-November	Hawthornes leave Lenox for West Newton, renting house from the Horace Manns
	18 or 20 December	*Snow Image* published
1852	**2 April**	Buys Bronson Alcott's house ("Hillside") in Concord and land across from it from Samuel Sewell and Ralph Waldo Emerson
	Late May	Hawthornes move to Concord; call house "Wayside"
	5 June	Franklin Pierce nominated for president; NH offers on 9 June to write his campaign biography
	14 July	*The Blithedale Romance* published
	27 July	Louisa Hawthorne killed in steamer fire near New York City
	11 September	*Life of Pierce* published
	2 November	Pierce elected
1853	**26 March**	NH's appointment as U.S. consul at Liverpool and Manchester confirmed by Senate, effective 1 August

	6 July	Hawthornes sail from Boston to Liverpool
	17 July	The Hawthornes, with William D. Ticknor, arrive in Liverpool
	Late July	The Hawthornes move from the Waterloo Hotel into Mrs. Blodget's boardinghouse, Duke Street
	1 August	Begins consulship
	6 August	The Hawthornes move from Mrs. Blodget's to Rock Ferry Hotel, Rock Ferry, Cheshire
	Late August	*Tanglewood Tales* published
	1 September	The Hawthornes move to Rock Park, Rock Ferry
1854	8–10 July	NH tours North Wales
	15–29 July	SPH and children spend two weeks at Douglas, Isle of Man; NH visits on two weekends
	7–20 September	SPH and children visit Rhyl, North Wales; NH joins them on 9–11 and 15–19 September
	18 September	Second edition of *Mosses from an Old Manse* published
1855	1 January	Dr. Nathaniel Peabody, SPH's father, dies
	1 March	Consular Bill, reducing NH's income, passes, to take effect 1 July
	19 June–2 July	The Hawthornes vacation at Lansdowne Crescent, Leamington

	2–7 July	NH visits Lichfield and Uttoxeter and returns to Liverpool
	9 July	NH leaves for Lake District
	30 July	NH returns to Liverpool; stays at Rock Ferry Hotel
	1 August	SPH and children return to Rock Ferry
	23–24 August	NH visits Bolton-le-Moors
	5 September	NH arrives in London for the first time
	15–22 September	NH returns to Mrs. Blodget's boardinghouse
	8 October	SPH, Rose, and Una sail to Lisbon
1856	20 March–10 April	NH visits London and environs
	2–8 May	NH visits Scotland
	22–23 May	NH visits Manchester
	17 June	NH moves from Castle Hotel, Southampton, to Clifton Villa, Shirley
	19 June	NH returns to Liverpool
	27 June	NH goes to Southampton
	1 July–30 August	NH stays at Blackheath, near London, except for returns to Liverpool on 14–26 July and 8–26 August
	30 August–4 September	SPH and NH tour Oxford and vicinity

	8 September	NH returns to Mrs. Blodget's with Julian
	13 September	SPH, Una, and Rose arrive at Mrs. Blodget's
	16 September	The Hawthornes move to Brunswick Terrace, Southport; NH commutes to Liverpool
1857	**13 February**	Writes formal letter of resignation of consulship to James Buchanan, to take effect 31 August 1857
	10–13 April	NH, SPH, and Julian travel to York, returning through Manchester
	22 May–3 June	NH, SPH, and Julian tour Lincoln, Boston, Peterborough, Nottingham, and Manchester
	26 June–13 July	NH, SPH, and Julian tour northern England and Scotland
	21 July	The Hawthornes move to Old Trafford, a suburb of Manchester; NH commutes to Liverpool
	8 September	The Hawthornes move to Lansdowne Circus, Leamington
	12 October	Nathaniel Beverley Tucker assumes the Liverpool consulship
	10 November	The Hawthornes move to Great Russell Street, London
1858	**5–6 January**	The Hawthornes travel to Paris via Boulogne and Amiens
	13–14 January	The Hawthornes travel to Marseilles via Lyons

	17–20 January	The Hawthornes travel to Rome via Genoa, Leghorn, and Civita Vecchia
	23 January	The Hawthornes move from hotel to Via Porta Pinciana
	24–31 May	The Hawthornes travel to Florence via Spoleto, Assisi, Perugia, and Arezzo
	1 June	The Hawthornes move into Casa del Bello
	1 August	The Hawthornes move to Villa Montauto, outside Florence
	13–16 October	The Hawthornes travel to Rome; move into Piazza Poli
	24 October	Una first becomes ill with malaria
1859	Early April	Una nearly dies from malaria
	25 May–24 June	The Hawthornes travel to London via Leghorn, Genoa, Marseilles, Avignon, Geneva, Lausanne, Paris, Havre, and Southampton; move into Mrs. Coxon's boardinghouse
	1–4 July	NH tours Brighton, Arundel, Farnboro, and Aldershott Camp
	14 July	The Hawthornes leave for Whitby, but are unable to find lodgings there
	22 July	The Hawthornes leave for Redcar; move onto High Street the next day
	5 October	The Hawthornes move to Bath Street, Leamington
1860	28 February	*The Marble Faun* published as *The Transformation* in Britain

	7 March	*The Marble Faun* published in America
	22 March	The Hawthornes move to Charles Street, Bath
	14–31 May	NH visits London, Cambridge, Blackheath
	ca. 3 June	The Hawthornes move to Mrs. Blodget's boardinghouse, Liverpool
	16 June	The Hawthornes depart for America with James and Annie Fields
	28 June	The Hawthornes arrive in Boston, and at the "Wayside," Concord
	30 June	Banquet in NH's honor given by Ticknor and Fields, publishers
	Early August	Vacations with Una and sister Elizabeth at Montserrat; remodeling of "Wayside" begins
	6–15 September	With Una, visits Horatio Bridge in Portsmouth
	Mid-September	Una has recurrence of malaria
1861	**27 July–10 August**	Vacations with Julian at Pride's Crossing, Beverly
1862	**6 March**	Leaves with William D. Ticknor on a trip to Washington via New York and Philadelphia
	13 March	Meets Abraham Lincoln at the White House
	15 March	Visits Harper's Ferry, Virginia
	ca. 17–18 March	Visits Fortress Monroe and Newport News
	28 March	Tours Manassas battlefield, and, on the 30th with Vice President Hannibal Hamlin, Fortress Monroe

	10 April	Arrives back in Concord
	5 August–	Vacations with Julian in West
	4 September	Gouldsborough, Maine
1863	**19 September**	*Our Old Home* published
1864	**29 March**	Leaves with William D. Ticknor for a trip to New York and perhaps Cuba
	10 April	Ticknor dies in Philadelphia; NH returns to Concord on the 14th
	12 May	Leaves with Pierce for a tour of northern New England
	18 May	Dies in the Pemigewasset House, Plymouth, New Hampshire

BIOGRAPHIES

Alcott, Amos Bronson (1799–1888): Teacher at the progressive Temple School in Boston, he moved to Concord in 1840, then co-founded the short-lived Fruitlands communal experiment at Harvard, Massachusetts, during the last half of 1843. The Alcotts permanently settled in Concord in 1857. The Hawthornes bought the Alcotts' home, "Hillside," in 1852, and renamed it "Wayside."

Bancroft, George (1800–1891): An historian, Bancroft was active in Democratic politics, serving as ambassador to England (1846–49). Hawthorne obtained his post in the Salem Custom House partly through Bancroft's efforts.

Bennoch, Francis (1812–90): London politician, businessman, and poet, Bennoch was, according to Hawthorne, one of his two best friends in England. He traveled with the Hawthornes, and he maintained a close friendship with them after Nathaniel's death.

Bradford, George Partridge (1807–90): A Harvard Divinity School graduate, Bradford was a member of the Brook Farm community and a good friend of Alcott, Emerson, Hawthorne, and Thoreau.

Bridge, Horatio (1806–93): A friend of Hawthorne's from their days at Bowdoin College, Bridge was a lawyer and naval officer. He put up money to guarantee the publication of *Twice-Told Tales*. Hawthorne edited his *Journal of an African Cruiser* (1845). Bridge's *Personal Recollections of Nathaniel Hawthorne* (1893) memorializes their friendship.

Bright, Henry Arthur (1830–84): A businessman and man of letters from Liverpool, Bright was, according to Hawthorne, one of his two best friends in England. Bright read *The Marble Faun* in manuscript and commented on it; Hawthorne later presented him with the completed manuscript as a token of friendship. He accompanied Hawthorne on his travels in England and helped to open the doors of society to him.

Brook Farm: A social experiment begun in 1841 by George Ripley and his wife, Sophia, in West Roxbury, near Boston, to see if there was an alternative to an ever-increasing materialistic way of life. Brook Farm failed when a new central building, under construction, burned down in 1847, and there was no insurance on it. Hawthorne, who was a resident there in 1841, considered it as a place where he and Sophia could live after their marriage, but he discovered that the farmwork left him no time for writing. He invested $1,500 in the project, which he sued to recover; and even though the judgment was in his favor, he never received any of the money.

Curtis, George William (1824–92): A resident of Brook Farm, reformer, and travel writer, Curtis co-edited *Putnam's Monthly Magazine* (1853–57). His depiction of Hawthorne in *Homes of American Authors* (1853) helped to convince the public of Hawthorne's personal aloofness.

Duyckinck, Evert Augustus (1816–78): An important New York literary figure who helped edit Wiley and Putnam's *Library of American Books,* the *Literary World* (1847–53), and the *Cyclopædia of American Literature* (1855), Duyckinck worked with Hawthorne on *Journal of an African Cruiser* (1845) and *Mosses from an Old Manse* (1846). He helped introduce Hawthorne to Herman Melville in 1850.

Emerson, Ralph Waldo (1803–82): The leading figure of the Transcendentalist movement, Emerson was Hawthorne's close neighbor in Concord; indeed, he had sold him in 1852 the farmland across from "Hillside." He and Hawthorne did not have a close relationship, and Emerson confessed that he did not enjoy reading Hawthorne's books.

Fields, James Thomas (1817–81): An influential member of the firm Ticknor and Fields (which later evolved into Houghton, Mifflin), he became Hawthorne's publisher in 1850, when he encouraged him to publish *The Scarlet Letter.* James and his wife, Annie Adams Fields (1834–1915), ran a popular literary salon in Boston, and both were personal friends of the Hawthornes. He published a biography of Hawthorne in 1876.

Fuller, Sarah Margaret (1810–50): A major figure among the Transcendentalists, Fuller was an occasional visitor to Concord and to the Brook Farm community (where one of the cottages was named after her). From the time he met her in 1839, Hawthorne had ambivalent feelings about Fuller: he admired her intellect but shrunk from what he considered her non-feminine assertiveness in many matters. She served as a partial model for Zenobia in *The Blithedale Romance.*

Goodrich, Samuel Griswold (1793–1860): Editor and author, Goodrich published Hawthorne's works in his annual *The Token,* engaged him as editor of the *American Magazine of Useful and Entertaining Knowledge* (1836) but never paid him his full salary, and convinced him and Louisa to write *Peter Parley's Universal History, on the Basis of Geography* (1836).

Hawthorne, Elizabeth Manning (1802–83): Also known as Ebe and Abby, she was Hawthorne's older sister. Elizabeth was well read and contributed much material to the *American Magazine of Useful and Entertaining Knowledge* during her brother's editorship (1836) and helped him to write *Peter Parley's Universal History, on the Basis of Geography* (1836).

Hawthorne, Julian (1846–1934): Sophia and Nathaniel's son, Julian grew up to become a prolific author. He attended Franklin Benjamin Sanborn's school in Concord and (briefly) Harvard College. Although Julian was an unreliable biographer, his *Nathaniel Hawthorne and His Wife* (1884) and *Hawthorne and His Circle* (1903) are still valuable.

Hawthorne, Maria Louisa (1808–52): Hawthorne's younger sister, Louisa was less intellectual but more social than her older sister Elizabeth. She died during a steamboat accident.

Hawthorne, Rose (1851–1926): She was called Rosebud or Pessima by her father. In 1871, Rose married the writer George Parsons Lathrop (who would write a biography of Hawthorne in 1876). The couple separated in 1895, and Rose dedicated her life to helping cancer patients. A Roman Catholic convert, she became Sister Mary Alphonsa in 1900.

Hawthorne, Sophia Amelia Peabody (1809–71): One of the famous Peabody sisters of Salem (along with Mary, who married Horace Mann, and Elizabeth), Sophia was ill a great deal of the time but still managed to study art under such painters as Washington Allston. She met Hawthorne in 1837, and two years later they began an extended correspondence. Sophia illustrated a separate publication of Hawthorne's story "The Gentle Boy" in 1839, the year in which they secretly became engaged. They were married in 1842. After Hawthorne's death, Sophia edited censored editions of his *American Note-Books* (1868), *English Note-Books* (1870), and *French and Italian Note-Books* (1871), and herself wrote *Notes in England and Italy* (1870). She died in London.

Hawthorne, Una (1844–77): Sophia and Nathaniel's daughter is thought to be a model for Pearl in *The Scarlet Letter*. Her near-death from malaria in Rome from 1858 to 1859 greatly upset her parents: Sophia stayed with her nearly all the time and Nathaniel stopped writing in his journal. After Hawthorne's death, she traveled with her mother overseas, staying abroad most of the time until her own death.

Hillard, George Stillman (1808–79): Lawyer and man of letters, Hillard was one of Hawthorne's closest friends, renting rooms to him in Boston, representing him in his suit against Brook Farm, and serving as executor of his estate.

Longfellow, Henry Wadsworth (1807–82): The most popular poet in mid-nineteenth-century America, Longfellow was at Bowdoin College with Hawthorne. The two became good friends, even unsuccessfully attempting some literary collaborations in the 1830s. He was a pallbearer at Hawthorne's funeral.

Mann, Mary Tyler Peabody (1806–87): Sophia's sister, Mary was a writer of children's books, cookbooks, translations, and a novel. She married the educational reformer Horace Mann in 1843. The Hawthornes rented their house in West Newton from 1851 to 1852.

Manning, Richard (1782–1831): Hawthorne's uncle, he lived in Raymond, Maine, where he ran a store.

Manning, Robert (1784–1842): Hawthorne's uncle, he also lived in Raymond, Maine, where he was a successful businessman and pomologist. After 1813, he was the informal guardian of Hawthorne and his sisters.

Melville, Herman (1819–91): Melville first met Hawthorne at a literary picnic in the Berkshires in 1850, and they were mutually attracted. In August, Melville (writing as "A Virginian") published "Hawthorne and His Mosses" in the *Literary World,* and the following year he dedicated *Moby-Dick* to Hawthorne. Their friendship cooled after Hawthorne left Lenox, though Melville did briefly visit Hawthorne in England.

O'Sullivan, John Louis (1813–95): Co-founder and editor of the *United States Magazine and Democratic Review* (1837–46), which published many stories by Hawthorne, and editor of the *New York Morning News* (1844–46), O'Sullivan was appointed by Franklin Pierce as chargé d'affaires in Portugal (1854–58).

Peabody, Elizabeth Palmer (1804–94): An educational and social reformer, she assisted Alcott in the Temple School, operated a book store and circulating library in Boston, and, under her own imprint, published Hawthorne's *Grandfather's Chair, Famous Old People,* and *Liberty Tree.*

Pierce, Franklin (1804–69): One of Hawthorne's closest friends from their days at Bowdoin College, Pierce was elected President in 1852. Hawthorne wrote a campaign biography of him, *Life of Franklin Pierce* (1852). Pierce appointed Hawthorne consul at Liverpool. Hawthorne dedicated *Our Old Home* to him, over the objections of many who disagreed with Pierce's defense of the Compromise of 1850, the Fugitive Slave Law, and states' rights. Hawthorne died while on a trip with Pierce.

Ripley, George (1802–80): Ripley and his wife, Sophia, founded the Brook Farm community in 1841. He turned to journalism when Brook Farm failed in 1847, most notably as literary critic of the *New York Tribune*. Hawthorne sued Ripley in 1845 to recover the $1,500 he had invested in Brook Farm; and although he was awarded $585.70 in 1846, none of the money was collected.

Sanborn, Franklin Benjamin (1831–1917): A second-generation Transcendentalist, he taught school in Concord, was a member of John Brown's "secret six," and later became an indefatigable chronicler of the Transcendental period. Julian entered his school in 1862.

Thoreau, Henry David (1817–62): Hawthorne's neighbor in Concord, Thoreau became a good friend of the Hawthornes. He and Hawthorne often went boating together, and Thoreau later sold his own boat to him. Hawthorne often tried to promote Thoreau's writings to publishers and reviewers.

Ticknor, William Davis (1810–64): Partner with James T. Fields in Ticknor and Fields, he was Hawthorne's publisher and friend from 1850 on. He traveled with the Hawthornes in Europe and frequently went on journeys with just Hawthorne. He died while on a trip with Hawthorne in 1864.

Whipple, Edwin Percy (1819–86): Scholar and critic, Whipple became friends with Hawthorne after reviewing *The Scarlet Letter* in the May 1850 *Graham's Magazine*. He helped select the title for *The House of the Seven Gables*, and read and commented upon the manuscript of *The Blithedale Romance*.

PHOTOGRAPHS

Nathaniel Hawthorne's birthplace in Salem
Reproduced by permission of the Peabody Essex Museum

Oil painting of Hawthorne (1840) by Samuel Osgood
Reproduced by permission of the Peabody Essex Museum

Oil painting of Sophia Amelia Peabody (ca. 1830) by Chester Harding
Louise Hall Tharp, *The Peabody Sisters of Salem* (1950)

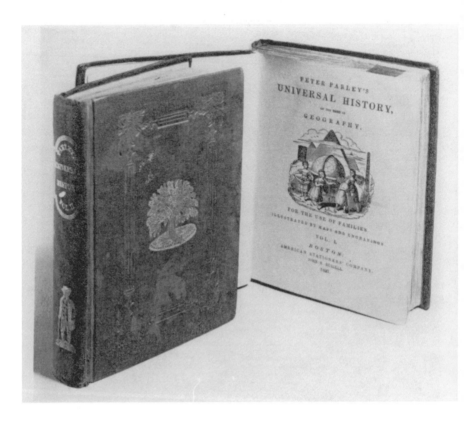

Peter Parley's Universal History (1837)
Kirkland sale, Parke-Bernet Galleries, 13–14 March 1962, item 214

[NUMBER 222]

Hawthorne to George S. Hillard, 16 July 1841, written from Brook Farm
Hogan sale, Parke-Bernet Gallaries, 23–24 January 1945, item 222

Hawthorne to Epes Sargent, 21 October 1842, introducing Henry David Thoreau
By Permission of St. Lawrence University (Ulysses Sumner Milburn
Collection of Hawthorneana)

The Old Manse, Concord
Collection of Joel Myerson

9

" Sundry citizens of this good land, meaning well, and hoping well, prompted by a certain something in their nature, have trained themselves to do service in various Essays, Poems, Histories, and books of Art, Fancy, and Truth."

ADDRESS OF THE AMERICAN COPY-RIGHT CLUB.

WILEY AND PUTNAM'S

LIBRARY OF AMERICAN BOOKS.

NO. XVII.

MOSSES FROM AN OLD MANSE.

BY NATHANIEL HAWTHORNE.

PART I.

NEW YORK AND LONDON.

WILEY AND PUTNAM, 161 BROADWAY: 6 WATERLOO PLACE.

Price, Fifty Cents.

Front wrapper for *Mosses from an Old Manse* (1846)

Hawthorne's surveyor stencil from the Salem Custom House
Reproduced by permission of the Peabody Essex Museum

Oil portrait of Hawthorne (1850) by Cephas Thompson
Courtesy of the Grolier Club, New York

Etching of Sophia Peabody Hawthorne by S. A. Schoff
Collection of Joel Myerson

The Wayside, Concord
Collection of Joel Myerson

The House of the Seven Gables, Salem
Reproduced by permission of the Peabody Essex Museum

15

DEPARTMENT OF STATE,
WASHINGTON, *april 17th 1853*

Nathaniel Hawthorne, Esq.

Appointed Consul of the United States for *the Port of
Liverpool, England.*

SIR:

THE PRESIDENT, by and with the advice and consent of the Senate,
having appointed you Consul of the United States for *the Port
of Liverpool in England, to take
effect from and after July 20th, 1853,*
I transmit to you a printed copy of the General Instructions to Consuls,
to the 1st and 2d Chapters of which your immediate attention is called;
a form of the Consular bond; and other documents for the use of your
Consulate, of which a list is subjoined. Among them will be found a
circular of July 30th, 1840, which contains a copy of an act of the 20th
of that month not embodied in the Instructions, and with the provisions
of which it is important you should be fully acquainted.

Your Commission will be sent to the Legation of the United States
at *London* with instructions to apply to
the *British* Government for the usual Exequatur,
which, when obtained, will be forwarded to you with the Commission.

You will communicate to the department the name of the State or
Country in which you were born: and if you have ever resided *in
Liverpool.*

I am, Sir,
Your obedient servant,

Wm. L. Marcy.

DOCUMENTS TRANSMITTED.

General Instructions, Blank bond, List of Ministers, Consuls, &c., Forms
of Returns and Statement of Fees. Ink lines, Circulars of

Document appointing Hawthorne as Consul at Liverpool
By Permission of St. Lawrence University (Ulysses Sumner Milburn
Collection of Hawthorneana)

16

Sophia Peabody Hawthorne (1855)
Lloyd R. Morris, *The Rebellious Puritan: Portrait of Mr. Hawthorne* (1927)

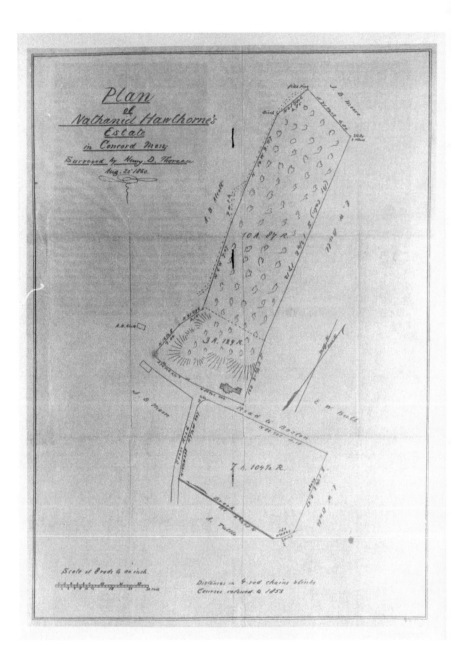

Thoreau's survey map for the Hawthornes' Wayside (1860)
Nathaniel Hawthorne 1804–1864 (New York: Grolier Club, 1964); courtesy of
the Grolier Club

18

James T. Fields, Hawthorne, and William D. Ticknor (1861 or 1862)
James T. Fields, *Yesterday with Authors* (1900 ed.)

19

Sophia Peabody Hawthorne (1861)
Reproduced by permission of the Peabody Essex Museum

Una, Julian, and Rose Hawthorne (1861)
Reproduced by permission of the Peabody Essex Museum

Nathaniel Hawthorne (1861)
Collection of Joel Myerson

THE LETTERS

TO ROBERT MANNING

Salem Thursday December 9 1813

Dear Uncle

I hope you are well and I hope Richard is too My foot is no better[1] Louisa has got so well that she has begun to go school but she did not go this forenoon because it snowd Maam[2] is going to send for Doctor Kitridge to day when William Cross comes home at 12o clock and maybe he will do some good for Doctor Barstow has not and I don't know as Doctor Kitridge will it is now 4 weeks Yesterday, since I have been to school and I dont know but it will be 4 weeks longer before I go again I have been out in the office two or three times and have set down on the step of the door and once I hopped out into the street. Yesterday I went out in the office and had 4 cakes Hannah carried me out once but not then Elizabeth and Louisa send their love to you I hope you will write to me soon but I have nothing more to write so good bye dear Uncle your affectionate Nephew.

Nathaniel Hathorne.[3]

1. NH's foot had been injured playing ball on 10 November, and his lameness continued for fourteen months, requiring crutches. [CE]
2. NH's mother, Elizabeth Clarke Manning Hathorne.
3. NH later added the "w" to the spelling of the family's name.

TO LOUISA HATHORNE

Salem Tuesday Sept 28 1819

Dear Sister

We are all well and hope you are the same.
I do not know what to do with myself here. I shall never be contented here I am sure. I now go to a 5 dollar school, I, that have been to a 10 dollar one. "Oh Lucifer, son of the morning, how art thou fallen!"[1] I wish I was but in Raymond

and I should be happy. But "twas light that ne'er shall shine again on lifes dull stream."[2] I have read Waverly, The Mysteries of Udolpho, The Adventures of Ferdinand Count Fathom, Roderick Random, and the first vol. of Arabian Nights.

Oh earthly pomp is but a dream
And like a meteor's short lived gleam
And all the sons of glory soon
Will rest beneath the mould'ring stone

And Genius is a star whose light
Is soon to sink in endless night
And heavenly Beauty's angel form
Will bend like flower in winter's storm

Though those are my rhymes, yet they are not exactly my thoughts. I am full of scraps of poetry[,] can't keep it out of my brain

I saw where in his lowly grave
Departed Genius lay.
And mournful yew trees oer it wave
To hide it from the day.

I could vomit up a dozen pages more if I was a mind to so turn over.

Oh do not bid me part from thee
For I will Leave thee never
Although thou throwst thy scorn on me
Yet I will love forever.

There is no heart within my breast
for it has flown away
And till I knew it was thy guest
I sought it night and day

Tell Ebe she's not the only one of the family whose works have appeared in the papers.[3] The knowledge I have of your honour and good sense Louisa gives me full confidence that you will not show this letter to anybody. you may to mother though
My respects to Mr and Mrs Ham.

I remain your humble servant and affectionate brother

N H

Your's to Uncle received

1. Isaiah 14:12.
2. Thomas Moore, "Love's Young Dream," in *Irish Melodies* (1808).
3. Elizabeth, Julian Hawthorne reported, told him that NH had at the age of sixteen sent poems "to a Boston newspaper." These have not yet been identified. [*CE*]

TO ELIZABETH C. HATHORNE

Salem Tuesday March 7th 1820

Dear Mother,

As we received no letter last week, we are in anxiety about your health. All of us are well. Mrs Forrester & Mrs Crowninshield are better. I have left school, and have begun to fit for College under Benjm L. Oliver, Lawyer. So you are in great danger of having one learned man in your family. Mr. Oliver thought I could enter College next commencement, but Uncle Robert is afraid I should have to study too hard. I get my lessons at home, and recite them to him at 7 oclock in the morning. I am extremely homesick. Aunt Mary is continually scolding at me.[1] Grandmaam hardly ever speaks a pleasant word to me.[2] If I ever attempt to speak a word in my defence, they cry out against my impudence. However I guess I can live through a year and a half more, and then I shall leave them. One good effect results from their eternal finding-fault. It gives me some employment in retaliating, and that keeps up my spirits. Mother I wish you would let Louisa board with Mrs Dike if she comes up here to go to school. Then Aunt M. can't have her to domineer over. I hope, however, that I shall see none of you up here very soon. Shall you want me to be a Minister, Doctor or Lawyer? A Minister I will not be. I beleive M. Louisa has not written one letter to me. Well, I will not write to her till she does. Oh how I wish I was again with you, with nothing to do but to go a gunning. But the happiest days of my life are gone. Why was I not a girl that I might have been pinned all my life to my Mother's apron. After I have got through college I will come down and learn Ebe. Latin and Greek. I rove from one subject to another at a great rate.

I remain your affectionate and dutiful son, and most obedient and most humble servant, and most respectful, and most hearty well-wisher.

Nathaniel Hathorne.

1. Mary Manning, the sister of NH's mother.
2. Miriam Lord Manning.

TO ELIZABETH C. HATHORNE AND ELIZABETH M. HATHORNE

Salem October 31st 1820

Dear Mother,

Your Letter & Uncle Richard's were received. We are all well. If Uncle Robert's Letter was not rec'd last week, he wishes you to send to Mr. Coburn's for 3 Bundles Trees & bushes (Freight Paid,) and to Dr Dupee's for 14 trees. They must be planted immediately with 2 shovels of Manure to each tree. The Bushes are to be planted in the Borders with Manure. I am happy to hear that the Storm did no damage to our territories. Uncle Robert says he shall bring me down the next time he comes. I do not know how soon that will be. It is nearly a Year now since I saw you.[1] I still continue to write for Uncle William,[2] and find my Salary quite convenient for many purposes. Please to present my respects to Richard Manning Esquire and Lady, and to Elizabeth T. Manning.[3]

I remain Your Affectionate Son
Nathaniel Hathorne

I shall expect a letter from you this week or next.

Dear Sister,

I am very angry with you for not sending me some of your Poetry, which I consider as a great piece of Ingratitude. You will not see one line more of mine, untill You return the confidence which I have placed in you. I have bought the

Lord of the Isles, and intend either to send or to bring it to you. I like it as well as any of Scott's other Poems. I have read Hoggs Tales, Caleb Williams, St Leon & Mandeville. I admire Godwin's Novels, and intend to read them all. I shall read the Abbot by the Author of Waverly as soon as I can hire it. I have read all Scott's Novels except that. I wish I had not, that I might have the pleasure of reading them again. Next to these I like Caleb Williams. I have almost given up writing Poetry. No Man can be a Poet & a Book Keeper at the same time. I do find this place most horribly "dismal." And have taken to chewing tobacco with all my might, which I think raises my spirits. Say nothing of it in your letters, nor of the Lord of the Isles. Louisa seems very well contented. I do not think I shall ever go to College. I can scarcely bear the thought of living upon Uncle Robert for 4 years longer. How happy I should feel, to be able to say, "I am Lord of myself."[4]

You may cut off this part of my letter, and show the other to Uncle Richard. Do write me some Letters in Skimmed Milk.[5] I must conclude as I am in a "monstrous" Hurry.

Your Affectionate Brother
Nath. Hathorne.

P.S. the most beautiful Poetry I think I ever saw, begins

> "She's gone to dwall in Heaven, my Lassie,
> She's gone to dwall in Heaven;
> Yer'e owre pure quo' a voice aboon,
> For dwalling out of Heaven."[6]

It is not the words but the thoughts. I hope you have read it, as I know you would admire it.

---

1. NH's mother lived in Raymond, Maine, while he was attending school in Salem.

2. William Manning, the brother of NH's mother.

3. Elizabeth Tarbox Manning had been adopted by Richard Manning and his wife, Susannah, in 1820.

4. John Oldham, "A Satire addressed to a friend That is about to leave the University, and Come Abroad in the World" (1683).

5. An elementary form of invisible writing, which could be revealed by heating the paper. [*CE*]

6. The first stanza of a pseudo-traditional ballad by Allan Cunningham published in R. H. Cromek's *Remains of Nithdale and Galloway Song* (1810).

TO WILLIAM MANNING

Brunswick, [Maine] Octr. 9th. 1821.

Dear Uncle,

I suppose you have heard that I have entered College.[1] I passed through my examination as well as most of the Candidates. I am very well contented with my situation, and do not wish to come back to Salem this some time. My Chum is the Son of the Hon. Mr. Mason of Portsmouth. He has money enough, which is perhaps unfortunate for me, as it is absolutely necessary that I should make as good an appearance as he does. The Students supply the Furniture for their own Rooms, buy their own wood, and pay 2 dollars a term for washing, 1 dollar for sweeping and bed making besides various other expences.

I board at Professor Newman's with three other Students. The Laws of the College are not at all too strict, and I do not have to study near so hard as I did in Salem.

The 5 dollars you gave me, has been of great use to me, and I did not tell Uncle Robert that I had it, so that I was richer when he left me than he supposed. I hope I shall have no occasion to call upon you for any more this term. If I should be in want of any, I shall confidently apply to you.

If Elizabeth has returned from Andover, I should like to have her write to me. I hope that Grandmother, Aunt Mary, Mr. & Mrs. Dike, Uncle Sam, Aunt Eunice & Ruth, and all my other friends are well.

I remain
Your affectionate Nephew,
Nathaniel Hathorne.

1. NH attended Bowdoin College in Brunswick, Maine.

TO ELIZABETH M. HATHORNE

Brunswick [Maine], Octr. 28th. 1821

Dear Sister,

As Mr McKeen offers to carry a Letter for me, I will endeavour to find some subject for one. I am very well contented with my situation, and like a College Life much better than I expected. I have not yet been under the necessity of studying more than 3 hours a Day, though by the Laws of the College I should study 7. The Lessons are so short that I want employment the greatest part of the time. Yet I generally make the time pass very tolerably, by dint of playing Cards, at which all the Students are great adepts, and other unlawful occupations, which are made more pleasant by the fines attached to them if discovered. The Laws of the College are not very strict, and they are not half of them obeyed. Some of them are peculiarly repugnant to my feelings, such as, to get up at sunrise every morning to attend prayers, which law the Students make it a custom to break twice a week. But the worst of all is to be compelled to go to meeting every Sunday, and to hear a red hot Calvinist Sermon from the President, or some other dealer in fire and brimstone. Our President is a short, thick little lump of a man, with no talents, and, as I have been told, no extraordinary learning. He is quite an inoffensive little animal, and causes me no trouble except to put my hand to my hat when I meet him.

The College is a much more civilized place than one would expect to find in this wilderness. There are two Societies composed of the Students, one containing 1200 and the other 600 volumes. The Books are generally well chosen, and they have many of the best English Authors. There is also a theological Society and Library, into which, owing to a fib of my Chum's who said that I was religious, I should have been elected, had I not rescued myself by taking the name of the Devil in vain, which had a very great and marvellous effect. The peculiarly pious expression of my countenance, which was so much noticed in Andover, has caused me many inconveniences in this place, insomuch that it is with great difficulty I can keep clear of Conferences, and other meetings of the Righteous. By far the greater proportion of the Members of College are yet in the "bond of bitterness and the gall of iniquity,"[1] but there is a considerable congregation of Saints.—The first bell rings and I must dress myself to attend meeting.

Afternoon—Meeting for this day is over. We have had a Minister from the Andover Mill, and he "dealt damnation round"[2] with an unsparing hand, and finished by consigning us all to the Devil.

I suppose Caroline Archer is married before this time. If you should have any thoughts of entering into the Holy State yourself, I hope you will ask my advice. I noticed that Mr. L. looked very remarkably well, considering that he has been "crossed in hopeless Love."[3]

The winter Vacation will commence on the 19th. of December, and continue 7 weeks. I am sorry that you will not be in Raymond this winter, as that would add much to the happiness I expect to enjoy. I suppose you will go to the Assemblies, and in the round of pleasure and dissipation lose all remembrance of the Friends you have left. I do not wish however to have you think that I have grown sentimental for I was never in better spirits in my life, than since I have been here.

I must close my letter as I have a Bible Lesson to get to recite after prayers. I believe it is not the custom in any other College to recite Lessons from the bible, and I think it a very foolish one.

I hope you will remember that no letter has been sent me since I have been here, which is now nearly a month. I do not think you can have any excuse for not writing, as you must have sufficient time.

Praying that you may in time arrive in safety at the end of this letter I take my leave,

Your Affectionate Brother,
Nathaniel Hathorne.

I need not caution you not to shew this.

1. See Acts 8:22–23.
2. See Alexander Pope, "Universal Prayer" (1738).
3. A conflation of two famous lines from Richard Brinsley Sheridan's farce *The Critic* (1779).

TO LOUISA HATHORNE

Brunswick [Maine]. April 14th. 1822.

My Dear Sister,

I received your Letter of April 10th, and also one which was dated the 20th of March. How it could have been so long on the road, I cannot conceive. I hope you will excuse my neglect in writing to Mother and you so seldom, but still I beleive there is but one Letter due from me to you, as I wrote about the middle of March. My health during this term has been as good as usual, except that I am sometimes afflicted with the Sunday Sickness,[1] and, as that happens to be the case to day, I employ my time in writing to you.

My occupations this term have been much the same as they were last, except that I have, in a great measure, discontinued the practice of playing cards. One of the Students has been suspended lately for this Offence, and 2 of our Class have been fined. I narrowly escaped detection myself, and mean for the future to be more careful.

I beleive our loss by the fire is or will be nearly made up.[2] I sustained no damage by it, except having my Coat torn, but it luckily happened to be my old one. The repairs on the Building are begun, and will probably be finished by next commencement.

I suppose Uncle Robert has arrived at Raymond. I think I shall not want my pantaloons this term, the end of which is only three weeks from Wednesday. I look forward with great pleasure to the Vacation, though it is so short, that I shall scarcely have time to get home. A great part of the Students intend to remain here.

I hope [*manuscript torn*] will endeavour to answer. I received a letter from Elizabeth last week, and wrote one to her. I was very much surprised to hear of Mr. Carlile's failure.

I have some cash at present, but was much in want of it the first part of the term. I suppose that you have heard that a Letter containing money which Uncle Robert sent me some time ago, was lost. I have since received some by Joseph McKean. I believe Mother has written me but one Letter this term. I shall expect both of you to write me before the end of the term. Excuse my bad writing.

I remain,
Your affectionate brother
Nath Hathorne.

You need not show this.

---

1. NH's euphemism for being too lazy or unconcerned with attending Sunday services.
2. Maine Hall was destroyed by fire on 4 March. NH roomed privately until it was rebuilt.

TO ELIZABETH C. HATHORNE

Brunswick [Maine] May 30th 1822

My Dear Mother,

I hope you have safely arrived in Salem. I have nothing particular to inform you of, except that all the Card Players in College have been found out, and my unfortunate self among the number. One has been dismissed from College, two suspended, and the rest, with myself, have been fined 50 cts. each. I beleive the President intends to write to the friends of all the delinquents. Should that be the case you must show the letter to nobody. If I am again detected I shall have the honour of being suspended. When the President asked what we played for, I thought proper to inform it was 50 cts. although it happened to be a Quart of Wine, but if I had told him of that he would probably have fined me for having a blow. There was no untruth in the case, as the wine cost 50 cts. I have not played at all this term.

I have not drank any kind of spirit or wine this term, and shall not till the last week.

I remain
N H.

I must have some money, for I have none left, except about 75 cts.

Do not show this.

TO LOUISA HATHORNE

Brunswick [Maine]. August 11th. 1824.

My dear Louisa,

I have just received your Letter, and you will no doubt wonder at my punctuality in answering it. The occasion of this miracle is, that I am in a terrible hurry to get home, and your assistance is necessary for that purpose. In the first place I will offer a few reasons why it is expedient for me to return to Salem immediately, and then proceed to show how your little self can be instrumental in effecting this purpose.

Firstly—I have no clothes in which I can make a decent appearance, as the weather in this part of the world is much too cold for me to wear my thin clothes often, and I shall therefore be compelled to stay at home from meeting all the rest of the term, and perhaps to lie in bed the whole of the time. In this case my fines would amount to an enormous sum.

Secondly—If I remain in Brunswick much longer I shall spend all my money, for, though I am extremely prudent, I always feel uneasy when I have any cash in my pocket. I do not feel at all inclined to spend another vacation in Brunswick, but if I stay much longer I shall inevitably be compelled to, for want of means to get home.

Thirdly—Our senior examination is now over, and many of our class have gone home. The studies are now of little importance, and I could obtain leave of absence much easier than at any other time.

Fourthly—It is so long since I saw the land of my birth that I am almost dead of homesickness, and am apprehensive of serious injury to my health, if I am not soon removed from this place.

Fifthly—The Students have now but little to do, and mischief, you know, is the constant companion of idleness. The latter part of the term preceding commencement is invariably spent in dissipation, and I am afraid that my stay here will have an ill effect upon my moral character, which would be a cause of great grief to Mother & you.

I think that by the preceding arguments I have clearly shown that it is very improper for me to remain longer in Brunswick, and we will now consider the means of my deliverance. In order to effect this you must write me a letter, stating that Mother is desirous for me to return home, and assigning some reason for it. The letter must be such a one as is proper to be read by the president, to whom it will be necessary to show it. You must write immediately upon the receipt of this, and I shall receive your letter on Monday. I shall start the next morning, and be in Salem on Wednesday. You can easily think of a good excuse. Almost any one will do. I beseech you not to neglect it, and if Mother has any objections your eloquence will easily persuade her to consent. I can get no good by remaining here, and earnestly desire to be at home.

If you are at a loss for an excuse, say that Mother is out of health, or that Uncle R. is going a journey on account of his health, and wishes me to attend him, or that Elizabeth is on a visit at some distant place and wishes me to come and bring her

home. Or that George Archer has just arrived from sea, and is to sail again immediately, and wishes to see me before he goes. Or that some of my relations are to die
or be married, and my presence is necessary on the occasion. And lastly, if none of
these excuses will suit you, and you can think of no other, write, and order me to
come home without any. If you do not, I shall certainly forge a letter, for I will be
at home within a week. Write the very day that you receive this. If Elizabeth were
at home she would be at no loss for a good excuse.

If you will do as I tell you I shall be

Your affectionate Brother, Nath. Hathorne.

My want of decent clothes will prevent my calling at Mrs. Sutton's. Write
immediately. Write immediately. Write immediately.

Haste, Haste, Post haste, ride and run, until these shall be delivered. You must
and shall and will do as I desire. If you can think of a true excuse, send it, if not,
any other will answer the same purpose. If I do not get a letter by Monday, or
Tuesday at farthest, I will leave Brunswick without liberty.

TO SAMUEL GRISWOLD GOODRICH

Salem, Decr 20th, 1829

Dear Sir,

I am obliged to you for your willingness to aid me in my affairs, though I perceive that you do not anticipate much success. Very probably you may be in the
right, but I have nevertheless concluded to trouble you with some of the tales.
These which I send have been completed (except prefixing the titles) a considerable time. There are two or three others, not at present in a condition to be sent.
If I ever finish them, I suppose they will be about upon a par with the rest.

You will see that one of the stories is founded upon the superstitions of this
part of the country. I do not know that such an attempt has hitherto been made;
but, as I have thrown away much time in listening to such traditions, I could not
help trying to put them into some shape. The tale is certainly rather wild and
grotesque, but the outlines of many not less so might be picked up hereabouts.

Before returning the tales, (for such, I suppose, is the most probable result) will you have the goodness to write to me, and await my answer? I have some idea that I shall be out of town, and it would be inconvenient to have them arrive during my absence.

I am &c,
Nath. Hawthorne.

P.S. None of the pieces are shorter than the one first sent you. If I write any of the length you mention, I will send them to you; but I think I shall close my literary labours with what I have already begun.

TO CAREY & LEA, PUBLISHERS

Salem (Mass.) Januy 27th. 1832

Gentlemen,

I am the author of some tales (My Kinsman Major Molineaux, Roger Malvin's Burial, & the Gentle Boy) published in the Token for the present year.[1] I do not know whether they attracted your notice; but the object of this letter is to inquire whether you would choose to insert an article from me in the next Souvenir?—and if so, what number of pages?—and whether there is any mode of transmitting the manuscript to Philadelphia, except by mail?
I should not wish to be mentioned as the author of those tales.[2]

Very Respectfully
Nath. Hawthorne.

Messrs. Carey & Lea.

1. Henry C. Carey and Isaac Lea of Philadelphia had been publishing an annual giftbook, the *Atlantic Souvenir,* since 1826, the final volume of which was published in 1832. The following year, Goodrich absorbed their title into his *Token and Atlantic Souvenir,* published by Gray and Bowen in Boston.
2. NH published four stories in the *Token* for 1831 and six in the *Token* for 1832.

TO ELIZABETH M. HAWTHORNE

Boston, Feby 10th, 1836.

E——

Uncle Robert cannot call on me anywhere but at Mr. Fessenden's;[1] as I never stay at the Company's office, and do all my writing and other business at my own room—which is up nearer to Heaven than he is ever likely to climb. If he comes, he will have the pleasure of seeing Mrs. Fessenden and the gentleman and lady boarders; and that will doubtless be very agreeable. I have generally called at the stage-office on Saturdays, and shall continue to do so. Was he in Boston at the presentation of the plate?[2]

I don't know but I have copy (as the printers call it) enough to make up this number; but you may extract every thing good that you come across—provided always it be not too good; and even if it should be, perhaps it will not quite ruin the Magazine; my own selections being bad enough to satisfy any body.[3] I can't help it. The Bewick Co. are a damned sneaking set, or they would have a share in Athenaeum for the use of the Editor *ex officio*.[4] I have now the liberty of reading there but not taking out books. I have given the Puritan an enormous puff— knowing nothing in the world about it, except from those extracts.[5] Finish your life of Hamilton. I wish you would write a biography of Jefferson to fill about 4 magazine pages and be ready in a month or six weeks.—If you don't, I must; and it is not a subject that suits me. Say whether you will or not. In regard to ordinary biographical subjects, my way is to take some old magazine and make an abstract—you can't think how easy it is.

Nath. Hawthorne.

1. Thomas Green Fessenden, poet and editor of the *New England Farmer*.

2. Robert Manning had been presented a silver pitcher by the Massachusetts Horticultural Society, "for his meritorious exertions in advancing the cause of Pomological science, and for procuring and distributing new varieties of fruits from Europe." [*CE*]

3. NH edited and (with his sister Elizabeth) was the major contributor (primarily of filler material) to the *American Magazine of Useful and Entertaining Knowledge* between March and August 1836. NH received only twenty dollars of the $500 per year he had been promised as editor by Goodrich. His contributions have been published as *Hawthorne as Editor: Selections from*

His Writings in The American Magazine of Useful and Entertaining Knowledge, ed. Arlin Turner (Baton Rouge: Louisiana State University Press, 1941).

4. The Boston Athenæum, a subscription library and probably the best available library in Boston at the time.

5. Elizabeth had sent three excerpts from John Oldburg (pseudonym for Leonard Withington), *The Puritan: A Series of Essays Critical, Moral, and Miscellaneous* (1836). NH printed these in the March issue. [*CE*]

TO LOUISA HAWTHORNE

Boston, Feby 15th, 1836

L———

For the Devil's sake, if you have any money, send me a little. It is now a month since I left Salem, and not a damned cent have I had, except five dollars that I borrowed of Uncle Robert—and out of that I paid my stage fare and other expenses. I came here trusting to Goodrich's positive promise to pay me 46 dollars as soon as I arrived; and he has kept promising from one day to another; till I do not see that he means to pay me at all. I have now broke off all intercourse with him, and never think of going near him. In the first place, he had no business ever to have received the money. I never authorized Bowen to pay it to him; and he must have got it by telling some lie. My mind is pretty much made up about this Goodrich. He is a good-natured sort of man enough; but rather an unscrupulous one in money matters, and not particularly trustworthy in anything. I don't feel at all obliged to him about this Editorship; for he is a stockholder and director in the Bewick Co; and of course it was his interest to get the best man he could; and I defy them to get another to do for a thousand dollars what I do for 500; and furthermore, I have no doubt that Goodrich was authorized to give me 600. He made the best bargain with me he could, and a hard bargain too. This world is as full of rogues as Beelzebub is of fleas.[1]

I don't want but two or three dollars. Till I receive some of my own, I shall continue to live as I have done. It is well that I have enough to do; or I should have had the blues most damnably here; for of course I have no amusement. My present stock is precisely 34 cts. You must pay for the letter, as my pockets may be entirely empty when it comes. They made me pay for the trunk. Send also more extracts and concoctions. I shall come down when I am rich enough. All that I have spent in Boston, except for absolute necessaries has been 9 cents on the first day I came—6 for a glass of wine and three for a cigar. Don't send more than 2 or 3 dollars. Unless I receive a supply, I can send again.

Nath Hawthorne.

P.S. If Goodrich should not finally pay me, I shall still have a claim on Bowen, who is a fair man.

1. Beelzebub, the Hawthornes' cat, was named for the Philistine god of flies, placed by John Milton in *Paradise Lost* second only to Satan.

TO ELIZABETH M. HAWTHORNE

Boston March 22d [23] 1836

You need proceed no further with Hamilton. As the press was in want of him, I have been compelled to finish his life myself, this forenoon. I did not receive the packet till last night (Tuesday.) I should have given you earlier notice; but did not know myself that the engraving was coming into this number. I seldom have more than a day or two's notice. I approve of your life; but have been obliged to correct some of your naughty notions about arbitrary government. You should not make quotations; but put other people's thoughts into your own words, and amalgamate the whole into a mass. You may go on concocting and extracting and send me some more of both varieties, as soon as convenient. I shall probably send my valise the latter part of the week. I don't know that I shall need any extracts till then. Those ridiculous Gazette people were in such a hurry to puff me, that they puffed poor Mr. Bradford.[1] They could not possibly have seen the March number when that notice was inserted.

Nath Hawthorne

1. The *American Magazine* had been commented upon favorably in the 11 March *Salem Gazette*.

TO HENRY WADSWORTH LONGFELLOW

Salem, March 7th, 1837

Dear Sir,

The agent of the American Stationers Company will send you a copy of a book entitled 'Twice-told Tales'—of which, as a classmate, I venture to request your acceptance.[1] We were not, it is true, so well acquainted at college, that I can plead an absolute right to inflict my 'twice-told' tediousness upon you; but I have often regretted that we were not better known to each other, and have been glad of your success in literature, and in more important matters. I know not whether you are aware that I have made a good many idle attempts in the way of Magazine and Annual scribblings. The present volume contains such articles as seemed best worth offering to the public a second time; and I should like to flatter myself that they would repay you some part of the pleasure which I have derived from your own Outre Mer.[2]

Your obedient servant
Nath. Hawthorne.

Prof. H. W. Longfellow.

1. *Twice-Told Tales* was published on 6 or 7 March 1837.
2. *Outre-Mer; A Pilgrimage Beyond the Sea* (1835), a collection of essays and sketches.

TO HENRY WADSWORTH LONGFELLOW

Salem, June 4th. 1837.

Dear Sir,

Not to burthen you with my correspondence, I have delayed a rejoinder to your very kind and cordial letter, until now. It gratifies me to find that you have occasionally felt an interest in my situation; but your quotation from Jean Paul, about the 'lark-nest,' makes me smile.[1] You would have been much nearer the truth, if you had pictured me as dwelling in an owl's nest; for mine is about as dismal, and, like the owl, I seldom venture abroad till after dusk. By some witchcraft or other—for I really cannot assign any reasonable why and wherefore—I have been carried apart from the main current of life, and find it impossible to get back again. Since we last met—which, I remember, was in Sawtell's room, where you read a farewell poem to the relics of the class—ever since that time, I have secluded myself from society; and yet I never meant any such thing, nor dreamed what sort of life I was going to lead. I have made a captive of myself and put me into a dungeon; and now I cannot find the key to let myself out—and if the door were open, I should be almost afraid to come out. You tell me that you have met with troubles and changes. I know not what they may have been; but I can assure you that trouble is the next best thing to enjoyment, and that there is no fate in this world so horrible as to have no share in either its joys or sorrows. For the last ten years, I have not lived, but only dreamed about living. It may be true that there have been some unsubstantial pleasures here in the shade, which I should have missed in the sunshine; but you cannot conceive how utterly devoid of satisfaction all my retrospects are. I have laid up no treasure of pleasant remembrances, against old age; but there is some comfort in thinking that my future years can hardly fail to be more varied, and therefore more tolerable, than the past.

You give me more credit than I deserve, in supposing that I have led a studious life. I have, indeed, turned over a good many books, but in so desultory a way that it cannot be called study, nor has it left me the fruits of study. As to my literary efforts, I do not think much of them—neither is it worth while to be ashamed of them. They would have been better, I trust, if written under more favorable circumstances. I have had no external excitement—no consciousness that the public would like what I wrote, nor much hope nor a very passionate desire that they should do so. Nevertheless, having nothing else to be ambitious of, I have felt considerably interested in literature; and if my writings had made any decided impression, I should probably have been stimulated to greater exertions; but there has been no warmth of approbation, so that I have always written with benumbed fingers. I have another great difficulty, in the lack of materials; for I have seen so little of the world, that I have nothing but thin air to concoct my stories of, and it is not easy to give a lifelike semblance to such shadowy stuff. Sometimes, through a peep-hole, I have caught a glimpse of the real world; and the two or three articles, in which I have portrayed such glimpses, please me better than the others.

I have now, or soon shall have, one sharp spur to exertion, which I lacked at an earlier period; for I see little prospect but that I must scribble for a living. But this troubles me much less than you would suppose. I can turn my pen to all sorts of drudgery, such as children's books &c, and by and bye, I shall get some editorship that will answer my purpose. Frank Pierce, who was with us at college, offered me his influence to obtain an office in the Exploring Expedition;[2] but I believe that he was mistaken in supposing that a vacancy existed. If such a post were attainable, I should certainly accept it; for, though fixed so long to one spot, I have always had a desire to run round the world.

The copy of my Tales was sent to Mr. Owen's, the bookseller's in Cambridge. I am glad to find that you had read and liked some of the stories. To be sure, you could not well help flattering me a little, but I value your praise too highly not to have faith in its sincerity. When I last heard from the publishers—which was not very recently—the book was doing pretty well. Six or seven hundred copies had been sold.[3] I suppose, however, these awful times have now stopped the sale.[4]

I intend, in a week or two, to come out of my owl's nest, and not return to it till late in the summer—employing the interval in making a tour somewhere in New-England. You, who have the dust of distant countries on your "sandal-shoon,"[5] cannot imagine how much enjoyment I shall have in this little excursion. Whenever I get abroad, I feel just as young as I did ten years ago. What a letter am I inflicting on you! I trust you will answer it.

Yours sincerely, Nath Hawthorne

1. For Longfellow's use of Jean Paul Friedrich Richter's "idea of happiness," see *CE*, 15:253–54n.
2. Both Bridge and Pierce tried unsuccessfully to have NH appointed to the United States Exploring Edition of 1838–39 to the South Seas and Antarctica.
3. The first printing of *Twice-Told Tales* was 1,000 copies, for which NH received $100.
4. NH refers to the economic depression that followed upon the financial panic of 1837.
5. See *Hamlet*, IV, v, 23–26, where Ophelia sings "How should I your true love know / From another one? / By his cockle hat and staff, / And his sandal shoon."

TO CAROLINE GILMAN

Salem, September 25th, 1837.

Mr. N. Hawthorne has recently been favored with a number of the Southern Rose, containing a very favorable notice of his 'Twice-told Tales.'[1] He feels far too much gratification in praise from such a source, not to maintain a sturdy faith in the correctness of the judgement there passed, although modesty might whisper him that the writer has been greatly more kind than critical. But the truth is, he has himself been so much delighted with certain productions from the pen, as he believes, of the Editor of the Rose, that he feels as if he might accept all the approbation that she can possibly bestow on him, and still leave her in his debt. He particularly remembers, in perusing the Recollections of a Housekeeper, a year or two since, how hopelessly he compared his own writings with the nature and truth of that little work.[2]

Mr. Hawthorne has delayed this acknowledgement, in the hope of being able to offer a tale or sketch for publication in the Rose; but anxieties of various kinds have kept his pen idle, and his fancy produces no flowers, nor hardly a weed that looks like one. In conclusion, he begs permission to express his high respect for the Editor, and for one whom the inhabitants of Salem are proud to claim as a native townsman.[3]

Editor of the Southern Rose.

1. Caroline Howard Gilman was born in Boston but settled in Charleston, South Carolina, after her marriage to the minister Samuel Gilman in 1819. She edited the *Southern Rose* both as a magazine for children (1832–33) and for adults (1833–39). The review of NH appeared in the 8 July 1837 issue.
2. A reference to Caroline Gilman's first book, a humorous account of early married life.
3. Samuel Gilman had been born in Gloucester and had spent his boyhood in Salem.

TO JOSEPH B. BOYD

Salem, Novr 7th. 1837

Dear Sir,

Your letter addressed to *Samuel* Hawthorne, lay some time in the Post-Office of this city, before I could feel myself justified in receiving it from the Postmaster. But as I know of no other person who spells the family name in the same manner, and as *Samuel* has somewhat of a scriptural affinity to *Nathaniel*, I at length ventured to break the seal. Even now, I scarcely know whether to consider the letter as intended for myself, being too justly conscious of my slender pretensions to literary merit, to presume that my autograph would be a valuable item in your collection.[1] But as I really happen to be the author of a volume entitled "Twice-told Tales," and may therefore claim at least a humble rank among American writers, I have deemed it no more than a proper courtesy to make this reply to your letter. Begging you to accept my thanks for your expressions of approbation, (if indeed I may appropriate them to myself,) and with my best wishes for your welfare,

> I remain, Sir,
> Respectfully,
> Your obd't servt,
> Nath. Hawthorne

Joseph B. Boyd, Esq
Cincinnati, Ohio

1. Writing famous people for their autograph was quite popular in the nineteenth century. This was NH's first "fan letter" of this sort.

TO HENRY WADSWORTH LONGFELLOW

> Salem, March 21st. 1838.

My dear Longfellow,

I was sorry that you did not come to dinner on Sunday; for I wanted to hold a talk with you about that book of fairy tales, which you spoke of at a previous interview.[1] I think it a good idea, and am well inclined to do my part towards the execution of it—provided I have time—which seems more probable now than it did a few months since. Not but what I am terribly harassed with magazine scribbling, and moreover have had overtures from two different quarters, to perpetrate childrens' histories and other such iniquities. But it seems to me that your book will be far more creditable, and perhaps quite as profitable; nor need it impede any other labors. Possibly we may make a great hit, and entirely revolutionize the whole system of juvenile literature. I wish you would shape out your plan distinctly, and write to me about it. Ought there not to be a slender thread of story running through the book, as a connecting medium for the other stories? If so, you must prepare it. If I recollect right, it was your purpose to select some of the stories; but I should deem it preferable to have them all either original or translated—at least, for the first volume of the series. I would not have it a very bulky book—say two or three hundred 18mo pages,[2] of large print; it being merely an experiment. You shall be the Editor, and I will figure merely as a contributor; for, as the conception and system of the work will be yours, I really should not think it honest to take an equal share of the fame which is to accrue. Seriously; I think that a very pleasant and peculiar kind of reputation may be acquired in this way— we will twine for ourselves a wreath of tender shoots and dewy buds, instead of such withered and dusty leaves as other people crown themselves with; and what is of more importance to me, though of none to a Cambridge Professor,[3] we may perchance put money in our purses. Think about it, and write to me; and let us get our baby-house ready by October.

I am going to study German.[4] What dictionary had I better get? Perhaps you can procure me a second-hand one without trouble—which, as perhaps it is a large and costly work, would be quite a considerable favor. But it is no great matter; for I am somewhat doubtful of the stability of my resolution to pursue the study.

I mean to come to Boston, within a month, and will endeavor to see you.

Your friend,
(in much of a hurry)
Nath. Hawthorne.

P.S. If you have any reminiscences about Cilley, impart them to me. It has fallen to my lot to write a biographical sketch of him; and I fear it will be a thorny affair to handle.[5]

1. A proposed collaboration of Longfellow and NH to be called "The Boys' Wonder-Horn" after *Des Knabens Wunderhorn* (1805–8), the famous collection of German folksongs by Ludwig Achim von Arnim and Clemens Brentano. [*CE*]

2. NH probably means "16mo," a book with a page height of about 6 3/4".

3. Longfellow became Smith Professor of French and Spanish Languages at Harvard in 1836.

4. This suggested course of language study, apparently made by Elizabeth Palmer Peabody, lasted only a few months.

5. Jonathan Cilley, NH's classmate at Bowdoin and a member of Congress, had been killed in a duel in 1838. NH published "Biographical Sketch of Jonathan Cilley" in the September 1838 *United States Magazine and Democratic Review.*

TO GEORGE BANCROFT

Salem, Jany 11th, 1839

Sir,

After due reflection, I have determined to accept the office which you had the goodness to offer me, in the Inspector's department of the Custom-House.[1] On enquiry of Gen. McNeel and Mr. Jameson, I find that the post vacated by Mr. Harris is considered more laborious and responsible than an ordinary Inspectorship; and they were both of opinion that I should prefer the duties of the latter. From November to April, however, the Inspectorships are all on the same footing; so that it would not be necessary to decide immediately as to the eligibility of Mr Harris's post.

I hope to be able to remove to Boston within a fortnight; and it would then be agreeable to me to enter upon office.

With much obligation,
Very Respectfully Yours,
Nath. Hawthorne.

George Bancroft, Esq.
Boston.

1. NH's appointment, aided through the offices of Elizabeth Palmer Peabody, Orestes A. Brownson, and Bancroft's wife, Elizabeth, was effective 21 January 1839 at an annual salary of $1,500.

TO GEORGE P. MORRIS

[Salem, ca. 11 January 1839]

Dear Sir:

It will give me great pleasure to comply with your proposition in regard to contributions for the Mirror, so far as it may be in my power.[1] I think I can furnish the five articles within the year, at furthest—and perhaps much sooner. Just at the moment I am undergoing somewhat of a metamorphosis; for Mr. Bancroft has formed so high an opinion of my capacity for business as to offer me the post of Inspector in the Boston Custom House—and as I know nothing to the contrary of my suitableness for it (knowing nothing about the matter), I have determined to accept. I understand that I shall have a good deal of leisure time, the greater part of which I mean to employ in writing books for the series projected by the Board of Education, which, I think, promises to be more profitable than any other line of literary labour.[2] Still I shall not utterly lay by the story-telling trade, and shall be happy to come before the public through such a medium as the *Mirror*. It rejoices me to hear of its high repute, under your management.
How is our friend Mr. Benjamin?[3]

Very truly yours,
Nathaniel Hawthorne

Geo. P. Morris

1. George Pope Morris published the *New-York Mirror,* a popular and well-regarded magazine, from 1823 to 1842. No contribution by NH has been noted in the *New-York Mirror*.
2. Nahum Capen, publisher of Hawthorne's first novel *Fanshawe* (1838), and Horace Mann, Secretary to the Massachusetts Board of Education, were planning a series of books for use in the district school libraries.
3. Park Benjamin was the literary editor of the *New-Yorker*.

TO HENRY WADSWORTH LONGFELLOW

Salem, Jany 12th. 1839

My dear Longfellow,

I was nowise to blame for going down the steps of the Tremont, almost at the moment that you were coming up; inasmuch as I did not receive your letter, appointing the rendezvous, till I reached Salem that evening. Those little devils in your hollow teeth had made you oblivious,[1] and caused you to carry the epistle in your pocket at least a week, before putting it into the Post-Office. But never mind; for, please God, we will meet in future often enough to make up for lost time. It has pleased Mr. Bancroft (knowing that what little ability I have is altogether adapted for active life) to offer me the post of Inspector in the Boston Custom-House; and I am going to accept it, with as much confidence in my suitableness for it, as Sancho Panza had in his gubernatorial qualifications.[2] I have no reason to doubt my capacity to fulfil the duties; for I don't know what they are; but, as nearly as I can understand, I shall be a sort of Port-Admiral, and take command of vessels after they enter the harbor, and have control of their cargoes. Pray Heaven I may have opportunities to make defalcation![3] They tell me that a considerable portion of my time will be unoccupied; the which I mean to employ in sketches of my new experience, under some such titles as follow:—"Passages in the life of a Custom-House Officer"—"Scenes in Dock"—"Voyages at Anchor"—"Nibblings of a Wharf-Rat"—"Trials of a Tide-Waiter"—"Romance of the Revenue Service"—together with an ethical work in two volumes on the subject of Duties—the first volume to treat of moral and religious Duties; and the second, of the Duties imposed by the Revenue Laws, which I already begin to consider as much the most important class.

Thus you see I have abundance of literary labor in prospect; and this makes it more tolerable that you refuse to let me blow a blast upon the "Wonder-Horn." Assuredly, you have a right to make all the music on your own instrument; but I should serve you right were I to set up an opposition—for instance, with a corn-stalk fiddle, or a pumpkin vine trumpet. Really I do mean to turn my attention to writing for children, either on my own hook, or for the series of works projected by the Board of Education—to which I have been requested to contribute. It appears to me that there is a very fair chance of profit.

I received a letter, the other day, from Bridge, dated at Rome, November 3d. He speaks of the Consul, Mr. Greene—"an old friend of Longfellow's." Bridge seems to be leading a very happy life. I wish some one of the vessels, which are to be put under my command, would mutiny, and run away with the worshipful Inspector to the Mediterranean. Well—I have a presentiment that I shall be there one day.

I shall remove to Boston in the course of a fortnight; and, most sincerely, I do not know that I have any pleasanter anticipation than that of frequently meeting you. I saw Mr. Sparks' at Miss Silsbee's, some time since; and he said you were thinking of a literary paper.[4] Why not? Your name would go a great way towards insuring its success; and it is intolerable that there should not be a single belles-lettres journal in New-England. And whatever aid a Custom-House officer could afford, should always be forthcoming. By the way, "The Inspector" would be as good a title for a paper as "The Spectator."

If you mean to see me in Salem, you must come pretty quick.

Yours truly,
Nath. Hawthorne.

1. Longfellow had been suffering from a toothache and a swollen jaw.

2. In Miguel de Cervantes's *Don Quixote:* "As I see it, in this matter of governments, everything depends on the kind of start you make; and it may be that after I've been governor for a couple of weeks, I'll have my hand in and will be better at the job than at work in the fields, which I was brought up to do" (part 2, chapter 33). [*CE*]

3. Defalcation, deducting a part.

4. Jared Sparks, an editor and historian, had become McLean Professor of Ancient and Modern History at Harvard in the previous year. For more on the aborted scheme of a "literary paper," see *CE,* 15:289n.

TO SOPHIA PEABODY

[Boston] Wednesday Afternoon, March 6th, 1839

My dearest Sophie,

I had a parting glimpse of you, Monday forenoon, at your window—and that image abides by me, looking pale, and not so quiet as is your wont. I have reproached myself many times since, because I did not show my face, and then we should both have smiled; and so our reminiscences would have been sunny instead of shadowy. But I believe I was so intent on seeing you, that I forgot all about the desirableness of being myself seen. Perhaps, after all, you did see me—at least you knew that I was there. I fear that you were not quite well that morning. Do grow better and better—physically I mean, for I protest against any spiritual improvement, until I am better able to keep pace with you—but do be strong, and full of life—earthly life—and let there be a glow in your cheeks. And sleep soundly the whole night long, and get up every morning with a feeling as if you were newly created; and I pray you to lay up a stock of fresh energy every day till we meet again; so that we may walk miles and miles, without your once needing to lean upon my arm. Not but what you shall lean upon it, as much as you choose—indeed, whether you choose or not—but I would feel as if you did it to lighten my footsteps, not to support your own. Am I requiring you to work a miracle within yourself? Perhaps so—yet not a greater one than I do really believe might be wrought by inward faith and outward aids. Try it, my Dove;[1] and be as lightsome on earth as your sister doves are in the air.

Tomorrow I shall expect a letter from you; but I am almost in doubt whether to tell you that I expect it; because then your conscience will reproach you, if you should happen not to have written. I would leave you as free as you leave me. But I do wonder whether you were serious in your last letter, when you asked me whether you wrote too often, and seemed to think that you might thus interfere with my occupations. My dear Sophie, your letters are no small portion of my spiritual food, and help to keep my soul alive, when otherwise it might languish unto death, or else become hardened and earth-incrusted, as seems to be the case with almost all the souls with whom I am in daily intercourse. They never interfere with my worldly business—neither the reading nor the answering them—(I am speaking of your letters, not of those "earth-incrusted" souls)—for I keep them to be the treasure of my still and secret hours, such hours as pious people spend in prayer; and the communion which my spirit then holds with yours has something of religion in it. The charm of your letters does not depend upon their intellectual value, though that is great, but on the spirit of which they are the utterance, and which is a spirit of wonderful efficacy. No one, whom you would deem worthy of your friendship, could enjoy so large a share of it as I do, without feeling the influence of your character throughout his own—purifying his aims and desires, enabling him to realize that there is a truer world than this feverish one around us, and teaching him how to gain daily entrance into that better world. Such, so far as I have been able to profit by it, has been your ministration to me. Did you dream what an angelic guardianship was entrusted to you?

March 7th. Your letter did come. You had not the heart to disappoint me, as I did you, in not making a parting visit, and shall again, by keeping this letter to send by Mary [Peabody]. But I disappoint you in these two instances, only that you may consider it a decree of Fate (or of Providence, which you please) that we shall not meet on the mornings of my departure, and that my letters shall not come oftener than on the alternate Saturday. If you will but believe this, you will be quiet. Otherwise I know that the Dove will flutter her wings, and often, by necessity, will flutter them in vain. Do forgive me, and let me have my own way, and believe (for it is true) that I never cause you the slightest disappointment without pain and remorse on my part. And yet, I know that when you wish me to do any particular thing, you will always tell me so, and that if my sins of omission or commission should ever wound your heart, you will by no means conceal it.

I did enjoy that walk infinitely—for certainly the enjoyment was not all finite. And what a heavenly pleasure we might have enjoyed this very day; the air was so delicious, that it seemed as if the dismal old Custom-House was situated in Paradise; and this afternoon, I sat with my window open, to temper the glow of a huge coal-fire. It almost seems to me, now, as if beautiful days were wasted and thrown away, when we do not feel their beauty and heavenliness through one another.

Your own friend,

N. H.

1. This first extant association of SPH with the dove seems to derive from the beginnings of their courtship in Boston, and to be memorialized by the description in the *Blithedale Romance*, which invests the bird with a "slight, fantastic pathos" (*CE*, 3:152).

TO SOPHIA PEABODY

Boston, April 30th. 6. P.M. 1839.

My beloved,

Your sweetest of all letters found me at the Custom-House, where I had almost just arrived, having been engaged all the forenoon in measuring twenty chaldrons of coal—which dull occupation was enlivened by frequent brawls and amicable discussions with a crew of funny little Frenchmen from Acadie. I know not whether your letter was a surprise to me—it seems to me that I had a prophetic faith that the Dove would visit me—but at any rate, it was a joy, as it always is; for my spirit turns to you from all trouble and all pleasure. This forenoon I could not wait, as I generally do, to be in solitude before opening your letter; for I expected to be busy all the afternoon, and was already tired with working yesterday and to day; and my heart longed to drink your thoughts and feelings, as a parched throat for cold water. So I pressed the Dove to my lips (turning my head away, so that nobody saw me) and then broke the seal. I do think it is the dearest letter you have written; but I think so of each successive one; so you need not imagine that you have outdone yourself in this instance. How did I live before I knew you—before I possessed your affection! And my dearest, how can you speak as if there were no possibility of remaining best friends! I reckon upon your love as something that is to endure when everything that can perish has perished—though my trust is sometimes mingled with fear, because I feel myself unworthy of your love. But if I am worthy of it, you will always love me; and if there be anything good and pure in me, it will be proved by my always loving you.

After dinner, I had to journey over to East Cambridge, expecting to measure a cargo of Coal there; but the vessel had stuck in the mud on her way thither, so that nothing could be done till tomorrow morning. It must have been my guardian angel that steered her upon that mud-bank; for I really needed rest. Did you lead the vessel astray, my Dove? I did not stop to inquire into particulars, but returned home forthwith, and locked my door, and threw myself on the bed, with your letter in my hand. I read it over slowly and peacefully, and then folding it up, I rested my heart upon it, and fell fast asleep.

Friday, May 3d. 5 P.M. My dearest, ten million occupations, and interruptions, and intrusions, have kept me from going on with my letter; but my spirit has visited you continually, and yours has come to me. I have had to be out a good deal in the east-winds; but your spell has proved sovereign against all harm, though sometimes I have shuddered and shivered for your sake. How have you borne it, my poor dear little Dove? Have you been able to flit abroad on to-day's west wind, and go to Marblehead, as you designed? You will not have seen Mrs. Hooper, because she came up to Boston in the cars, on Monday morning. I had a brief talk with her, and we made mutual inquiries, she about you, and I about little Annie. I will not attempt to tell you how it rejoices me that we are to spend a whole month together in the same city. Looking forward to it, it seems to me as if that month would never come to an end, because there will be so much of eternity in it.

I wish you had read that dream-letter through, and could remember its contents. I am very sure that it could not have been written by me, however, because I should not think of addressing you as "My dear Sister"—nor should I like to have you call me brother—nor ever should have liked it, from the very first of our acquaintance. We are, I trust, kindred spirits, but not brother and sister. And then what a cold and dry annunciation of that awful contingency—the "continuance or not of our acquaintance." Mine own Dove, you are to blame for dreaming such letters, or parts of letters, as coming from me. It was you that wrote it—not I. Yet I will not believe that it shows a want of faith in the steadfastness of my affection, but only in the continuance of circumstances prosperous to our earthly and external connection. Let us trust in GOD for that.[1] Pray to GOD for it, my Dove—for you know how to pray better than I do. Pray, for my sake, that no shadows of earth may ever come between us; because my surest hope of being a good man, and my only hope of being a happy man, depends upon the permanence of our union. I have great comfort in such thoughts as those you suggest— that our hearts have been drawn towards one another so naturally—that we have not cultivated our friendship, but let it grow,—that we have thrown ourselves upon one another with such perfect trust;—and even the deficiency of worldly wisdom, that some people would ascribe to us in following the guidance of our hearts so implicitly, is proof to me that there is a deeper wisdom within us. Oh, let us not think but that all will be well! And even if, to worldly eyes, it should appear that our lot is not a fortunate one, still we shall have glimpses, at least—and I trust a pervading sunshine—of a happiness that we could never have found, if we had unquietly struggled for it, and made our own selection of the means and species of it, instead of trusting all to something diviner than our reason.

My Dove, there were a good many things that I meant to have written in this letter; but I have continually lapsed into fits of musing, and when I have written, the soul of my thought has not readily assumed the earthly garments of language. It is now time to carry the letter to Mary. I kiss you, dearest—did you feel it?

Your own friend
Nath. Hawthorne, Esqr.

Dear me! What an effect that Esquire gives to the whole letter!

1. The spelling of God in capitals was a gesture to SPH, who habitually used that form. [CE]

TO SOPHIA PEABODY

Salem, May 26th. 1839

Mine own self,

I felt rather dismal yesterday—a sort of vague weight on my spirit—a sense that something was wanting to me here. What or who could it have been that I so missed? I thought it not best to go to your house last evening; so that I have not yet seen Elizabeth—but we shall probably attend the Hurley-Burley to-night.[1] Would that my Dove might be there! It seems really monstrous that here, in her own home—or what was her home, till she found another in my arms—she should no longer be. Oh, my dearest, I yearn for you, and my heart heaves when I think of you—(and that is always, but sometimes a thought makes me know and feel you more vividly than at others, and that I call "thinking of you")—heaves and swells (my heart does) as sometimes you have felt it beneath you, when your head or your bosom was resting on it. At such moments it is stirred up from its depths. Then our two ocean-hearts mingle their floods.

I do not believe that this letter will extend to three pages. My feelings do not, of their own accord, assume words—at least, not a continued flow of words. I write a few lines, and then I fall a-musing about many things, which seem to have no connection among themselves, save that my Dove flits lightly through them all. I feel as if my being were dissolved, and the idea of you were diffused throughout it. Am I writing nonsense? That is for you to decide. You know what is Truth— "what is what"—and I should not dare to say to you what I felt to be other than the Truth—other than the very "what." It is very singular (but I do not suppose I can express it) that, while I love you so dearly, and while I am so conscious of the deep embrace of our spirits, and while this is expressed by our every embrace of our hearts, still I have an awe of you that I never felt for anybody else. Awe is not the word, either; because it might imply something stern in you—whereas—but you must make it out for yourself. I do wish that I could put this into words—not so much for your satisfaction (because I believe you will understand) as for my own. I suppose I should have pretty much the same feeling if an angel were to come from Heaven and be my dearest friend—only the angel could not have the tenderest of human natures too, the sense of which is mingled with this senti-ment. Perhaps it is because in meeting you, I really meet a spirit, whereas the obstructions of earth have prevented such a meeting in every other case. But I leave the mystery here. Sometime or other, it may be made plainer to me.

But methinks it converts my love into religion. And then it is singular, too, that this awe (or whatever it be) does not prevent me from feeling that it is I who have the charge of you, and that my Dove is to follow my guidance and do my bidding. Am I not very bold to say this? And will not you rebel? Oh no; because I possess this power only so far as I love you. My love gives me the right, and your love consents to it.

Since writing the above, I have been asleep; and I dreamed that I had been sleeping a whole year in the open air; and that while I slept, the grass grew around me. It seemed, in my dream, that the very bed-clothes which actually covered me were spread beneath me, and when I awoke (in my dream) I snatched them up, and the earth under them looked black, as if it had been burnt—one square place, exactly the size of the bed clothes. Yet there was grass and herbage scattered over this burnt space, looking as fresh, and bright, and dewy, as if the summer rain and the summer sun had been cherishing them all the time. Interpret this for me, my Dove—but do not draw any sombre omens from it. What is signified by my nap of a whole year? (it made me grieve to think that I had lost so much of eternity)—and what was the fire that blasted the spot of earth which I occupied, while the grass flourished all around? and what comfort am I to draw from the fresh herbage amid the burnt space? But it is a silly dream, and you cannot expound any sense out of it. Generally, I cannot remember what my dreams have been—only there is a confused sense of having passed through adventures, pleasurable or otherwise. I suspect that you mingle with my dreams, but take care to flit away just before I awake, leaving me but dimly and doubtfully conscious of your visits. [*excision*] Do you never start so suddenly from a dream that you are afraid to look round the room, lest your dream-personages (so strong and distinct seemed their existence, a moment before) should have thrust themselves out of dreamland into the midst of realities? I do, sometimes.

I wish I were to see you this evening. How many times have you thought of me to-day? All the time?—or not at all? Did you ever read such a foolish letter as this? Here I was interrupted, and have taken a stroll down on the Neck—a beautiful, beautiful, beautiful sunshine, and air, and sea. Would that my Dove had been with me. I fear that we shall perforce lose some of our mutual intimacy with Nature—we walk together so seldom that she will seem more like a stranger.

Would that I could write such sweet letters to mine own self, as mine own self writes to me. Good bye, dearest self. Direct yours to

Nath. Hawthorne, Esq.
Custom-House, Boston

1. NH is punning on the witches' use of "hurlyburly" at the beginning of *Macbeth* (I, i, 3), and the name of his friend Susan Burley.

TO SOPHIA PEABODY

Boston, July 3d. 1839.

Most beloved Amelia,[1]

I shall call you so sometimes in playfulness, and so may you; but it is not the name by which my soul recognizes you. It knows you as Sophie, but I doubt whether that is the inwardly and intensely dearest epithet either. I believe that "Dove" is the true word after all; and it never can be used amiss, whether in sunniest gaiety or shadiest seriousness. And yet it is a sacred word, and I should not love to have anybody hear me use it, nor know that GOD has baptized you so— the baptism being for yourself and me alone. By that name, I think, I shall greet you, when we meet in Heaven. Other dear ones may call you 'daughter,' 'sister,' 'Sophia'; but when, at your entrance into Heaven, or after you have been a little while there, you hear a voice say 'Dove!' then you will know that your kindred spirit has been admitted (perhaps for your sake) to the mansions of rest. That word will express his yearning for you—then to be forever satisfied; for we will melt into one another, and be close, close together then. The name was inspired; it came without our being aware that you were thenceforth to be my Dove, now and through eternity. I do not remember how nor when it alighted on you; the first I knew, it was in my heart to call you so.

Good night now, my Dove. It is not yet nine oclock; but I am somewhat aweary, and prefer to muse about you till bedtime, rather than write.

July 5th. ½ past seven P.M. I must, somehow or other, finish this letter tonight, my dearest—or else it could not be sent tomorrow; and then I fear our head would ache, naughty head that it is. My heart yearns to communicate to you; but if it had any other means at hand, it certainly would not choose to communicate by the scratchings of an iron pen, which I am now compelled to use. This must and will inevitably be a dull letter. Oh how different from yours, which I received to day. You are absolutely inspired, my Dove; and it is not my poor stupid self that inspires you; for how could I give what is not in me. I wish I could write to you in the morning, before my toils begin; but that is impossible, unless I were to write before day-light. At eventide, my mind has quite lost its elasticity—my heart, even, is weary—and all that I seem capable of doing is to rest my head on its pillow, its own pillow, and there lay down the burthen of life. I do not mean to imply that I am unhappy or discontented; for this is not the case; my life is only a burthen, in the same way that it is so to every toilsome man, and mine is a healthy weariness, such as needs only a night's sleep to remove it. But from henceforth forever, I shall be entitled to call the sons of toil my brethren, and shall know how to sympathize with them, seeing that I, likewise, have risen at the dawn, and borne the fervor of the mid-day sun, nor turned my heavy footsteps homeward till eventide. Years hence, perhaps, the experience that my heart is acquiring now will flow out in truth and wisdom.

You ask me a good many questions, my Dove, and I will answer such of them as now occur to me, and the rest you may ask me again, when we meet. First as to your letters. My beloved, you must write whenever you will, in all confidence that I can never be otherwise than joyful to receive your letters. Do not get into the habit of trying to find out, by any method save your own intuition, what is pleasing and what displeasing to me. Whenever you need my counsel, or even my reproof, in any serious matter, you will not fail to receive it; but I wish my Dove to be as free as a Bird of Paradise. Now, as to this affair of the letters, I have sometimes been a little annoyed at the smiles of my brother measurers, who, notwithstanding the masculine fist of the direction, seem to know that such delicately sealed and folded epistles can come only from a lady's small and tender hand.[2] But this annoyance is not on my own account; but because it seems as if the letters were prophaned by being smiled at—but this is, after all, a mere fantasy, since the smilers know nothing about my Dove, not that I really have a Dove; nor can they be certain that the letters come from a lady, nor, especially, can they have the remotest imagination what heavenly letters they are. The sum and substance is, that they are smiling at nothing; and so it is no matter for their smiles. I would not give up one letter to avoid the "world's dread laugh,"[3]—much less to shun the good-natured raillery of three or four people who do not dream of giving pain. Why has my Dove made me waste so much of my letter in this talk about nothing?

My dearest, did you really think that I meant to express a doubt whether we should enjoy each other's society so much, if we could be together all the time. No, no; for I always feel, that our momentary and hurried interviews scarcely afford us time to taste the draught of affection that we drink from one another's hearts. There is a precious portion of our happiness wasted, because we are forced to enjoy it too greedily. But I thought, as you do, that there might be more communication of intellect, as well as communion of hearts, if we could be oftener together.

Your picture gallery of auxiliary verbs is an admirable fantasy. You are certainly the first mortal to whom it was given to behold a verb; though, it seems as if they ought to be visible, being creatures whose office it is (if I remember my Grammar aright) "to be, to do, and to suffer." Therein is comprehended all that we mortals are capable of. No; for, according to this definition, verbs do not feel, and cannot enjoy—they only exist, and act, and are miserable. My Dove and I are no verbs—or if so, we are passive verbs, and therefore happy ones. [*excision*]

1. This is the only known letter in which NH addresses SPH by her middle name. [*CE*]

2. At NH's request, SPH uses a heavier, more "masculine" hand to address her envelopes, so that his co-workers would not think that they were messages from her.

3. James Thompson, *The Seasons: Autumn* (1730).

TO SOPHIA PEABODY [FRAGMENT]

Boston, July 24th, 1839—8 oclock. P.M.

Mine own,

I am tired this evening, as usual, with my long day's toil; and my head wants its pillow—and my soul yearns for the friend whom God has given it—whose soul He has married to my soul. Oh, my dearest, how that thought thrills me! We are married! I felt it long ago; and sometimes, when I was seeking for some fondest word, it has been on my lips to call you—'Wife!' I hardly know what restrained me from speaking it—unless a dread (for that would have been an infinite pang to me) of feeling you shrink back from my bosom, and thereby discovering that there was yet a deep place in your soul which did not know me. Mine own Dove, need I fear it now? Are we not married? God knows we are. Often, while holding you in my arms, I have silently given myself to you, and received you for my portion of human love and happiness, and have prayed Him to consecrate and bless the union. And any one of our innocent embraces—even when our lips did but touch for a moment, and then were withdrawn—dearest, was it not the symbol of a bond between our Souls, infinitely stronger than any external rite could twine around us? Yes—we are married; and as God Himself has joined us, we may trust never to be separated, neither in Heaven nor on Earth. We will wait patiently and quietly, and He will lead us onward hand in hand (as He has done all along) like little children, and will guide us to our perfect happiness—and will teach us when our union is to be revealed to the world. My beloved, why should we be silent to one another—why should our lips be silent—any longer on this subject? The world might, as yet, misjudge us; and therefore we will not speak to the world; but when I hold you in my arms, why should we not commune together about all our hopes of earthly and external, as well as our faith of inward and eternal union? Farewell for to-night, my dearest—my soul's bride! Oh, my heart is thirsty for your kisses; they are the dew which should restore its freshness every night, when the hot sunshiny day has parched it. Kiss me in your dreams; and perhaps my heart will feel it.

July 25th. 8 oclock. P.M. How does my Dove contrive to live and thrive, and keep her heart in cheerful trim, through a whole fortnight, with only one letter from me? It cannot be indifference; so it must be heroism—and how heroic! It does seem to me that my spirit would droop and wither like a plant that lacked rain and dew, if it were not for the frequent shower of your gentle and holy thoughts. But then there is such a difference in our situations. My Dove is at home—not, indeed, in her home of homes—but still in the midst of true affections; and she can live a spiritual life, spiritual and intellectual. Now, my intellect, and my heart and soul, have no share in my present mode of life—they find neither labor nor food in it; every thing that I do here might be better done by a machine. I am a machine, and am surrounded by hundreds of similar machines;—or rather, all of the business people are so many wheels of one great machine—and we have no more love or sympathy for one another than if we were made of wood, brass, or iron, like the wheels of other pieces of complicated machinery. Perchance—but do not be frightened, dearest—the soul would wither and die within me, leaving nothing but the busy machine, no germ for immortality, nothing that could taste of heaven, if it were not for the consciousness of your deep, deep love, which is renewed to me with every letter. Oh, my Dove, I have really thought sometimes, that God gave you to me to be the salvation of my soul.

TO SOPHIA PEABODY

[Boston] Custom-House, August 8th. 1839

Your letter, my beloved wife, was duly received into your husband's heart, yesterday. I found it impossible to keep it all day long, with unbroken seal, in my pocket; and so I opened and read it on board of a salt vessel, where I was at work, amid all sorts of bustle, and gabble of Irishmen, and other incommodities. Nevertheless its effect was very blessed, even as if, I had gazed upward from the deck of the vessel, and beheld my wife's sweet face looking down upon me from a sun-brightened cloud. Dearest, if your dove-wings will not carry you so far, I beseech you to alight upon such a cloud, sometimes, and let it bear you to me. True it is, that I never look heavenward without thinking of you, and I doubt whether it would much surprise me to catch a glimpse of you among those upper regions. Then would all that is spiritual within me so yearn towards you, that I should leave my earthy incumbrances behind, and float upward and embrace you in the heavenly sunshine. Yet methinks I shall be more content to spend a lifetime of earthly and heavenly happiness intermixed. So human am I, my beloved, that I would not give up the hope of loving and cherishing you by a fireside of our own, not for any unimaginable bliss of higher spheres. Your influence shall purify me and fit me for a better world—but it shall be by means of our happiness here below. In my present state of spiritual life, I cannot conceive my bliss without the privilege of pressing my lips to yours—of pillowing my head upon your bosom. Dearest wife, shall there be no holy kisses in the sky?—shall I not still hold you in my arms, when we are angels together?

Was such a rhapsody as the foregoing ever written in the Custom-House before? I have almost felt it a sin to write to my Dove here; because her image comes before me so vividly, and the place is not worthy of it. Nevertheless, I cast aside my scruples, because, having been awake ever since four oclock this morning (now thirteen hours) and abroad since sunrise, I shall feel more like holding intercourse in dreams than with my pen, when secluded in my room. I am not quite hopeless, now, of meeting you in dreams. Did you not know, beloved, that I dreamed of you, as it seemed to me, all night long, after that last blissful meeting? It is true, when I looked back upon the dream, it immediately became confused; but it had been vivid, and most happy, and left a sense of happiness in my heart. Come again, sweet wife! Force your way through the mists and vapors that envelope my slumbers—illumine me with a radiance that shall not vanish when I awake. I throw my heart as wide open to you as I can. Come and rest within it, my Dove. Where else should you rest at night, if not in your husband's arms—and quite securely in his heart.

Oh, how happy you make me by calling me your husband—by subscribing yourself my Wife. I kiss that word when I meet it in your letters; and I repeat over and over to myself, "she is my Wife—I am her Husband." Dearest, I could almost think that the institution of marriage was ordained, first of all, for you and me, and for you and me alone; it seems so fresh and new—so unlike anything that the people around us enjoy or are acquainted with. Nobody ever had a wife but me—nobody a husband, save my Dove. Would that the husband were worthier of his wife; but she loves him—and her wise and prophetic heart could never do so if he were utterly unworthy.

At My own Room. August 9th.—about 10. A.M. It is so rare a thing for your husband to find himself in his own room in the middle of the forenoon, that he cannot help advising his Dove of that remarkable fact. By some misunderstanding, I was sent on a fruitless errand to East-Cambridge, and have stopped here, on my return to the Custom-House, to rest and refresh myself—and what can so rest and refresh me as to hold intercourse with my darling wife? It must be but a word and a kiss, however—a written word and a shadowy kiss. Good bye, dearest. I must go now to hold controversy, I suppose, with some plaguy little Frenchman about a peck of coal more or less; but I will give my beloved another word and kiss, when the day's toil is over.

About 8 oclock P.M.—I received your letter, your sweet, sweet letter, my sweetest wife, on reaching the Custom-House. Now as to that swelled face of ours—it had begun to swell when we last met; but I did not tell you, because I knew that you would associate the idea of pain with it; whereas, it was attended with no pain at all. Very glad am I, that my Dove did not see me when one side of my face was swollen as big as two; for the image of such a monstrous onesidedness, or doublesidedness, might have haunted her memory through the whole fortnight. Dearest, is it a weakness that your husband wishes to look tolerably comely always in your eyes?—and beautiful if he could!! My Dove is beautiful, and full of grace; she should not have an ugly mate. But to return to this "naughty swelling"—it began to subside on Tuesday, and has now, I think, entirely disappeared, leaving my visage in its former admirable proportion. Nothing is now the matter with me, save that my heart is as much swollen as my cheek was—swollen with love, with pent-up love, which I would fain mingle with the heart-flood of mine own sweet wife. Oh, dearest, how much I have to say to you!—how many fond thoughts die before their birth!

Dearest, I dare not give you permission to go out in the east-winds. The west-wind will come very often, I am sure, if it were only for the sake of my Dove. Have nothing to do with that hateful East-Wind, at least not till I can shelter you in my arms, and render you invulnerable with kisses. Oh, Dove, how I wish you were to rest this night in the bosom of your own, ownest husband!

TO SOPHIA PEABODY

Boston, September 23d 1839. ¹/₂ past 6. P.M.

Belovedest little wife—sweetest Sophie Hawthorne—what a delicious walk that was, last Thursday! It seems to me, now, as it I could really remember every footstep of it. It is almost as distinct as the recollection of those walks, in which my earthly form did really tread beside your own, and my arm uphold you; and, indeed, it has the same character as those heavenly ramblings;—for did we tread on earth even then? Oh no—our souls went far away among the sunset clouds, and wherever there was ethereal beauty, there were we, our true selves; and it was there we grew into each other, and became a married pair. Dearest, I love to date our marriage as far back as possible; and I feel sure that the tie had been formed, and our union had become indissoluble, even before we sat down together on the steps of the "house of spirits." How beautiful and blessed those hours appear to me! True; we are far more conscious of our relation, and therefore infinitely happier, now, than we were then; but still those remembrances are among the most precious treasures of my soul. It is not past happiness; it makes a portion of our present bliss. And thus, doubtless, even amid the Joys of Heaven, we shall love to look back to our earthly bliss, and treasure it forever in the sum of our infinitely accumulating happiness. Perhaps not a single pressure of the hand, not a glance, not a sweet and tender tone, not one kiss, but will be repeated sometime or other in our memory.

[*excision*] Oh, dearest, blessedest Dove, I never felt sure of going to Heaven, till I knew, that you loved me; but now I am conscious of God's love in your own. And now good bye for a little while, mine own wife. I thought it was just on the verge of supper-time when I began to write—and there is the bell now. I was beginning to fear that it had rung unheard, while I was communing with my Dove. Should we be the more ethereal, if we did not eat? I have a most human and earthly appetite.

Mine own wife, since supper I have been reading over again (for the third time, the two first being aboard my salt-ship—the Marcia Cleaves—) in your letter of yesterday and a dearest letter it is—and meeting with Sophie Hawthorne twice, I took the liberty to kiss her very fervently. Will she forgive me? Do know yourself by that name, dearest, and think of yourself as Sophie Hawthorne. It thrills my heart to write it, and still more, I think, to read it in the fairy letters of your own hand. Oh, you are my wife, my dearest, truest, tenderest, most beloved wife. I would not be disjoined from you for a moment, for all the world. And how strong, while I write, is the consciousness that I am truly your husband! Dove, come to my bosom—it yearns for you as it never did before. I shall fold my arms together, after I am in bed, and try to imagine that you are close to my heart. Naughty wife, what right have you to be anywhere else? How many sweet words I should breathe into your ear, in the quiet night—how many holy kisses would I press upon your lips—whenever I [*excision verso*] consciousness of my bliss. But I should [*excision verso; excision*]

My little Dove, I have observed that butterflies—very broad-winged and magnificent butterflies—frequently come on board of the salt ships where I am at
work. What have these bright strangers to do on Long Wharf, where there are no
flowers nor any green thing—nothing but brick stores, stone piers, black ships,
and the bustle of toilsome men, who neither look up to the blue sky, nor take note
of these wandering gems of air. I cannot account for them, unless, dearest, they
are the lovely fantasies of your mind, which you send hither in search of me. There
is the supper-bell. Goodbye, darling.

Sept 25th. Morning.—Dove, I have but a single moment to embrace you. Tell
Sophie Hawthorne I love her. Has she a partiality for your own, own,

Husband.

TO SOPHIA PEABODY

Boston, October 3d 1839, ¹/₂ past 7. P.M.

Ownest Dove,

Did you get home safe and sound, and with a quiet and happy heart! How
could you go without another press of lips? Providence acted lovingly towards us
on Tuesday evening, allowing us to meet in the wide desert of this world, and mingle our spirits in a conjugal embrace. How strangely we should have felt, had we
been compelled to meet and part without the pressure of one another's lips! It
would have seemed all a vision then; now we have the symbol of its reality. You
looked like a vision, beautifullest wife, with the width of the room between us—
so spiritual that my human heart wanted to be assured that you had an earthly
vesture on, and your warm kisses gave me that assurance. What beautiful white
doves those were, on the border of the vase! Are they of mine own Dove's kindred?
Do you remember a story of a cat who was changed into a lovely lady?—and on
her bridal night, a mouse happened to run across the floor; and forthwith the cat-
wife leaped out of bed to catch it. What if mine own Dove, in some woeful hour
for her poor husband, should remember her dove-instincts, and spread her wings
upon the western breeze, and return to him no more! Then would he stretch out
his arms, poor wingless biped, not having the wherewithal to fly, and cry aloud—
'Come back, naughty Dove!—whither are you going?—come back, and fold your

wings upon my heart again, or it will freeze!' And the Dove would flutter her wings, and pause a moment in the air, meditating whether or no she should come back; for in truth, as her conscience would tell her, this poor mortal had given her all he had to give—a resting-place on his bosom—a home in his deepest heart. But then she would say to herself—'my home is in the gladsome air—and if I need a resting place, I can find one on any of the sunset-clouds. He is unreasonable to call me back; but if he can follow me, he may!' Then would the poor deserted husband do his best to fly in pursuit of the faithless Dove; and for that purpose would ascend to the top-mast of a salt-ship, and leap desperately into the air, and fall down head-foremost upon the deck, and break his neck. And there should be engraven on his tombstone—"Mate not thyself with a Dove, unless thou hast wings to fly."

Now will my Dove scold at me for this foolish flight of fancy;—but the fact is, my goose-quill flew away with me. I do think that I have gotten a bunch of quills from the silliest flock of geese on earth. But the rest of the letter shall be very sensible. I saw Mr. Howes in the reading-room of the Athenaeum, between one and two oclock to day; for I happened to have had leisure for an early dinner, and so was spending a half hour turning over the periodicals. He spoke of the long time since your husband had been at his house; and so I promised, on behalf of that respectable personage, that he would spend an evening there on his next visit to Salem. But if I had such a sweetest wife as your husband has, I doubt whether I could find in my heart to keep the engagement. Now good night, truest Dove in the world. You will never fly away from me; and it is only the infinite impossibility of it that enables me to sport with the idea. I want you very much in my arms to-night. I mean to dream of you with might and main. How sweet those kisses were, on Tuesday evening! Dearest, there was an illegible word in your yesterday's note. I have bored over it, but cannot make it out. Your words are too precious to be thus hidden under their own vesture. Good night, darlingest wife!

October 4th.—5 or thereabout. P.M.—Mine own Dove, I dreamed the queerest dreams last night, about being deserted, and all such nonsense—so you see how I was punished for that naughty romance of the Faithless Dove. It seems to me that any dreams are generally about fantasies, and very seldom about what I really think and feel. You did not appear visibly in my last night's dreams; but they were made up of desolation; and it was good to awake, and know that my spirit was forever and irrevocably linked with the soul of my truest and tenderest Dove. You have warmed my heart, mine own wife; and never again can I know what it is to be cold and desolate, save in dreams. You love me dearly—don't you?

And so my Dove has been in great peril since we parted. No—I do not believe she has; it was only a shadow of peril, not a reality. My spirit cannot anticipate any harm to you; and I trust you to God with securest faith. I know not whether I could endure actually to see you in danger; but when I hear of any risk—as for instance when your steed seemed on the point of dashing you to pieces (but I do quake a little at that thought) against a tree—my mind does not seize upon it as if it had any substance. Believe me, dearest, the tree would have stood aside to let you pass, had there been no other means of salvation. Nevertheless, do not drive your steed against trees wilfully. Mercy on us, what a peril that was of the fat woman, when she "smashed herself down" beside my Dove! Poor Dove! Did you not feel as if an avalanche had all but buried you. I can see my Dove at this moment, my slender, little delicatest white Dove, squeezed almost out of Christendom by that great mass of female flesh—that ton of woman—that beef-eater and beer guzzler, whose immense cloak, though broad as a ship's mainsail, could not be made to meet in front—that picture of an alewife—that triple, quadruple, dozen-fold old lady.

Will not my Dove confess that there is a little *nonsense* in this epistle? But be not wroth[1] with me, darling wife;—my heart sports with you because it loves you.

If you happen to see Sophie Hawthorne, kiss her cheek for my sake. I love her full as well as I do mine own wife. Will that satisfy her, do you think? If not, she is a very unreasonable little person.

It is my chiefest pleasure to write to you, dearest.

Your ownest Husband.

1. Wroth, angry or exasperated.

TO SOPHIA PEABODY

Boston, October 23d 1839—$^1/_2$ past 7. P.M.

Dear little Dove,

Here sits your husband, comfortably established for the evening in his own domicile, with a cheerful coal-fire making the room a little too warm. I think I like to be a very little too warm. And now if my Dove were here, she and that naughty Sophie Hawthorne, how happy we all three—two—one—(how many are there of us?)—how happy might we be! Dearest, it will be a yet untasted bliss, when, for the first time, I have you in a domicile of my own, whether it be in a hut or a palace, a splendid suit of rooms or an attic chamber. Then I shall feel as if I had brought my wife home at last. Oh, beloved, if you were here now, I do not think I could possibly let you go till morning—my arms should imprison you—I would not be content, unless you nestled into my very heart, and there slept a sweet sleep with your own husband. My blessed Dove, how I long to hear your gentle breathing, as you lie asleep in my arms. Which of us do you think will fall asleep first? I hope it will be my Dove, because then she will arrange a dream of pictorial magnificence and heavenly love, and by and bye, her husband will enter beneath the dusky veil of sleep and find himself in the midst of her enchantments. Shall Sophie Hawthorne be there too? Shall she share our nuptial couch? Yes, mine own Dove, whether you like it or no, that naughty little person must share our pillow. You would wonder, were I to tell you how absolutely necessary she has contrived to render herself to your husband. His heart stirs at her very name—even at the thought of her unspoken name. She is his sunshine—she is a happy smile on the visage of his Destiny, causing that stern personage to look as benign as Heaven itself. And were Sophie Hawthorne a tear instead of a smile, still your foolish husband would hold out his heart to receive that tear within it, and doubtless would think it more precious than all the smiles and sunshine in the world. But Sophie Hawthorne has bewitched him—for there is great reason to suspect that she deals in magic. Sometimes, while your husband conceives himself to be holding his Dove in his arms, lo and behold! there is the arch face of Sophie Hawthorne peeping up at him. And again, in the very midst of Sophie Hawthorne's airs, while he is meditating what sort of chastisement would suit her misdemeanors, all of a sudden he becomes conscious of his Dove, with her wings folded upon his heart to keep it warm. Methinks a woman, or angel (yet let it be a woman, because I deem a true woman holier than an angel)—methinks a woman, then, who should combine the characteristics of Sophie Hawthorne and my Dove would be the very perfection of her race. The heart would find all it yearns for, in such a woman, and so would the mind and the fancy;—when her husband was lightsome of spirit, her merry fantasies would dance hand in hand with his; and when he was overburthened with cares, he would rest them all upon her bosom—and his head, too. Oh, that my head were to rest upon such a bosom to-night!

Dearest, your husband was called on by Mr. Hillard yesterday, who said that he intended soon to take a house in Boston, and, in that case, would like to take your respectable spouse to lodge and breakfast. What thinks my Dove of this? Your husband is quite delighted, because he thinks matters may be managed so, that once in a while he may meet his own wife within his own premises. Might it not be so?

Or would his wife—most preposterous idea!—deem it a sin against decorum to pay a visit to her husband? Oh, no, belovedest. Your unreserve, your out-gushing frankness, is one of the loveliest results of your purity, and innocence, and holiness. And now good night, wife worshipful and beloved. Amid many musings, nine oclock has surprised me at this stab of my epistle, and I have but time to give you the fondest imaginable kiss, and go to bed. Oh! will not you come, too?

October 24th.—$^1/_2$ past 6. P.M. Dearest Dove, your letter came to day; and I do think it the sweetest of all letters—but you must not therefore suppose that you have excelled yourself; for I think the same of each successive one. My dearest, what a delightful scene was that between Sophie Hawthorne and my Dove, when the former rebelled so stoutly against Destiny, and the latter, with such meek mournfulness, submitted. Which do I love the best, I wonder—my Dove, or my little Wild-Flower? I love each best, and both equally; and my heart would inevitably wither, and dry up, and perish utterly, if either of them were torn away from it. Yet, truly, I have reason to apprehend more trouble with Sophie Hawthorne than with my Dove [*excision*] that Sophie Hawthorne's patience will be worn quite threadbare, before his visit is at end. Sweetest wife, I fold you in my arms—can't you feel my heart throbbing against yours? Oh, kiss your husband.

TO SOPHIA PEABODY

                                        Boston, Nov 29th. 1839.—6 or 7 P.M.

Blessedest wife,

Does our head ache this evening?—and has it ached all or any of the time to-day? I wish I knew, dearest, for it seems almost too great a blessing to expect, that my Dove should come quite safe through the trial which she has encountered. Do, mine own wife, resume all your usual occupations as soon as possible—your sculpture, your painting, your music (what a company of sister-arts is combined in the little person of my Dove!)—and above all, your riding and walking.[1] Write often to your husband, and let your letters gush from a cheerful heart; so shall they refresh and gladden me, like draughts from a sparkling fountain, which leaps from some spot of earth where no grave has ever been dug. Dearest, for some little time to come, I pray you not to muse too much upon your brother, even though such musings should be untinged with gloom, and should appear to make you happier.[2]

In the eternity where he now dwells, it has doubtless become of no importance to himself whether he died yesterday, or a thousand years ago; he is already at home in the celestial city—more at home than ever he was in his mother's house. Then, my beloved, let us leave him there for the present; and if the shadows and images of this fleeting time should interpose between us and him, let us not seek to drive them away, for they are sent of God. By and bye, it will be good and profitable to commune with our brother's spirit; but so soon after his release from mortal infirmity, it seems even ungenerous towards himself to call him back by yearnings of the heart and too vivid picturings of what he was.

Little Dove, why did you shed tears the other day, when you supposed that your husband thought you to blame for regretting the irrevocable past? Dearest, I never think you to blame; for you positively have no fault. Not that you always act wisely, or judge wisely, or feel precisely what it would be wise to feel, in relation to this present world and state of being; but it is because you are too delicate and exquisitely wrought in heart, mind, and frame, to dwell in such a world—because, in short, you are fitter to be in Paradise than here. You needed, therefore, an interpreter between the world and yourself—one who should sometimes set you right, not in the abstract (for there you are never wrong) but relatively to human and earthly matters;—and such an interpreter is your husband, who can sympathise, though inadequately, with his wife's heavenly nature, and has likewise a portion of shrewd earthly sense, enough to guide us both through the labyrinth of time. Now, dearest, when I criticise any act, word, thought, or feeling of yours, you must not understand it as a reproof, or as imputing anything wrong, wherewith you are to burthen your conscience. Were an angel, however holy and wise, to come and dwell with mortals, he would need the guidance and instruction of some mortal; and so will you, my Dove, need mine—and precisely the same sort of guidance that the angel would. Then do not grieve, nor grieve your husband's spirit, when he essays to do his office; but remember that he does it reverently, and in the devout belief that you are, in immortal reality, both wiser and better than himself; though sometimes he may chance to interpret the flitting shadows around us more accurately than you. Hear what I say, dearest, in a cheerful spirit, and act upon it with cheerful strength. And do not give an undue weight to my judgment, nor imagine that there is no appeal from it, and that its decrees are not to be questioned. Rather, make it a rule always to question them and be satisfied of their correctness;—and so shall my Dove be improved and perfected in the gift of a human understanding, till she become even *earthly-wiselier* than her sagacious husband. Undine's husband gave her an immortal soul;[3] my beloved wife must be content with an humbler gift from me, being already provided with as high and pure a soul as ever was created.

God bless you, belovedest. I bestow three kisses on the air—they are intended for your eyelids and brow, to drive away the head-ache.—

Your ownest.

1. Information on SPH, her art, and her extant works, is in Patricia Dunlavy Valenti, "Sophia Peabody Hawthorne: A Study of Artistic Influence," *Studies in the American Renaissance 1990,* ed. Joel Myerson (Charlottesville: University Press of Virginia, 1990), 1–21.

2. George Francis Peabody died in 1839. He had dropped out of Harvard and was an unsuccessful businessman.

3. In Friedrich de La Motte-Fouqué's *Undine* (1811), the title character is a water-sprite, adopted by a poor fisherman and his wife, who falls in love with a knight. Upon their marriage, she acquires a soul.

TO SOPHIA PEABODY

Boston Jany 1st. 1840. 6 oclock, P.M.

Belovedest wife

Your husband's heart was exceedingly touched by that little backhanded note, and likewise by the bundle of allumettes—half a dozen of which I have just been kissing with great affection.[1] Would that I might kiss that poor dear finger of mine! Kiss it for my sake, sweetest Dove—and tell naughty Sophie Hawthorne to kiss it too. Nurse it well, dearest; for no small part of my comfort and cheeriness of heart depends upon that beloved finger. If it be not well enough to bear its part in writing me a letter within a few days, do not be surprised if I send down the best surgeon in Boston to effect its speedy cure. Nevertheless, darlingest wife, restrain this good little finger, if it show any inclination to recommence its labors too soon. If your finger be pained in writing, your husband's heart ought to (and I hope would) feel every twinge.

Belovedest, I have not yet wished you a Happy New Year! And yet I have— many, many of them; as many, mine own wife, as we can enjoy together—and when we can no more enjoy them together, we shall no longer think of Happy New Years on earth, but look longingly for the New-Year's Day of eternity. What a year the last has been! Dearest, you make the same exclamation; but my heart originates it too. It has been the year of years—the year in which the flower of our life has bloomed out—the flower of our life and of our love, which we are to wear in our bosoms forever. Oh, how I love you, blessedest wife!—and how I thank God that He has made me capable to know and love you! Sometimes I feel, deep, deep down in my heart, how dearest above all things you are to me; and those are blissful moments. It is such a happiness to be conscious, at last, of something real! All my life hitherto, I have been walking in a dream, among shadows which could not be pressed to my bosom; but now, even in this dream of time, there is something that takes me out of it, and causes me to be a dreamer no more. Do you not feel, dearest, that we live above time and apart from time, even while we seem to be in the midst of time? Our affection diffuses eternity round about us.

My carefulest little wife will rejoice to know that I have been free to sit by a good fire all this bitter cold day—not but what I have a salt-ship on my hands, but she must have some ballast, before she can discharge any more salt; and ballast cannot be procured till the day after tomorrow. Are not these details very interesting? I have a mind, some day, to send my dearest a journal of all my doings and sufferings, my whole external life, from the time I awake at dawn, till I close my eyes at night. What a dry, dull history would it be! But then, apart from this, I would write another journal of my inward life throughout the self-same day—my fits of pleasant thought, and those likewise which are shadowed by passing clouds—the yearnings of my heart towards my Dove—my pictures of what we are to enjoy together. Nobody would think that the same man could live two such different lives simultaneously. But then, as I have said above, the grosser life is a dream, and the spiritual life a reality.

Very dearest, I wish you would make out a list of books that you would like to be in our library; for I intend, whenever the cash and the opportunity occur together, to buy enough to fill up our new bookcase; and I want to feel that I am buying them for both of us. When I next come to Salem, you shall read the list, and we will discuss it, volume by volume. I suppose the bookcase will hold about two hundred volumes; but you need not calculate upon making such a vast collection all at once. It shall be accomplished in small lots; and then we shall price every volume, and receive a separate pleasure from the acquisition of it.

Does it seem a great while since I left you, dearest? Truly, it does to me. These separations lengthen our earthly lives by at least nine-tenths; but then, in our brief seasons of communion, there is the essence of a thousand years. Was it Thursday that I told my Dove would be the day of my next appearance?—or Friday? "Oh, Friday, certainly," says Sophie Hawthorne. Well; it must be as naughty Sophie says.

Oh, belovedest, I want you in my arms. My head desires very much to rest on your bosom. You have given me a new feeling, blessedest wife—a sense that, strong as I may have deemed myself, I am insufficient for my own support; and that there is a tender little Dove, without whose help I cannot get through this weary world at all. God bless you, ownest wife.

Your ownest husband.

1. SPH's letter, one of the few that survives, is printed in Julian Hawthorne, *Nathaniel Hawthorne and His Wife*, 2 vols. (Boston: James R. Osgood, 1884), 1:208–9. Her allumettes (or matches) were made from twists of paper, used for lighting candles or lamps with a flame from the fireplace.

TO SOPHIA PEABODY [FRAGMENT]

[Boston, ca. 21 January 1840]

Have the Strophe and Antistrophe made up their quarrel yet?[1] There is an unaccountable fascination about that Sophie Hawthorne—whatever she chooses to do or say, whether reasonable or unreasonable, I am forced to love her the better for it. Not that I love her better than my Dove; but then it is right and natural that the Dove should awaken infinite tenderness, because she is a bird of Paradise, and has a perfect and angelic nature—so that love is her inalienable and unquestionable right. And yet my wayward heart will love this naughty Sophie Hawthorne;—yes, its affection for the Dove is doubled, because she is inseparably united with naughty Sophie. I have one love for them both, and it is infinitely intensified, because they share it together. But Sophie must remember that my Dove is the tenderest of creatures, and that it is her own appointed office to cheer and sustain her.

Dearest, I cannot yet tell how soon your husband will clasp you to his breast. Colonel Hall is not well yet, and does not feel able to come to the Custom-House every day. I wish—unless it involve too long a separation—to defer my coming until I can spend another week, or several days at least, with mine own wife. Perhaps I may come on Saturday—possibly not quite so soon. Do not, belovedest, delay to send the pictures, one moment after they are quite ready. I do yearn for them. Never were such precious pictures painted.

1. Perhaps a phonetic pun on "Sophie" and "Dove." [*CE*]

TO SOPHIA PEABODY

Boston, Feby 11th. 1840—7. P.M.

Belovedest,

Your letter, with its assurance of your present convalescence, and its promise (to which I shall hold you fast) that you will never be sick any more, cause me much joy.[1]—Dearest, George Hillard came in just as I had written the first sentence; so we will begin on a new score.

Your husband has been measuring coal all day, on board of a black little British schooner, in a dismal dock at the north end of the city. Most of the time, he paced the deck to keep himself warm; for the wind (north-east, I believe it was) blew up through the dock, as if it had been the pipe of a pair of bellows. The vessel lying deep between two wharves, there was no more delightful prospect, on the right hand and on the left, than the posts and timbers, half immersed in the water, and covered with ice, which the rising and falling of successive tides had left upon them; so that they looked like immense icicles. Across the water, however, not more than half a mile off, appeared the Bunker Hill monument;[2] and what interested me considerably more, a church-steeple, with the dial of a clock upon it, whereby I was enabled to measure the march of the weary hours. Sometimes your husband descended into the dirty little cabin of the schooner, and warmed himself by a red-hot stove, among biscuit-barrels, pots and kettles, sea-chests, and innumerable lumber of all sorts—his olfactories, meanwhile, being greatly refreshed by the odour of a pipe, which, the captain or some of his crew were smoking. But at last came the sunset, with delicate clouds, and a purple light upon the islands; and your husband blessed it, because it was the signal of his release; and so he came home to talk with his dearest wife. And now he bids her farewell, because he is tired and sleepy. God bless you, belovedest. Dream happy dreams of me to-night.

February 12th—Evening—All day long again, best wife, has your poor husband been engaged in a very black business—as black as a coal; and though his face and hands have undergone a thorough purification, he feels as if he were not altogether fit to hold communication with his white Dove. Methinks my profession is somewhat akin to that of a chimney-sweeper; but the latter has the advantage over me, because, after climbing up through the darksome flue of the chimney, he emerges into the midst of the golden air, and sings out his melodies far over the heads of the whole tribe of weary earth-plodders. My dearest, my toil to-day has been cold and dull enough; nevertheless your husband was neither cold nor dull; for he kept his heart warm and his spirit bright with thoughts of his belovedest wife. I had strong and happy yearnings for you to-day, ownest Dove— happy, even though it was such an eager longing, which I knew could not then be fulfilled, to clasp you to my bosom. And now here I am in our parlour, aweary— too tired, almost, to write—just tired enough to feel what bliss it would be could I throw myself on the sofa and rest my head on its own pillow. Blessedest, I want you to "help our sleep" to-night. That is your own idea. What a sweet one!

Well, dearest, my labors are over for the present. I cannot, however, come home just at present—three of the Measurers being now absent; but you shall see me very soon. Naughtiest, why do you say that you have scarcely seen your husband, this winter? Have there not, to say nothing of shorter visits, been two eternities of more than a week each, which were full of blessings for us? My Dove has quite forgotten these. Ah, well! If visits of a week long be not worth remembering, I shall alter my purpose of coming to Salem for another like space;—otherwise I might possibly have been there, by Saturday night, at furthest. Dear me, how sleepy I am! I can hardly write, as you will discover by the blottings and scratchings. So good-bye now, darlingest:—and I will finish in the freshness of the morning.

February 13th.—Past 8. A.M. Belovedest, how very soon this letter will be in your hands. It brings us much closer together, when the written words of one of us can come to the heart of the other, in the very same day that they flowed from the heart of the writer. I mean to come home to our parlour early to-day; so, when you receive this letter, you can imagine me there, sitting in front of the Isola.[3] I have this moment interrupted myself to go and look at that precious production. How I wish that naughty Sophie Hawthorne could be induced to turn her face towards me! Nevertheless, the figure is her veritable self, and so would the face be, only that she deems it too beauteous to be thrown away on her husband's gaze. I have not dared to kiss her yet. Will she abide it?

My dearest, do not expect me very fervently till I come. I am glad you were so careful of your inestimable eyes as not to write to me yesterday. Mrs. Hillard says that Elizabeth made her a call. Good-bye. I am very well to day, and unspeakably happy in the thought that I have a dearest little wife, who loves me pretty well. God bless her.

1. SPH had a history of illness, often forcing her to retire to her room for extended periods of time.

2. The monument at Bunker Hill in Charlestown, overlooking Boston, commemorating the battle fought there on 16 June 1775, would be dedicated on 17 June 1843.

3. "Isola," SPH's painting of Lake Como, Italy, shows a lone female figure in the foreground, with her back to the viewer.

TO SOPHIA PEABODY

Boston, April 15th. 1840 Afternoon.

Belovedest—since writing this word, I have made a considerable pause; for, dearest, my mind has no activity to-day. I would fain sit still, and let thoughts, feelings, and images of thee, pass before me and through me, without my putting them into words, or taking any other trouble about the matter. It must be that thou dost not especially and exceedingly need a letter from me; else I should feel an impulse and necessity to write. I do wish, most beloved wife, that there were some other method of communing with thee at a distance; for really this is not a natural one to thy husband. In truth, I never use words, either with the tongue or pen, when I can possibly express myself in any other way; and how much, dearest, may be expressed without the utterance of a word! Is there not a volume in [*excision*] many of our glances?—even in a pressure of the hand? And when I write to thee, I do but painfully endeavor to shadow into words what has already been expressed in those realities. In heaven, I am very sure, there will be no occasion for words;—our minds will enter into each other, and silently possess themselves of their mutual riches. Even in this world, I think, such a process is not altogether impossible—we ourselves have experienced it—but words come like an earthy wall betwixt us. Then our minds are compelled to stand apart, and make signals of our meaning, instead of rushing into one another, and holding converse in an infinite and eternal language. Oh, dearest, have not the moments of our oneness been those in which we were most silent? It is our instinct to be silent then, because words could not adequately express the perfect concord of our hearts, and therefore would infringe upon it. Well, ownest, good bye till tomorrow; when perhaps thy husband will feel a necessity to use even such a wretched medium as words, to tell thee how he loves thee. No words can tell it now.

April 16th. Afternoon—Most dear wife, never was thy husband gladder to receive a letter from thee than to-day. And so thou didst perceive that I was rather out of spirits on Monday. Foolish and faithless husband that I was, I supposed that thou wouldst not take any notice of it; but the simple fact was, that I did not feel quite so well as usual; and said nothing about it to thee, because I knew thou wouldst desire me to put off my departure, which (for such a trifle) I felt it not right to do—and likewise, because my Dove would have been naughty, and so perhaps have made herself ten times as ill as her husband. Dearest, I am quite well now—only very hungry; for I have thought fit to eat very little for two days past; and I think starvation is a remedy for almost all physical evils. You will love

Colonel Hall, when I tell you that he has not let me do a [*excision verso*] return; and even to-day he has sent me home to my room, although I assured him that I was perfectly able to work. Now, dearest, if thou givest thyself any trouble and torment about this past indisposition of mine, I shall never dare to tell thee about my future incommodities; but if I were sure thou wouldst estimate them at no more than they are worth, thou shouldst know them all, even to the slightest prick of my finger. It is my impulse to complain to thee in all griefs, great and small; and I will not check that impulse, if thou wilt sympathize reasonably, as well as most lovingly. And now, ownest wife, believe that thy husband is well;—better, I fear, than thou, who art tired to death, and hast even had the headache. Naughtiest, dost thou think that all the busts in the world, and all the medallions and other forms of sculpture, would be worth creating, at the expence of such weariness and headache to thee. I would rather that thy art should be annihilated, than that thou shouldst always pay this price for its exercise. But perhaps, when thou hast my bosom to repose upon, thou wilt no longer feel such overwhelming weariness. I am given thee to repose upon, that so my most tender and sensitivest little Dove may be able to do great works.

And dearest, I do by no means undervalue thy works, though I cannot estimate all thou hast ever done at the price of a single throb of anguish to thy belovedest head. But thou hast achieved mighty things. Thou hast called up a face which was hidden in the grave—hast re-created it, after it was resolved to dust—and so hast snatched from Death his victory.[1] I wonder at thee, my beloved. Thou art a miracle thyself, and workest miracles. I could not have believed it possible to do what thou hast done, to restore the lineaments of the dead so perfectly that even she who loved him so well can require nothing more;[2]—and this too, when thou hadst hardly known his living face.[3] Thou couldst not have done it, unless God had helped thee. This surely was inspiration, and of the holiest kind, and for one of the holiest purposes.

Dearest, I shall long to see thee exceedingly next Saturday; but having been absent from duty for two or three days past it will not be right for me to ask any more time so soon. Dost thou think it would?

How naughty was thy husband to waste the first page of this letter in declaiming against this blessed art of writing! I do not see how I could live without it;— thy letters are my heart's food; and oftentimes my heart absolutely insists upon pouring itself out on paper, for thy perusal. In truth, if the heart could do all the work, I should probably write to thee the whole time of my absence; but thou knowest that the cooperation of the hand and head are indispensable; and they, not being able to comprehend the infinite necessity of the heart's finding an utterance, are sometimes sluggish.

April 17th.—Before breakfast.—Ownest, I am perfectly well this morning, and want to give thee ten thousand kisses. Dost thou love me? Dearest, expect not another letter till Tuesday. Is thy weariness quite gone?

Thine ownest, ownest husband.

1. Emerson's brother Charles Chauncy Emerson died of tuberculosis in 1836. SPH modeled a clay bas-relief medallion of him, reprinted as the frontispiece in *Studies in the American Renaissance 1984*, ed. Joel Myerson (Charlottesville: University Press of Virginia, 1984).
2. Charles's fiancé, Elizabeth Hoar, never married and was treated by the Emerson family as a daughter. She would be a good friend of SPH's when the Hawthornes lived in Concord.
3. SPH saw Charles Emerson only once and worked from a pencil sketch she had made at that time.

TO HORACE CONOLLY [FRAGMENT?]

[Boston] May, 1840

The day after the great storm in March, I went with David Roberts to make a call on the Duchess at the old house in Turner Street, to learn how she weathered the gale. I had a more than ordinary pleasant visit, and among other things, in speaking of the old house, she said it has had in the history of its changes and alterations Seven Gables. The expression was new and struck me very forcibly; I think I shall make something of it.[1] I expressed a wish to go all over the house; she assented and I repaired to the Attic, and there was no corner or dark hole I did not peep into. I could readily make out five gables, and on returning to the parlour, I inquired where the two remaining gables were placed. The information I received was that the remaining gables were on the north side, and that when Col. Turner became the owner of the house, he removed the 'lean to' on which were the missing gables, and made amends by placing three gables on the L or addition which he made on the south side of the house; the mark of beams still remains in the studding to show precisely where they were. On my return after the exploration I had made of the old structure, the Duchess said to me, "Why don't you write something?"

"I have no subject to write about."

"Oh, there are subjects enough,—write about that old chair in the room; it is an old Puritan relict and you can make a biographical sketch of each old Puritan who became in succession the owner of the chair."

It was a good suggestion and I have made use of it under the name "Grandfather's Chair," finished and ready for the printer.[2] It will be a child's book, and I have nearly completed it, as you may see when you come from Philadelphia.

1. This is the apparent genesis of *The House of the Seven Gables* (1851). [*CE*]

2. Elizabeth Palmer Peabody co-published (on 3 December 1840) *Grandfather's Chair: A History for Youth*.

TO JAMES KIRKE PAULDING

Salem (Mass) May 31st, 1840.

Sir,[1]

I have been requested to appeal to you in behalf of a young man, James Cook by name, who is now serving as a common seaman in the navy. Mr. Cook had been one of the publishers of the Salem Advertiser (the leading Democratic paper in Essex county) from the time of its establishment till its transfer to other hands—a space of four or five years. My own acquaintance with him was but slight; but I know him to have been a man of education and ability, and much respected for his exemplary conduct. Some six or eight months since, he disappeared from home; and as his friends could gain no intelligence of him, he was generally supposed to have committed suicide in a fit of insanity—an idea which was strengthened by the singularity of his deportment, when last seen. Nothing had since been heard of him until very recently, when a letter was received by his parents, informing them of his enlistment in the navy, and that he is now at the Norfolk station, on board of the ship Delaware. There can be no doubt that he took this step under the influence of insanity, both because his previous demeanor indicated mental derangement, and because no reasonable motive is discoverable or imaginable; inasmuch as he thereby sacrificed very fair prospects, and gave up all the advantages of prosperous circumstances and an unstained character. If, on consideration of the facts, you should judge this a case where the rigid rule of the service may be relaxed, you would comfort the hearts of his aged parents, who are awaiting your decision with anxious hopes. I know not whether it be worth while to mention—yet perhaps I may say it to Mr. Paulding, if not to the Secretary of the Navy—that there is a young lady to whom Cook was engaged to be married, and who has kept both her faith and her hopes throughout the period of his absence.

It is with reluctance, Sir, that I have taken this liberty, as being unknown to you personally, nor perhaps by reputation; and yet, apart from your official character, I cannot but feel it one of my birth-rights to address Mr. Paulding, who has made himself the admired and familiar friend of every reader in the land.

Respectfully,
Your obedient serv
Nathaniel Hawthorne.

Hon. J. K. Paulding,
Secy of the Navy.

1. The author James Kirke Paulding served as secretary of the navy from 1838 to 1841.

TO SOPHIA PEABODY

Salem, October 4th 1840—$^1/_2$ past 10. A.M.

Mine ownest,

Here sits thy husband in his old accustomed chamber, where he used to sit in years gone by, before his soul became acquainted with thine. Here I have written many tales—many that have been burned to ashes—many that doubtless deserved the same fate. This deserves to be called a haunted chamber; for thousands upon thousands of visions have appeared to me in it; and some few of them have become visible to the world. If ever I should have a biographer, he ought to make great mention of this chamber in my memoirs, because so much of my lonely youth was wasted here; and here my mind and character were formed; and here I have been glad and hopeful, and here I have been despondent; and here I sat a long, long time, waiting patiently for the world to know me, and sometimes wondering why it did not know me sooner, or whether it would ever know me at all—at least, till I were in my grave. And sometimes (for I had no wife then to keep my heart warm) it seemed as if I were already in the grave, with only life enough to be chilled and benumbed. But oftener I was happy—at least, as happy as I then knew how to be, or was aware of the possibility of being. By and bye, the world found me out in my lonely chamber, and called me forth—not, indeed, with a loud roar of acclamation, but rather with a still, small voice;[1] and forth I went, but found nothing in the world that I thought preferable to my old solitude, till at length a certain Dove was revealed to me, in the shadow of a seclusion as deep as my own had been. And I drew nearer and nearer to the Dove, and opened my bosom to her, and she flitted into it, and closed her wings there—and there she nestles now and forever, keeping my heart warm, and renewing my life with her own. So now I begin to understand why I was imprisoned so many years in this lonely chamber, and why I could never break through the viewless bolts and bars; for if I had sooner made my escape into the world, I should have grown hard and rough, and been covered with earthly dust, and my heart would have become callous by rude encounters with the multitude; so that I should have been all unfit to shelter a heavenly Dove in my arms. But living in solitude till the fulness of time was come, I still kept the dew of my youth and the freshness of my heart, and had these to offer to my Dove.

Well, dearest, I had no notion what I was going to write, when I began; and indeed I doubted whether I should write anything at all; for after such intimate communion as that of our last blissful evening, it seems as if a sheet of paper could only be a veil betwixt us. Ownest, in the times that I have been speaking of, I used to think that I could imagine all passions, all feelings, all states of the heart and mind; but how little did I know what it is to be mingled with another's being! Thou only hast taught me that I have a heart—thou only hast thrown a light deep downward, and upward, into my soul. Thou only hast revealed me to myself; for without thy aid, my best knowledge of myself would have been merely to know my own shadow—to watch it flickering on the wall, and mistake its fantasies for my own real actions. Indeed, we are but shadows—we are not endowed with real life, and all that seems most real about us is but the thinnest substance of a dream—till the heart is touched. That touch creates us—then we begin to be—thereby we are beings of reality, and inheritors of eternity. Now, dearest, dost thou comprehend what thou hast done for me? And is it not a somewhat fearful thought, that a few slight circumstances might have prevented us from meeting, and then I should have returned to my solitude, sooner or later (probably now, when I have thrown down my burthen of coal and salt) and never should have been created at all! But this is an idle speculation. If the whole world had stood between us, we must have met—if we had been born in different ages, we could not have been sundered.

Belovedest, how dost thou do? If I mistake not, it was a southern rain yesterday, and, next to the sunshine of Paradise, *that* seems to be thy element. [*excision*]

1. I Kings 19:11.

TO SOPHIA PEABODY

Oak Hill,[1] April 13th. 1841

Ownest love,

Here is thy poor husband in a polar Paradise! I know not how to interpret this
aspect of Nature—whether it be of good or evil omen to our enterprise. But I
reflect that the Plymouth pilgrims arrived in the midst of storm and stept ashore
upon mountain snow-drifts; and nevertheless they prospered, and became a great
people—and doubtless it will be the same with us. I laud my stars, however, that
thou wilt not have thy first impressions of our future home from such a day as this.
Thou wouldst shiver all thy life afterwards, and never realize that there could be
bright skies, and green hills and meadows, and trees heavy with foliage, where now
the whole scene is a great snow-bank, and the sky full of snow likewise. Through
faith, I persist in believing that spring and summer will come in their due season;
but the unregenerated man shivers within me, and suggests a doubt whether I may
not have wandered within the precincts of the Arctic circle, and chosen my heritage
among everlasting snows. Dearest, provide thyself with a good stock of furs; and if
thou canst obtain the skin of a polar bear, thou wilt find it a very suitable summer
dress for this region. Thou must not hope ever to walk abroad, except upon snow-
shoes, nor to find any warmth, save in thy husband's heart.

Belovedest, I have not yet taken my first lesson in agriculture, as thou mayst well
suppose—except that I went to see our cows foddered, yesterday afternoon. We have
eight of our own; and the number is now increased by a transcendental heifer,
belonging to Miss Margaret Fuller. She is very fractious, I believe, and apt to kick over
the milk pail. Thou knowest best, whether, in these traits of character, she resembles
her mistress. Thy husband intends to convert himself into a milk-maid, this evening;
but I pray heaven that Mr. Ripley may be moved to assign him the kindliest cow in
the herd—otherwise he will perform his duty with fear and trembling.

Ownest wife, I like my brethren in affliction very well; and couldst thou see us sitting round our table, at meal-times, before the great kitchen-fire, thou wouldst call it a cheerful sight. Mrs. Barker is a most comfortable woman to behold; she looks as if her ample person were stuffed full of tenderness—indeed, as if she were all one great, kind heart. Wert thou but here, I should ask for nothing more—not even for sunshine and summer weather; for thou wouldst be both, to thy husband. And how is that cough of thine, my belovedest? Hast thou thought of me, in my perils and wanderings? Thou must not think how I longed for thee, when I crept into my cold bed last night,—my bosom remembered thee,—and refused to be comforted without thy caresses. I trust that thou dost muse upon me with hope and joy, not with repining. Think that I am gone before, to prepare a home for my Dove, and will return for her, all in good time.

Thy husband has the best chamber in the house, I believe; and though not quite so good as the apartment I have left, it will do very well. I have hung up thy two pictures; and they give me a glimpse of summer and of thee. The vase I intended to have brought in my arms, but could not very conveniently do it yesterday; so that it still remains at Mrs. Hillards, together with my carpet. I shall bring them the next opportunity.

Now farewell, for the present, most beloved. I have been writing this in my chamber; but the fire is getting low, and the house is old and cold; so that the warmth of my whole person has retreated to my heart, which burns with love for thee. I must run down to the kitchen or parlor hearth, where thy image shall sit beside me—yea be pressed to my breast. At bed-time, thou shalt have a few lines more. Now I think of it, dearest, wilt thou give Mrs. Ripley a copy of Grandfather's Chair and Liberty Tree;[2] she wants them for some boys here. I have several vols of Famous Old People.

April 14th. 10. A.M. Sweetest, I did not milk the cows last night, because Mr. Ripley was afraid to trust them to my hands, or me to their horns—I know not which. But this morning, I have done wonders. Before breakfast, I went out to the barn, and began to chop hay for the cattle; and with such "righteous vehemence" (as Mr. Ripley says) did I labor, that, in the space of ten minutes, I broke the machine. Then I brought wood and replenished the fires; and finally sat down to breakfast and ate up a huge mound of buckwheat cakes. After breakfast, Mr. Ripley put a four-pronged instrument into my hands, which he gave me to understand was called a pitch-fork; and he and Mr. Farley being armed with similar weapons, we all three commenced a gallant attack upon a heap of manure. This affair being concluded, and thy husband having purified himself, he sits down to finish this letter to his most beloved wife. Dearest, I will never consent that thou come within half a mile of me, after such an encounter as that of this morning.

Pray Heaven that this letter retain none of the fragrance with which the writer was imbued. As for thy husband himself, he is peculiarly partial to the odor; but that whimsical little nose of thine might chance to quarrel with it.

Belovedest, Miss Fuller's cow hooks the other cows, and has made herself ruler of the herd, and behaves in a very tyrannical manner. Sweetest, I know not when I shall see thee; but I trust it will not be longer than till the end of next week. I love thee! I love thee! I would thou wert with me; for then would my labor be joyful—and even now, it is not sorrowful. Dearest, I shall make an excellent husbandman. I feel the original Adam reviving within me.

1. A location in West Roxbury, near the site of Brook Farm, where NH is actually writing. [*CE*]

2. Elizabeth Palmer Peabody published both *Famous Old People: Being the Second Epoch of Grandfather's Chair* (on 18 January 1841) and *Liberty Tree: With the Last Words of Grandfather's Chair* (on March 1841).

TO SOPHIA PEABODY

Oak Hill, April 6th. ¹/₂ past 6. A.M. [1841]

Most beloved, I have a few moments to spare before breakfast; and perhaps thou wilt let me spend them in talking to thee. Thy two letters blessed me yesterday, having been brought by some private messenger of Mrs. Ripley's. Very joyful was I to hear from my Dove, and my heart gave a mighty heave and swell as thou hast sometimes felt it do while thou was resting upon it. That cough of thine—I do wish it would take its departure; for I cannot bear to think of thy tender little frame being shaken with it all night long. Thou dost need to be kissed, little Dove, every hour of thy life—that would be a sovereign remedy.

Dearest, since I last wrote thee, there has been an addition to our community of four gentlemen in sables, who promise to be among our most useful and respectable members. They arrived yesterday, about noon. Mr. Ripley had proposed to them to join us, no longer ago than that very morning. I had some conversation with them in the afternoon, and was glad to hear them express much satisfaction with their new abode, and all the arrangements. They do not appear to be very communicative, however—or perhaps it may be merely an external reserve, like that of thy husband, to shield their delicacy. Several of their prominent characteristics, as well as their black attire, lead me to believe that they are members of the clerical profession; but I have not yet ascertained, from their own lips, what has been the nature of their past lives. I trust to have much pleasure in their society, and, sooner or later, that we shall all of us derive great strength from our intercourse with them. I cannot too highly applaud the readiness with which these four gentlemen in black have thrown aside all the fopperies and flummeries, which have their origin in a false state of society. When I last saw them, they looked as heroically regardless of the stains and soils incident to our profession, as thy husband did when he emerged from the gold mine.[1]

Ownest wife, thy husband has milked a cow!!!

Belovedest, the herd have rebelled against the usurpation of Miss Fuller's cow; and whenever they are turned out of the barn, she is compelled to take refuge under our protection. So much did she impede thy husband's labors, by keeping close to him, that he found it necessary to give her two or three gentle pats with a shovel; but still she preferred to trust herself to my tender mercies, rather than venture among the horns of the herd. She is not an amiable cow; but she has a very intelligent face, and seems to be of a reflective cast of character. I doubt not that she will soon perceive the expediency of being on good terms with the rest of the sisterhood.

I have not yet been twenty yards from our house and barn; but I begin to perceive that this is a beautiful place. The scenery is of a mild and placid character, with nothing bold in its character; but I think its beauties will grow upon us, and make us love it the more, the longer we live here. There is a brook, so near the house that we shall be able to hear its ripple, in the summer evenings; and whenever we lie awake in the summer nights; but, for agricultural purposes, it has been made to flow in a straight and rectangular fashion, which does it infinite damage, as a picturesque object.

Naughtiest, it was a moment or two before I could think whom thou didst mean by Mr. Dismal View.[2] Why, he is one of the best of the brotherhood, so far as cheerfulness goes; for, if he do not laugh himself, he makes the rest of us laugh continually. He is the quaintest and queerest personage thou didst ever see—full of dry jokes, the humor of which is so incorporated with the strange twistifications of his physiognomy, that his sayings ought to be written down, accompanied with illustrations by Cruikshank.[3] Then he keeps quoting innumerable scraps of Latin, and makes classical allusions, while we are turning over the gold mine; and the contrast between the nature of his employment and the character of his thoughts is irresistibly ludicrous.

Sweetest, I have written this epistle in the parlor, while Farmer Ripley, and Farmer Farley, and Farmer Dismal View, are talking about their agricultural concerns, around the fire. So thou wilt not wonder if it is not a classical piece of composition, either in point of thought or expression. I shall have just time, before breakfast is ready—the boy has just come to call us now—but still I will tell thee that I love thee infinitely; and that I long for thee unspeakably, but yet with a happy longing. The rest of them have gone into the breakfast room; [*excision*]

1. "The gold mine" was George Ripley's name for the manure pile. [*CE*]
2. Probably Warren Burton, a Unitarian clergyman, a follower of the mystic Emmanuel Swedenborg, a reformer, and the author of a number of popular books, most notably *The District School As It Was* (1838).
3. George Cruikshank, English illustrator and caricaturist.

TO SOPHIA PEABODY

[Brook Farm] May 1st [1841]

Every day of my life makes me feel more and more how seldom a fact is accurately stated; how, almost invariably, when a story has passed through the mind of a third person, it becomes, so far as regards the impression that it makes in further repetitions, little better than a falsehood, and this, too, though the narrator be the most truth-seeking person in existence. How marvellous the tendency is! . . . Is truth a fantasy which we are to pursue forever and never grasp? . . .

My cold has almost entirely departed. Were it a sunny day, I should consider myself quite fit for labor out of doors; but as the ground is so damp, and the atmosphere so chill, and the sky so sullen, I intend to keep myself on the sick-list this one day longer, more especially as I wish to read Carlyle on Heroes. . . .[1]

There has been but one flower found in this vicinity,—and that was an anemone, a poor, pale, shivering little flower, that had crept under a stone wall for shelter. Mr Farley found it, while taking a walk with me. . . .

This is May-day! Alas, what a difference between the ideal and the real!

1. The American edition of *On Heroes, Hero-Worship, & the Heroic in History,* by the Scottish writer Thomas Carlyle, was published in April 1841.

TO LOUISA HAWTHORNE

Brook Farm, West Roxbury,

May 3d 1841

As the weather precludes all possibility of ploughing, hoeing, sowing, and other such operations, I bethink me that you may have no objection to hear something of my whereabout and whatabout. You are to know then, that I took up my abode here on the 12th ultimo, in the midst of a snowstorm, which kept us all idle for a day or two. At the first glimpse of fair weather, Mr. Ripley summoned us into the cow-yard, and introduced me to an instrument with four prongs, commonly called a dung-fork. With this tool, I have already assisted to load twenty or thirty carts of manure, and shall take part in loading nearly three hundred more. Besides, I have planted potatoes and pease, cut straw and hay for the cattle, and done various other mighty works. This very morning, I milked three cows; and I milk, two or three every night and morning. The weather has been so unfavorable, that we have worked comparatively little in the fields; but, nevertheless, I have gained strength wonderfully—grown quite a giant, in fact—and can do a day's work without the slightest inconvenience. In short, I am transformed into a complete farmer.

This is one of the most beautiful places I ever saw in my life, and as secluded as if it were a hundred miles from any city or village. There are woods, in which we can ramble all day, without meeting anybody, or scarcely seeing a house. Our house stands apart from the main road; so that we are not troubled even with passengers looking at us. Once in a while, we have a transcendental visitor, such as Mr. Alcott; but, generally, we pass whole days without seeing a single face, save those of the brethren. At this present time, our effective force consists of Mr. Ripley, Mr. Farley, (a farmer from the far west,) Rev. Warren Burton (author of various celebrated works) three young men and boys, who are under Mr. Ripley's care, and William Allen, his hired man, who has the chief direction of our agricultural labors. In the female part of the establishment there is Mrs Ripley, and two women folks. The whole fraternity eat together; and such a delectable way of life has never been seen on earth, since the days of the early Christians. We get up at half-past four, breakfast at half past six, dine at half past twelve, and go to bed at nine.

The thin frock, which you made for me, is considered a most splendid article; and I should not wonder if it were to become the summer uniform of the community. I have a thick frock, likewise; but it is rather deficient in grace, though extremely warm and comfortable. I wear a tremendous pair of cow-hide boots, with soles two inches thick. Of course, when I come to see you, I shall wear my farmer's dress.

We shall be very much occupied during most of this month, ploughing and planting; so that I doubt whether you will see me for two or three weeks. You have the portrait by this time, I suppose; so you can very well dispense with the original.[1] When you write to me (which I beg you will do soon) direct your letter to West Roxbury, as there are two Post Offices in the town. I would write more; but William Allen is going to the village, and must have this letter; so good bye.

Nath. Hawthorne,

Ploughman.

1. This oil portrait of NH by Charles Osgood is reproduced in Rita K. Gollin, *Portraits of Nathaniel Hawthorne* (DeKalb: Northern Illinois University Press, 1983), 21, and is now at the Peabody Essex Museum in Salem.

TO SOPHIA PEABODY

Brook Farm, June 1st. 1841—nearly 6 A.M.

Very dearest,

I have been too busy to write thee a long letter by this opportunity; for I think this present life of mine gives me an antipathy to pen and ink, even more than my Custom House experience did. I could not live without the idea of thee, nor without spiritual communion with thee; but, in the midst of toil, or after a hard day's work in the gold mine, my soul obstinately refuses to be poured out on paper. That abominable gold mine! Thank God, we anticipate getting rid of its treasurers, in the course of two or three days. Of all hateful places, that is the worst; and I shall never comfort myself for having spent so many days of blessed sunshine there. It is my opinion, dearest, that a man's soul may be buried and perish under a dung-heap or in a furrow of the field, just as well as under a pile of money. Well; that giant, Mr. George Bradford, will probably be here to-day; so that there will be no danger of thy husband being under the necessity of laboring more than he likes, hereafter. Meantime, my health is perfect, and my spirits buoyant, even in the gold mine.

And how art thou belovedest? Two or three centuries have passed since I saw thee; and then thou wast pale and languid. Thou didst comfort me in that little note of thine; but still I cannot help longing to be informed of thy present welfare. Thou art not a prudent little Dove, and writ naughty to come on such a day as thou didst; and it seems to me that Mrs. Ripley does not know how to take care of thee at all. Art thou quite well now.

Dearest wife, I intend to come and see thee either on Thursday or Friday— perhaps my visit may be deferred till Saturday, if the gold mine should hold out so long. I yearn for thee unspeakably. Good bye now; for the breakfast horn has sounded, sometime since. God bless thee, ownest.

Thy lovingest husband.

TO GEORGE S. HILLARD

Brook Farm, July 16th. 1841.

Dear Hillard,

I have not written that infernal story.[1] The thought of it has tormented me ever since I came here, and has deprived me of all the comfort I might otherwise have had, in my few moments of leisure. Thank God, it is now too late—so I disburthen my mind of it, now and forever.

You cannot think how exceedingly I regret the necessity of disappointing you; but what could be done? An engagement to write a story must in its nature be conditional; because stories grow like vegetables, and are not manufactured, like a pine table. My former stories all sprung up of their own accord, out of a quiet life. Now, I have no quiet at all; for when my outward man is at rest—which is seldom, and for short intervals—my mind is bothered with a sort of dull excitement, which makes it impossible to think continuously of any subject. You cannot make a silk purse out of a sow's ear; nor must you expect pretty stories from a man who feeds pigs.

My hands are covered with a new crop of blisters—the effect of raking hay; so excuse this scrawl.

Yours truly,
Nath. Hawthorne

1. NH had promised a contribution to the 1842 *Token,* which Hillard was editing.

TO DAVID MACK

Boston, July 18th, 1841.

My dear Sir,[1]

Your letter has this moment been put into my hands. I truly thank you for it, and wish to lose no time in correcting some misapprehensions which have been caused by your judging of my feelings through the medium of third persons—and partly from my brief and imperfect communications to you, last Sunday.

I have never felt that I was called upon by *Mr. Ripley* to devote so much of my time to manual labor, as has been done since my residence at Brook Farm; nor do I believe that others have felt constraint of that kind, from him personally. We have never looked upon him as a master, or an employer, but as a fellow laborer on the same terms as ourselves, with no more right to bid us perform any one act of labor, than we have to bid him. Our constraint has been merely that of circumstances, which were as much beyond his control as our own; and there was no way of escaping this constraint, except by leaving the farm at once; and, this step none of us were prepared to take, because (though attributing less importance to the success of this immediate enterprise than Mr. Ripley does) we still felt that its failure would be very inauspicious to the prospects of the community. For my own part, there are private and personal motives which, without the influence of those shared by us all, would still make me wish to bear all the drudgery of this one summer's labor, were it much more onerous than I have found it. It is true that I not infrequently regret that the summer is passing with so little enjoyment of nature and my own thoughts, and with the sacrifice of some objects that I had hoped to accomplish. Such were the regrets to which I alluded, last Sunday; but Mr. Ripley cannot be held responsible for the disagreeable circumstances which cause them.

I recollect speaking very despondingly, or perhaps despairingly, of the prospects of the institution. My views in this respect vary somewhat with the state of my spirits; but I confess that, of late, my hopes are never very sanguine. I form my judgment, however, not from anything that has passed within the precincts of Brook Farm, but from external circumstances—from the improbability that adequate funds will be raised, or that any feasible plan can be suggested, for proceeding without a very considerable capital. I likewise perceive that there would be some very knotty points to be discussed, even had we capital enough to buy an estate. These considerations have somewhat lessened the heartiness and cheerfulness with which I formerly went forth to the fields, and perhaps have interposed a medium of misunderstanding between Mr. Ripley and us all. His zeal will not permit him to doubt of eventual success; and he perceives, or imagines, a more intimate connection between our present farming operations and our ultimate enterprise, than is visible to my perceptions. But, as I said before, the two things are sufficiently connected, to make me desirous of giving my best efforts to the promotion of the former.

You will see, I think, from what I have now stated, that there was no pressing necessity for me, or my fellow laborers, to dishearten Mr. Ripley, by expressing dissatisfaction with our present mode of life. It is our wish to give his experiment a full and fair trial; and if his many hopes are to be frustrated, we should be loth to give him reason to attribute the failure to lack of energy and perseverance in his associates. Nevertheless, we did, several days since (he and myself, I mean) have a conversation on the subject; and he is now fully possessed of my feelings, in respect to personal labor.

Probably you have not yet heard of Mr. Burton's departure from Brook Farm. It occurred the night before last. It is an unfortunate event, in all its aspects. You will probably learn some of the circumstances which led to it, from Mr. Ripley, who, I doubt not, will render all justice to Mr. Burton, so far as his position may enable him to form a correct judgment. It is a subject not easily to be discussed in a letter; but I hope, at some future time, to communicate my view of the matter *viva voce.*[2]

I have written this letter in great haste; so that, very probably, it may fail to satisfy your mind on the subjects involved. I shall be happy, whenever an opportunity occurs, to talk at large, and with all frankness, about the interests which we have in common. This, however, cannot be done for a week or two, as I am about to accompany Mr. Farley to the seashore, at his own and Mr. Ripley's request. His health is such, that this step is deemed essential. [*excision*]

---

1. David Mack, a graduate of Yale University who had studied law before becoming a tutor, signed the articles of agreement for Brook Farm on 29 September 1841 but never became a member. He joined a community in Northampton, Massachusetts, in 1842.

2. *viva voce*, orally.

TO LOUISA HAWTHORNE

West Roxbury, Aug 3d. 1841

Dear Louze,

I have been to Monument Point, about seven miles from Plymouth, for nearly a fortnight past, fishing and otherwise enjoying myself after the arduous labors of the summer. I got back hither only this forenoon.

Furthermore, I have made an engagement with J. Munroe & Co. to write and edit a series of juvenile books, partly original and partly English books, to be adapted to our market. The first number is to be a new edition of Grandfather's Chair.[1] We expect to make a great deal of money. I wish Elizabeth would write a book for the series. She surely knows as much about children as I do, and ought to succeed as well. I do hope she will think of a subject—whether historical, scientific, moral, religious, or fanciful—and set to work. It will be a good amusement to her, and profitable to us all.

After the first of September, I shall cease laboring for my board, and begin to write.[2] I doubt whether you see me before that period; but I intend then to pay you a visit of a week or two. By the bye, you seem quite to have forgotten my existence. Why do you never write?

It is nearly milking time. Good bye.
Nath. Hawthorne.

Cannot your mother write a book?

1. *Biographical Stories for Children* was published on 12 April 1842, but by Tappan and Dennet, not Munroe.
2. NH would leave formal membership in the Brook Farm community. During his later residence there, he would become a paying boarder (at $4.00 per week) with no obligation to work or teach. [*CE*]

TO SOPHIA PEABODY

Salem, September 14th. 1841—A.M.

Ownest beloved, I know not whether thou dost expect a letter from thy husband; but I have a comfortable faith that it will not be altogether unwelcome; so I
boldly sit down to scribble. I love thee transcendantly; and nothing makes me
more sensible of the fact, than that I write thee voluntary letters, without any
external necessity. It is as if intense love should make a dumb man speak. (Alas! I
hear a knocking at the door, and suspect that some untimely person is about to
call me away from my Dove.)

Afternoon—Dearest, it was even as I suspected. How sad it is, that we cannot
be sure of one moment's uninterrupted communication, even when we are talking together in that same old chamber, where I have spent so many quiet years!
Well; thou must be content to lose some very sweet outpourings wherewith my
heart would probably have covered the first, and perhaps the second, page of this
sheet. The amount of all would have been, that I am somewhat partial to thee—
and thou hast a suspicion of that fact, already.

Belovedest, Master Cheever is a very good subject for a sketch[1]—especially if
thou doest portray him in the very act of executing judgment on an evil-doer. The
little urchin may be laid across his knee, and his arms and legs (and whole person,
indeed) should be flying all abroad, in an agony of nervous excitement and corporeal smart. The Master, on the other hand, must be calm, rigid, without anger
or pity, the very personification of that immitigable law, whereby suffering follows
sin. Meantime, the lion's head should have a sort of sly twist of one side of its
mouth, and wink of one eye, in order to give the impression, that, after all, the
crime and the punishment are neither of them the most serious things in the
world. I would draw this sketch myself, if I had but the use of thy magic fingers.
Why dost thou—being one and the same person with thy husband—unjustly
keep those delicate little instruments (thy fingers, to wit) all to thyself?

Then, dearest, the Acadians will do very well for the second sketch. Wilt thou
represent them as just landing on the wharf?—or as presenting themselves before
Governor Shirley, seated in the great chair?[2] Another subject (if this do not altogether suit thee) might be old Cotton Mather, venerable in a three cornered hat,
and other antique attire, walking the streets of Boston, and lifting up his hands to
bless the people, while they all revile him.[3] An old dame should be seen flinging
water or emptying some vials of medicine on his head, from the latticed window
of an old-fashioned house; and all around must be tokens of pestilence and

mourning—as a coffin borne along, a woman or children weeping on a door-step. Canst thou paint the tolling of the Old South bell?

If thou likest not this subject, thou canst take the military council, holden at Boston by the Earl of Loudoun, and other captains and governors—his lordship in the great chair, an old-fashioned military figure, with a star on his breast.[4] Some of Louis XV's commanders will give thee the costume. On the table and scattered about the room must be symbols of warfare, swords, pistols, plumed hats, a drum, trumpet, and rolled up banner, in one heap. It were not amiss that thou introduce the armed figure of an Indian Chief, as taking part in the council—or standing apart from the English, erect and stern.

Now for Liberty-tree—there is an engraving of that famous vegetable in Snow's History of Boston; but thou wilt draw a better one out of thine own head.[5] If thou dost represent it, I see not what scene can be beneath it, save poor Mr. Oliver taking the oath.[6] Thou must represent him with a bag wig, ruffled sleeves, embroidered coat, and all such ornaments, because he is the representative of aristocracy and artificial system. The people may be as rough and wild as thy sweetest fancy can make them;—nevertheless, there must be one or two grave, puritanical figures in the midst. Such an one might sit in the great chair, and be an emblem of that stern, considerate spirit, which brought about the revolution. But thou wilt find this a hard subject.

But what a dolt is thy husband, thus to obtrude his counsel in the place of thine own inspiration! Belovedest, I want room to tell thee how I love thee. Thou must not expect me till Saturday afternoon. I yearn infinitely to see thee. Heaven bless thee forever and forever.

Thine ownest.

1. Here and below NH refers to historical personages who appear in *Famous Old People*. For the classicist and schoolmaster Ezekial Cheever, see *True Stories from History and Biography, CE,* 6:84.

2. For Governor William Shirley, see *True Stories,* 6:127–28.

3. For the famous Puritan divine Cotton Mather, see *True Stories, CE,* 6:103–4.

4. For the Earl of Loudon's council, see *True Stories, CE,* 6:136–37.

5. Caleb Hopkins Snow, *A History of Boston* (1825).

6. For Andrew Oliver, see *True Stories,* 6:159–160. Oliver, who was involved in enforcing the Stamp Act, was hanged in effigy on the Liberty Tree in Boston by the colonists.

TO SOPHIA PEABODY

Brook Farm, Septr 27th. 1841 7 $^1/_2$ A.M.

Dearest love,

Thy two letters of business came both together, Saturday evening! What an acute and energetic personage is my little Dove! I say it not in jest (though with a smile) but in good earnest, and with a comfortable purpose to commit all my business transactions to thee, when we dwell together. And why dost thou seem to apprehend that thou mayst possibly offend me. Thou canst do so never, but only make me love thee more and more.

Now as to this affair with Munroe. I fully confide in thy opinion that he intends to make an unequal bargain with thy poor simple and innocent husband—never having doubted this, myself. But how is he to accomplish it? I am not, nor shall be, in the least degree in his power; whereas, he is, to a certain extent, in mine. He might announce his projected library, with me for the editor, in all the newspapers in the universe; but still I could not be bound *to* become the editor, unless by my own act; nor should I have the slightest scruple in refusing to be so, at the last moment, if he persisted in treating me with injustice. Then, as for his printing Grandfather's Chair, I have the copyright in my own hands, and could and would prevent the sale, or make him account to me for the profits, in case of need. Meantime, he is making arrangement for publishing this library, contracting with other booksellers, and with printers and engravers, and, with every step, making it more difficult for himself to draw back. I, on the other hand, do nothing which I should not do, if the affair with Munroe were at an end; for if I write a book, it will be just as available for some other publisher as for him. My dearest, instead of getting me within his power by this delay, he has trusted to my ignorance and simplicity, and has put himself in my power. Show the contrary, if thou canst.

He is not insensible of this. At our last interview, he himself introduced the subject of the bargain, and appeared desirous to close it. But thy husband was not prepared, among other reasons, because I do not yet see what materials I shall have for the republications in the library; the works that he had shown me being ill-adapted for that purpose; and I wish first to see some French and German books, which he has sent for to New York. And, belovedest, before concluding the bargain, I have promised George Hillard to consult him and let him do the business. Is not this consummate discretion? And is not thy husband perfectly safe?

Then why does my Dove put herself into a fever? Rather, let her look at the matter with the same perfect composure that I do, who see all round my own position, and know that it is impregnable.

Most sweet wife, *I* cannot write thee any more at present, as Mr. Ripley is going away instantaneously; but we will talk at large on Saturday, when God means to send me to thy arms. I love thee infinitely, and admire thee beyond measure, and trust thee in all things, and will never transact any business without consulting thee—though on some rare occasions, it may happen that I will have my own way, after all. I feel inclined to break off this engagement with Munroe, as thou advisest, though not for precisely the reasons thou urgest; but of this hereafter.

Thy most own husband.

TO SOPHIA PEABODY

Brook Farm, October 18th [16]. [1841] Saturday.

Most dear wife, I received thy letters and note, last night, and was much gladdened by them; for never has my soul so yearned for thee as now. But, belovedest, my spirit is moved to talk with thee to-day about these magnetic miracles, and to beseech thee to take no part in them.[1] I am unwilling that a power should be exercised on thee, of which we know neither the origin nor consequence, and the phenomena of which seem rather calculated to bewilder us, than to teach us any truths about the present or future state of being. If I possessed such a power over thee, I should not dare to exercise it; nor can I consent to its being exercised by another. Supposing that this power arises from the transfusion of one spirit into another, it seems to me that the sacredness of an individual is violated by it; there would be an intrusion into thy holy of holies—and the intruder would not be thy husband! Canst thou think, without a shrinking of thy soul, of any human being coming into closer communion with thee than I may?—than either nature or my own sense of right would permit me? I cannot. And, dearest, thou must remember, too, that thou art now a part of me, and that by surrendering thyself to the influence of this magnetic lady, thou surrenderest more than thine own moral and spiritual being—allowing that the influence is a moral and spiritual one. And, sweetest, I really do not like the idea of being brought, through thy medium, into such an intimate relation with Mrs. Park!

Now, ownest wife, I have no faith whatever that people are raised to the seventh heaven, or to any heaven at all, or, that they gain any insight into the mysteries of life beyond death; by means of this strange science. Without distrusting that the phenomena which thou tellest me of, and others as remarkable, have really occurred, I think that they are to be accounted for as the result of a physical and material, not of a spiritual, influence. *Opium* has produced many a brighter vision of heaven (and just as susceptible of proofs) than those which thou recountest. They are dreams, my love—and such dreams as thy sweetest fancy, either waking or sleeping, could lastly improve upon. And what delusion can be more lamentable and mischievous, than to mistake the physical and material for the spiritual? What so miserable as to lose the soul's true, though hidden, knowledge and consciousness of heaven, in the mist of an earth-born vision? Thou shalt not do this. If thou wouldst know what heaven is, before thou comest thither hand in hand with thy husband, then retire into the depths of thine own spirit, and thou wilt find it there among holy thoughts and feelings; but do not degrade high Heaven and its inhabitants into any such symbols and forms as those which Miss Larned describes—do not let an earthy effluence from Mrs. Park's corporeal system bewilder thee, and perhaps contaminate something spiritual and sacred. I should as soon think of seeking revelations of the future state in the rottenness of the grave—where so many do seek it.

Belovedest wife, I am sensible that these arguments of mine may appear to have little real weight; indeed, what I write does no sort of justice to what I think. But I care the less for this, because I know that my deep and earnest feeling upon the subject will weigh more with thee than all the arguments in the world. And thou wilt know that the view which I take of this matter is caused by no want of faith in mysteries, but from a deep reverence of the soul, and of the mysteries which it knows within itself, but never transmits to the earthly eye or ear. Keep thy imagination sane—that is one of the truest conditions of communion with Heaven.

Dearest, after these grave considerations, it seems hardly worth while to submit a merely external one; but as it occurs to me, I will write it. I cannot think, without invincible repugnance, of thy holy name being bruited abroad in connection with these magnetic phenomena. Some (horrible thought!) would pronounce my Dove an impostor; the great majority would deem thee crazed; and even the few believers would feel a sort of interest in thee, which it would be anything but pleasant to excite. And what adequate motive can there be for exposing thyself to all this misconception? Thou wilt say, perhaps, that thy visions and experiences would never be known. But Miss Larned's are known to all who choose to listen. Thy sister Elizabeth would like nothing so much as to proclaim thy spiritual experiences, by sound of trumpet.

October 19th [18]. Monday.—Most beloved, what a preachment have I made to thee! I love thee, I love thee, I love thee, most infinitely. Love is the true magnetism. What carest thou for any other? Belovedest, it is probable that thou wilt see thy husband tomorrow. Art thou magnificent. God bless thee. What a bright day is here, but the woods are fading now. It is time I were in the city, for the winter.[2]

Thine ownest.

1. Animal magnetism was a type of hypnosis. NH was sceptical of practitioners of this pseudoscience, such as Mrs. Park, mentioned below, because he felt they unnaturally invade and control their subjects.
2. NH left Brook Farm in late October.

TO CORNELIUS MATHEWS AND EVERT A. DUYCKINCK

Boston, Decr 22d, 1841.
54 Pinckney St.

Gentlemen,[1]

Your letter of the 16th. inst. has reached me only to-day. For about six months past, I have been meditating a letter to Arcturus, expressive of my very deep gratitude for the article in the May number,[2] and likewise for several other kind words, each and all of which are treasured up as among the most valuable recompenses of my literary toils. You would have heard from me long ago; but during the summer, my fingers were so stiff with exercising the hoe and other agricultural tools, that positively I could not write legibly. Latterly, I have deferred my letter of thanks, until I could accompany it with a new volume of Twice-told Tales, which Mr. Munroe has in press.[3]

I do not think it possible that any praise can be in store for me, which will give me so much pleasure as your article about my writings. Perhaps it would be decorous in me to decline some considerable part of the approbation there bestowed, as being quite beyond my deserts; but I cannot find in my heart to do it. It is true, the public will never ratify it; but at least, the writer felt what he expressed; and therefore I have a right to receive it as genuine testimony to the impression which

I have produced. And, certainly, I would far rather receive earnest praise from a single individual, than to be deemed a tolerably pleasant writer by a thousand, or a million.

I have mentioned that Mr. Munroe has a new volume of my tales in press—and also a second edition of the former volume. I fear, therefore, that the tales will not be of any value to you, as they will be offered to the public in another form. They are at your disposal. Several (which, for aught I know, are as good as the rest) will be left out of the new collection.[4] In the Token for 1832 are some of the first stories which I wrote—"The Wives of the Dead"—"Major Molineux"—"Roger Malvin's Burial."—in that for 1833, "The Canterbury Pilgrims"—for 1837, "the Man of Adamant," and "Monsieur du Miroir"—for 1838, "Sylph Etherege." In the New England Magazine is "Young Goodman Brown." I have burnt whole quires of manuscript stories, in past times—which, if I had them now, should be at your service. I do not believe that I shall ever write any more—at least, not like my past productions; for they grew out of the quietude and seclusion of my former life; and there is little probability that I shall ever be so quiet and secluded again. During the last three or four years, the world has sucked me within its vortex; and I could not get back to my solitude again, even if I would.

I shall not expect to be remunerated for any use that you may make of my articles. It would give me great pleasure to see them in a Magazine which I like so much as Arcturus—I will not say how much I like it, because I cannot praise you gracefully, after you have praised me so much.

If either of you should visit Boston this winter, it would make me very happy to see you. Mr. Duyckinck and myself are already personally known to each other; and I wish I could say the same of Mr. Mathews.

Very truly Yours,
Nath. Hawthorne.

1. Cornelius Mathews, New York poet and dramatist, edited Arcturus with Duyckinck for its entire run, December 1840–May 1842.

2. Duyckinck's "Nathaniel Hawthorne" appeared in the May 1841 Arcturus.

3. James Munroe of Boston published a new edition of Twice-Told Tales in December 1841.

4. The Arcturus did reprint four of NH's tales, only one of which had been reprinted in Twice-Told Tales (see CE, 15:601n).

TO SOPHIA PEABODY

Salem, Jany 20th, 1842—11 oclock A.M.

Truest Heart,

Here is thy husband in his old chamber, where he produced those stupendous works of fiction, which have since impressed the Universe with wonderment and awe! To this chamber, doubtless, in all succeeding ages, pilgrims will come to pay their tribute of reverence;—they will put off their shoes at the threshold, for fear of desecrating the tattered old carpet. "There," they will exclaim, "is the very bed in which he slumbered, and where he was visited by those ethereal visions, which he afterwards fixed forever in glowing words! There is the wash-stand, at which this exalted personage cleansed himself from the stains of earth, and rendered his outward man a fitting exponent of the pure, soul within. There, in its mahogany frame, is the dressing-glass, which often reflected that noble brow, those hyacinthine locks, that mouth, bright with smiles, or tremulous with feeling, that flashing or melting eye, that—in short, every item of the magnanimous phiz of this unexampled man! There is the pine table—there the old flag-bottomed chair—in which he sat, and at which he scribbled, during his agonies of inspiration! There is the old chest of drawers, in which he kept what shirts a poor author may be supposed to have possessed! There is the closet, in which was reposited his threadbare suit of black! There is the worn-out shoe-brush with which this polished writer polished his boots. There is—" but I believe this will be pretty much all;—so here I close the catalogue.

Most dear, I love thee beyond all limits, and write to thee because I cannot help it;—nevertheless writing grows more and more an inadequate and unsatisfactory mode of revealing myself to thee. I no longer think of saying anything deep, because I feel that the deepest and truest must remain unsaid. We have left expression—at least, such expression as can be achieved with pen and ink—far behind us. Even the spoken word has long been inadequate. Looks—pressures of the lips and hands, and the touch of bosom to bosom—these are a better language; but, bye-and-bye, our spirits will demand some more adequate expression even than these. And thus it will go on; until we shall be divested of these earthly forms, which are at once our medium of expression, and the impediments to full communion. Then we shall melt into another, and all be expressed, once and continually, without a word—without an effort.

Belovedest, my cold is very comfortable now. Mrs. Hillard gave me some homo—I don't know how to spell it—homeopathic medicine,[1] of which I took a dose last night; and shall not need another. Art thou likewise well? Didst thou weary thy poor little self to death, yesterday? I do not think that I could possibly undergo the fatigue and distraction of mind which thou dost. Thou art ten times as powerful as I, because thou art so much more etherereal.[2]

Sweetest, thy husband has recently been both lectured about and preached about, here in his native city. The preacher was Rev. Mr. Fox of Newburyport; but how he contrived to hook me into a sermon, I know not. I trust he took for his text that which was spoken of my namesake of old—"Behold an Israelite indeed, in whom there is no guile."[3] Belovedest, if ever thou shouldst happen to hear me lauded on any public occasion, I shall expect thee to rise, and make thine own and my acknowledgments, in a neat and appropriate speech. Wilt thou not? Surely thou wilt—inasmuch as I care little for applause, save as it shall please thee; so it is rather thy concern than mine.

Mine ownest, it is by no means comfortable to be separated from thee three whole days at a time. It is too great a gap in life. There is no sunshine in the days in which thou dost not shine on me. And speaking of sunshine, what a beautifullest day (to the outward eye, I mean) was yesterday; and to-day seems equally bright and *gladsome,* although I have not yet tasted the fresh air. I trust that thou hast flown abroad, and soared upward to the seventh heaven. But do not stay there, sweetest Dove! Come back for me; for I shall never get there, unless by the aid of thy wings.

Now God bless thee, and make thee happy and joyful, until Saturday evening, when thou must needs bear the infliction of

Thine ownest Husband.

1. Homeopathic medicine treats disease by giving the patient small amounts of medicine, which produce in a healthy person effects similar to the symptoms of the disease being treated, and which, if given in larger doses, would produce the same effects as the disease.

2. NH's invention to combine "ethereal" and "real." [*CE*]

3. John 1:47. No account of a sermon by the Reverend Thomas Bayley Fox of Newburyport, Massachusetts, which mentions NH has been found in the Salem newspapers.

TO SOPHIA PEABODY

Salem, Feby 27th. 1842—Forenoon.

Thou dearest Heart,

As it is uncertain whether I shall return to Boston tomorrow, I write thee a letter; for I need to commune with thee; and even if I should bring the scroll of my thoughts and feelings with me, perhaps thou wilt not refuse to receive it. It is awful, almost (and yet I would not have it otherwise, for the world) to feel how necessary thou hast become to my well-being, and how my spirit is disturbed at a separation from thee, and stretches itself out through the dimness and distance to embrace its other self. Thou art my quiet and satisfaction—not only my chiefest joy, but the condition of all other enjoyments. When thou art away, vague fears and misgivings sometimes steal upon me; there are heart-quakes and spirit-sinkings for no real cause, and which never trouble me when thou art pressed close to my breast.

Belovedest, I have thought much of thy parting injunction to tell my mother and sisters that thou art her daughter and their sister. I do not think thou canst estimate what a difficult task thou didst propose to me—not that any awful and tremendous effect would be produced by the disclosure; but because of the strange reserve, in regard to matters of feeling, that has always existed among us. We are conscious of one another's feelings, always; but there seems to be a tacit law, that our deepest heart-concernments are not to be spoken of. I cannot gush out in their presence—I cannot take my heart in my hand, and show it to them. There is a feeling within me (though I know it is a foolish one) as if it would be as indecorous to do so, as to display to them the naked breast, on which God is well pleased that thou shouldst lay thy head. And they are in the same state as myself. None, I think, but delicate and sensitive persons could have got into such a position; but doubtless this incapacity of free communion, in the hour of especial need, is meant by Providence as a retribution for something wrong in our early intercourse.

Then it is so hard to speak of thee—*really* of thee—to anybody! I doubt whether I ever have really spoken of thee, to any person. I have spoken the name of Sophia, it is true; but the idea in my mind was apart from thee—it embraced nothing of thine inner and essential self; it was an outward and faintly-traced shadow that I summoned up, to perform thy part, and which I placed in the midst of thy circumstances; so that thy sister Mary, or Mrs. Ripley, or even Margaret [Fuller], were deceived, and fancied that I was talking about thee. But there didst thou lie, thy real self, in my deepest, deepest heart, while far above, at the surface, this distant image of thee was the subject of talk. And it was not without an effort which few are capable of making, that I could even do so much; and even then I felt as if it were profane. Yet I spoke to persons from whom, if from any, I might expect true sympathy in regard to thee.

I tell thee these things, in order that my Dove, into whose infinite depths the sunshine falls continually, may perceive what a cloudy veil stretches over the abyss of my nature. Thou wilt not think that it is caprice or stubbornness that has made me hitherto resist thy wishes. Neither, I think, is it a love of secrecy and darkness. I am glad to think that God sees through my heart; and if any angel has power to penetrate into it, he is welcome to know everything that is there. Yes; and so may any mortal, who is capable of full sympathy, and therefore worthy to come into my depths. But he must find his own way there. I can neither guide him nor enlighten him. It is this involuntary reserve, I suppose, that has given the objectivity to my writings. And when people think that I am pouring myself out in a tale or essay, I am merely telling what is common to human nature, not what is peculiar to myself. I sympathize with them—not they with me.

Febr 28th—Forenoon.—Sweetest, thou shalt have this letter instead of thy husband, to-night. Dost thou love me? I shall not find any letter from thee at the Post Office, because thou dost expect to hear my footstep on thy staircase, at six oclock this evening. Oh, but another day will quickly pass; and then this yearning of the soul will be appeased, for a little while at least. I wonder, I wonder, I wonder, where on earth we are to set up our Tabernacle. God knows;—but I want to know too.

Dearest love, I am very well, and comfortable as I desire to be, in thy absence. After all, it is a happiness to need thee, to sigh for thee, to feel the nothingness of all things without thee. But do not thou think so—thou must be happy always, not independently of thy husband, but with a bliss equally pervading presence and absence.

Belovedest, I have employed much of my time here in collecting curiosities, and have so many on my hands that I begin to fear it will require a volume to contain the catalogue. I would we had such a museum in reality. And now good-bye, most true Heart. Methinks this is the longest letter that I have written thee for a great while. Shalt thou expect me to write during my journey to New York?—or, were it not better to allow thee to forget me entirely, during that interval of a week? God bless thee, thou unforgettablest and unforgettingest.

Thine ownest husband.

TO DAVID MACK

Boston, May 25th, 1842.

My dear Sir,

When I last met you, I expressed my purpose of coming to Northampton, in the course of the present month, in order to gain information as to the situation and prospects of your community. Since our interview, however, circumstances of various kinds have induced me to give up the design of offering myself as a member. As a matter of conscience, with my present impressions, I should hardly feel myself justified in taking such a step; for, though I have much faith in the general good tendency of institutions on this principle, yet I am troubled with many doubts (after my experience of last year) whether I, as an individual, am a proper subject for those beneficial influences. In an economical point of view, undoubtedly, I could not do so well anywhere else; but I feel that this ought not to be the primary consideration. A more important question is, how my intellectual and moral condition, and my ability to be useful, would be affected by merging myself in a community. I confess to you, my dear Sir, it is my present belief that I can best attain the higher ends of life, by retaining the ordinary relation to society.

With my best wishes for your prosperity and happiness,

I remain Yours sincerely,
Nath. Hawthorne.

TO LOUISA HAWTHORNE

Concord, July 10th, 1842.

Dear Louze,

The execution took place yesterday.[1] We made a christian end, and came, straight to Paradise, where we abide at this present writing. We are as happy as people can be, without making themselves ridiculous, and might be even happier; but, as a matter of taste, we choose to stop short at this point. Sophia is very well, and sends her love. We intend that you shall be our first guest (unless there should be a chance visiter) and shall beseech the honor and felicity of your presence, sometime in August. New married people, I believe, are not considered fit to be seen, in less time than several weeks.

I know you will be delighted with our home and the neighboring scenery; and I have a confident hope that you will be delighted with ourselves likewise. I intend to improve vastly by marriage—that is, if I can find any room for improvement. But all this remains to be seen. Meantime, I promise myself few greater pleasures than that of receiving you here; for, in taking to myself a wife, I have neither given up my own relatives, nor adopted others. Give my love to mother and Ebe.

Yours affectionately,
N. H.

P.S. We have not got a kitten—yet.[2]

1. SPH and NH married on 9 July and moved into the Old Manse, adjacent to the bridge and battleground at which the Battle of Concord had been fought on 19 April 1775. Emerson had lived there while writing his first book, *Nature*.
2. The Manse acquired a female kitten named "Megara, after one of the furies," SPH wrote to her mother 3 September; by 20 September it had been renamed "Moloch," she reported. The same cat became "Pigwiggen." [*CE*]

TO MARGARET FULLER

Concord, August 25th, 1842.

Dear Margaret,

Sophia has told me of her conversation with you, about our receiving Mr. Ellery Channing and your sister as inmates of our household.[1] I found that my wife's ideas were not altogether unfavorable to the plan—which, together with your own implied opinion in its favor, has led me to consider it with a good deal of attention; and my conclusion is, that the comfort of both parties would be put in great jeopardy. In saying this, I would not be understood to mean anything against the social qualities of Mr. and Mrs. Channing—my objection being wholly independent of such considerations. Had it been proposed to Adam and Eve to receive two angels into their Paradise, as *boarders*, I doubt whether they would have been altogether pleased to consent. Certain I am, that, whatever might be the tact, and the sympathies of the heavenly guests, the boundless freedom of Paradise would at once have become finite and limited by their presence. The host and hostess would no longer have lived their own natural life, but would have had a constant reference to the two angels; and thus the whole four would have been involved in an unnatural relation—which the whole system of boarding out essentially and inevitably is.

One of my strongest objections is the weight of domestic care which would be thrown upon Sophia's shoulders by the proposed arrangement. She is so little acquainted with it, that she cannot estimate how much she would have to bear. I do not fear any burthen that may accrue from our own exclusive relation, because skill and strength will come with the natural necessity; but I should not feel myself justified in adding one scruple to the weight. I wish to remove everything that may impede her full growth and development—which, in her case, it seems to me, is not to be brought about by care and toil, but by perfect repose and happiness. Perhaps she ought not to have any earthly care whatever—certainly none which is not wholly pervaded with love, as a cloud is with warm light. Besides, she has many visions of great deeds to be wrought on canvass and in marble, during the coming autumn and winter; and none of these can be accomplished, unless she can retain quite as much freedom from household drudgery as she enjoys at present. In short, it is my faith and religion not wilfully to mix her up with any earthly annoyance.

You will not consider it impertinent, if I express an opinion about the most advisable course for your young relatives, should they retain their purpose of boarding out. I think that they ought not to seek for delicacy of character, and nice tact, and sensitive feelings, in their hosts. In such a relation as they propose, these characteristics should never exist on more than one side; nor should there be any idea of personal friendship, where the real condition of the bond is, to supply food and lodging for a pecuniary compensation. They will be able to keep their own delicacy and sensitiveness much more inviolate, if they make themselves inmates of the rudest farmer's household in Concord, where there will be no nice sensibilities to manage, and where their own feelings will be no more susceptible of damage from the farmer's family than from the cattle in his barn-yard. There will be a freedom in this sort of life, which is not otherwise attainable, except under a roof of their own. They can then say explicitly what they want, and can battle for it, if necessary; and such a contest would leave no wound on either side. Now, where four sensitive people were living together, united by any tie save that of entire affection and confidence, it would take but a trifle to render their whole common life diseased and intolerable.

I have thought, indeed, of receiving a personal friend, and a man of delicacy, into my household, and have taken a step towards that object. But in doing so, I was influenced far less by what Mr. Bradford is, than by what he is not; or rather, his negative qualities seem to take away his personality, and leave his excellent characteristics to be fully and fearlessly enjoyed. I doubt whether he be not precisely the rarest man in the world. And, after all, I have had some misgiving as to the wisdom of my proposal to him.

This epistle has grown to greater length than I expected, and yet it is but a very imperfect expression of my ideas upon the subject. Sophia wished me to write; and, as it was myself that made the objections, it seemed no more than just that I should assume the office of stating them to you. There is nobody to whom I would more willingly speak my mind, because I can be certain of being thoroughly understood. I would say more,—but here is the bottom of the page.

Sincerely your friend,
Nath. Hawthorne.

1. William Ellery Channing, the namesake of his uncle, the famous Unitarian minister, would marry Ellen Kilshaw Fuller on 23 September. The next April, they moved to a house near Emerson's.

TO EPES SARGENT

Concord, October 21st. 1842.

My dear Sir,[1]

In compliance with your request for an article, I have corrected and added some finishing touches to a sketch of character from a private journal of mine.[2] Whether it have any interest must depend entirely on the sort of view taken by the writer, and the mode of execution. If it suit your purpose, I shall be very glad.

There is a gentleman in this town by the name of Thoreau, a graduate of Cambridge, and a fine scholar, especially in old English literature—but withal a wild, irregular, Indian-like sort of fellow, who can find no occupation in life that suits him. He writes; and sometimes—often, for aught I know—very well indeed. He is somewhat tinctured with Transcendentalism; but I think him capable of becoming a very valuable contributor to your Magazine. In the Dial for July, there is an article on the Natural History of this part of the country, which will give you an idea of him as a genuine and exquisite observer of nature—a character almost as rare as that of a true poet.[3] A series of such articles would be a new feature in Magazine-literature, and perhaps a popular one; and, not improbably, he might give them a more popular tone than the one in the Dial. Would it not be worth while to try Mr. Thoreau's pen? He writes poetry also—for instance, "To the Maiden in the East"—"The Summer Rain"—and other pieces, in the Dial for October, which seem to be very careless and imperfect, but as true as bird-notes.[4] The man has stuff in him to make a reputation of; and I wish that you might find it consistent with your interest to aid him in attaining that object. In common with the rest of the public, I shall look for character and individuality in the Magazine which you are to edit; and it seems to me that this Mr. Thoreau might do something towards marking it out from the ordinary catalogue of such publications.

With my best wishes for your success, I am

Very truly Yours,
Nath. Hawthorne.

Epes Sargent, Esqr.
New-York.

1. Epes Sargent, journalist, poet, and dramatist, had worked on Boston newspapers before going to New York in 1839, where he associated with the *Mirror* and the *World*. At the time of NH's writing to him, he was preparing his own publication, *Sargent's New Monthly Magazine*, which lasted from January to June 1843.

2. "The Old Apple-Dealer" appeared in the January 1843 *Sargent's*.

3. Thoreau's "Natural History of Massachusetts" appeared in the July 1842 *Dial*, the quarterly journal published by the Transcendentalists.

4. Thoreau contributed eight poems to the October 1842 *Dial*.

TO HENRY WADSWORTH LONGFELLOW

Concord, Novr 26th. 1842

Dear Longfellow,

I have been looking to receive somewhat in the shape of a letter of congratulation from you, on the great event of my marriage; but it does not seem to be forthcoming.[1] Perhaps it is the etiquette that I should congratulate on your return from Outre Mer. Be it done accordingly.

I exceedingly desire to see you; and the object of this present writing is, to intreat you to come to Concord and deliver a lecture before the Lyceum.[2] Mr. Emerson, who is one of the Curators, has mentioned it to me several times. I inquired what remuneration could be offered you; and he spoke of the magnificent sum of ten dollars—which he says is the highest amount paid by country Lyceums. Do come—if not for filthy lucre, yet to gratify the good people here, and to see my wife and me. Choose your own time, only I should like to have it as soon as possible.

I am very well, and very happy; so is my wife.

Truly your friend,
Nath. Hawthorne.

1. Longfellow had been abroad in Europe from late April through early November.
2. Longfellow did not lecture at the Concord Lyceum in 1842 or 1843.

TO MARGARET FULLER

Concord. Feby 1st. 1843.

Dear Margaret.

I ought to have answered your letter a great while ago; but I have an immense deal of scribbling to do—being a monthly contributor to three or four periodicals;

so that I find it necessary to keep writing without any period at all. Now as to our friend Charles Newcomb,[1] I heartily wish that I could have the privilege of his society, next summer; and were it less than an absolute impossibility, I would undertake to be his host—though with some misgivings, chiefly as to my own proper performance of the relative duties of our position. But it is not possible, for a reason at present undeveloped, but which, I trust, time will bring to light.[2] We should have been compelled to eject even the impersonal Mr. Bradford, had he become our inmate. So here is a second negative. How strange, when I should be so glad to do everything that you had the slightest wish for me to do, and when you are so incapable of wishing any thing that ought not to be! Whether or no you bear a negative more easily than other people, I certainly find it easier to give you one; because you do not peep at matters through a narrow chink, but can take my view as perfectly as your own. I hope Charles Newcomb will not give up the idea of coming to Concord. There are many roofs besides mine; and Mr. Emerson, and Mr. Thoreau, and I, and everybody that is blessed with the knowledge of him, would gladly exert ourselves to find some proper whereabout for his reception. I should delight to anticipate long days with him on the river and in the woods.

We have been very happy this winter; we go on continually learning to be happy, and should consider ourselves perfectly so now, only that we find ourselves making advances all the time. I do suppose that nobody ever lived, in one sense, quite so selfish a life as we do. Not a footstep, except our own, comes up the avenue for weeks and weeks; and we let the world alone as much as the world does us. During the greater part of the day, we are separately engaged at our respective avocations; but we meet in my study in the evening, which we spend without any set rule, and in a considerable diversity of method—but on looking back, I do not find anything to tell of or describe. The essence would flit away out of the description, and leave a very common-place residuum; whereas the real thing has a delicate pungency. We have read through Milton's Paradise Lost, and other famous books; and it somewhat startles me to think how we, in some cases, annul the verdict of applauding centuries, and compel poets and prosers to stand another trial, and receive condemnatory sentence at our bar. It is a pity that there is no period after which an author may be safe. Forever and ever, he is to be tried again and again, and by everybody that chooses to be his judge; so that, even if he be honorably acquitted at every trial, his ghost must be in everlasting torment.

I have skated like a very schoolboy, this winter. Indeed, since my marriage, the circle of my life seems to have come round, and brought back many of my school-day enjoyments; and I find a deeper pleasure in them now than when I first went over them. I pause upon them, and taste them with a sort of epicurism, and am boy and man together. As for Sophia, I keep her as tranquil as a summer-sunset.

As regards both of us, the time that we spend together seems to spread over all the time that we are apart; and consequently we have the idea of being in each other's society a good deal more than we are. I wonder, sometimes, how she is able to dispense with all society but mine. In my own case, there is no wonder—indeed, in neither of our cases; and it is only when I get apart from myself, and take another person's view of the matter, that I think so.

I have missed Ellery Channing very much in my skating expeditions. Has he quite deserted us for good and all? How few people in this world know how to be idle!—it is a much higher faculty than any sort of usefulness or ability. Such rare persons, if the world knew what was due to them or good for itself, would have food and raiment as free as air, for the sake of their inestimable example. I do not mean to deny Ellery's ability for any sort of vulgar usefulness; but he certainly *can* lie in the sun.

I wish you might begin at the end of this scrawl instead of at the usual extremity; because then you would profit by the advice which I here give—not to attempt to decypher it. Sophia wants to read it, but I have too much regard for her to consent. She sends her love. Of course, you will be in Concord when the pleasant weather comes, for a month, or a week, or a day; and you must spend a proportionable part of the time at our house.

Your friend,
Nath Hawthorne.

1. Charles King Newcomb, from Providence, Rhode Island, a close friend of Emerson and Fuller, had known NH at Brook Farm. [*CE*]
2. A reference to SPH's first pregnancy.

TO SAMUEL COLMAN

Concord Septr 27th. 1843.

Dear Sir,[1]

I cannot in conscience keep 'Marco Paulo,'[2] because I am not connected with any public Journal or Magazine in such away, as to enable me to review it.

I am afraid that I cannot find time to write a regular series of articles for the 'Boys & Girls' Magazine.[3] It would give me pleasure to comply with your request; but it could not be done without interrupting other pursuits, and at a greater sacrifice than the real value of my articles. If I saw a probability of deriving a reasonable profit from juvenile literature, I would willingly devote myself to it for a time, as being both easier and more agreeable (by way of variety) than literature for grown people. But my experience hitherto has not made me very sanguine on this point. In fact, the business has long been overdone. Mr Abbot and other writers have reaped the harvest; and the gleanings seem to be scarcely worth picking up.

In any interval of leisure, I shall be happy to send you an occasional article. As to payment, I doubt not that the price offered by yourself is as much as my articles are worth to you, and shall therefore demand no more, either for my future contributions or the one already sent.

Truly Yours,
Nath. Hawthorne.

1. Samuel Colman, a Maine bookseller and publisher of Longfellow.
2. *Marco Paul's Adventures in Pursuit of Knowledge* (1843) by Jacob Abbott, prolific writer of children's stories, especially the famous Rollo Books.
3. "Little Daffydowndilly" appeared in the August 1843 *Boys and Girls Magazine,* edited by Colman's wife.

TO EVERT A. DUYCKINCK

Concord, Novr 26th. 1843.

My dear Sir,

I thank you for your friendly letter, with the extract from the Review—which, but for your good offices, I should probably never have seen.[1] Praise is sweeter to me now than ever it was, because I enjoy it through the medium of another, whose eyes are brightened by anything that is kindly (and, as she thinks, fitly) said of her husband. It is very pleasant to have a second self, to whom we may refer such matters as we cannot modestly deal with in our proper person. But what gives me a deeper pleasure than this foreign praise (not that I undervalue a voice from over the sea) is the earnest kindness which has induced you to communicate it. My tales and essays were letters that I wrote, in my solitary chamber, and threw them forth, without direction, into the infinite; and by some miracle, they have found their way to the very friends for whom they were intended. This is my feeling, when I meet with such a response as your's.

If you visit Boston next summer, you must come and spend a day or two with me. I live in an old parsonage, the most quiet place, I believe, in the whole world, with woods close at hand, and a river at the bottom of my orchard, and an old battle-field right under my window.[2] Everybody that comes here falls asleep, there is such an unearthly quiet; but for my own part, I feel as if, for the first time in my life, I was awake. I have found a reality, though it looks very much like some of my old dreams. In short, I have nothing to wish for—except, perhaps, that Providence would make it somewhat more plain to my apprehension how I am to earn my bread, after a year or two. But it will be time enough for that, when the necessity comes. Possibly my copyrights may increase in value. At present, they are not worth a sixpence.

I am very sorry that your monster of a city has swallowed up Mr. Beekman's residence.[3] He told me that there was peril of it, and it has often occurred to me since. Methinks it is a fit subject for a tale.

Truly your friend,
Nath. Hawthorne.

1. G. P. R. James reviewed *Twice-Told Tales* in the October 1843 *Foreign and Colonial Quarterly Review*.

2. For more on the Old Manse, see 10 July 1842, note 1.

3. James William Beekman had to move his home in New York City at great expense when 51st Street was extended.

TO LOUISA HAWTHORNE

Concord, March 3d (Sunday) 1844.

Dear Louse,

You and Elizabeth are aunts, and our mother is grandmother, to a little girl, who came head-first into this world at $^1/_2$ past 9 o clock this morning, after being ten awful hours in getting across the threshold. I have not yet seen the baby, and am almost afraid to look at it. Mrs. Peabody says it is *lovely*. Dr. Bartlett has the audacity to say that it looks like him, and has *red* hair. Mary O'Brien says it is a very pretty baby, but does not testify as to the color of the hair. Mrs. Prescott says it is a very fine baby indeed, and that, whatever may be the color of its hair now, it will speedily become dark. Of my own personal knowledge I can say nothing, except that it already roars very lustily. It is averred by all to be in the finest possible condition.

Sophia had a terrible time, but is now quite comfortable and perfectly happy. I will write more in a few days, but having had no sleep all night, do not feel competent to a longer epistle at present.

Your brother,
N. H.

P.S. In your reply, on no account say a word about the *red hair*. We had a name ready—Una![1] Is not it pretty! Una Hawthorne! Una Hawthorne!! It is very pretty.

---

1. Una represents Truth in Edmund Spenser's *The Faerie Queen* (1590–96), the first part of which SPH's mother had published a children's version of in 1836.

TO JOHN FROST

Concord (Mass) March 11th. 1844

Dear Sir,[1]

Considering it good policy in a writer to extend and vary his audience as much as possible, I comply with your request for an article.[2] It will make, I suppose, five, or perhaps six, pages of the Lady's Book. It is difficult to regulate the length of an article precisely according to order; as every story has its natural developement, and will be maimed and imperfect, if cut short of it.

By two or three editors, I have been offered twenty-five dollars for articles of such length as might suit myself. As I find it a delicate point to set a price on my own productions, you may have this story at the same valuation, though I do not care to become a regular contributor at that rate. I should have asked the same had it been shorter; and it is less than I could obtain elsewhere for the same amount of matter.

Should either the price or the article fail to satisfy you, have the kindness to send the latter to J. L. O'Sullivan, Esqr. (Editor of the Democratic Review) New York City.

Truly Yours
Nath. Hawthorne.

John Frost, Esqr.
Philadelphia.

1. John Frost had edited *The Young People's Book* from 1841 through 1842 and was now apparently an assistant editor for the popular and influential *Godey's Magazine and Lady's Book*. 2. "Drowne's Wooden Image" appeared in the July 1844 *Godey's*.

TO GEORGE S. HILLARD

Concord, August 19th, 1844.

Dear Hillard,

I do not see the use of any further lenity[1] with Loring.[2] I learn on good authority that he might pay his debts—this debt, at least—but will not. He was probably an honest fellow once, but has become demoralized by difficult circumstances and evil connections; so that he has no longer any principle about such matters. If he will not consent to pay the debt by instalments of $20 per month, commencing with the first of September, I do wish (unless you have insuperable objections) that you would put him under the screw. It strikes me as hardly fair, that a debtor should keep a horse for his private pleasure, (as our friend sees fit to do,) while the creditor trudges about with a hole in his cowhide boot—as will be my own case, when I take this letter to the Post Office. His pay is nearly $100 per month, and he can spare me a fifth part of it.

Muzzy has likewise regained his situation in the Custom House.[3] As he has paid $35 (if I mistake not) of the debt, you will not probably think it worth while to press him for the remainder; but if you choose, I have no objections—nor to the suing of a hundred more such, if it were my misfortune to have demands against so many scoundrels.

I do not ask you to come with Mrs. Hillard to see us, just now; because we are at present help-less—having lost our Irish damsel.[4] But I hope you will not let all the beautiful season pass without a visit. I heard, the other day, by accident, that Longfellow has a son. Present my congratul[a]tions.

Your friend, Nath Hawthorne.

P.S. I retain the manuscripts for the present, rather than send it by mail; being unwilling to subject you to double postage on so weighty a pacquet.

1. Lenity, mildness of temper.
2. William P. Loring, to whom NH had earlier loaned money.
3. John Muzzy regained his role as an inspector.
4. Mary Bryan left the Hawthornes' employ near the end of June, after a dispute about her honesty. [CE]

TO EVERT A. DUYCKINCK

Concord, March 2d 1845.

Dear Sir,

I can offer you nothing of which I claim to be the author; but, for some weeks past, I have been employed in arranging a journal, kept by a friend during a recent cruise on the West Coast of Africa.[1] As he gave me pretty large license, I have re-modelled the style, where it seemed necessary, and have developed his ideas, where he failed to do it himself, and have put on occasional patches of sentimental embroidery—at the same time avoiding to tamper with his facts, or to change the tenor of his observations upon them; so that the work has not become otherwise than authentic, in my hands. Much of the ground which the author traverses will be new to most readers; embracing principally Liberia, with sketches likewise of the Cape de Verde, Madeira, Sierra Leone, and various places that I had never heard of before. I think it makes a very respectable book; though, as he cares nothing for such matters himself, and only wrote the Journal at my request, it did not come into my hands as a very artistic production—nor will go out of them as such.

But it has good material, and is the work of a man of some cultivation, good feeling, and excellent practical sense. At present, the conclusion of the work is suspended, until I can have an interview with the author. This will take place about the middle of the month; and I will send you the manuscript in a week or two thereafter. Should your judgment of it be favorable, I shall be glad to have it come before the public through your medium.

Truly Yours,
Nath. Hawthorne.

1. NH edited Bridge's account of his travels on the west coast of Africa as *Journal of an African Cruiser*. It appeared on 20 June 1845 as the first number in Wiley and Putnam's *Library of American Books*, a series that would soon include Poe's *Tales*, Margaret Fuller's *Papers on Literature and Art*, Melville's *Typee*, and NH's *Mosses from an Old Manse*.

TO POMROY JONES

Concord, (Masstts) June 28th 1845.

Dear Sir,

I was absent from home when your epistle of 6th inst. arrived, with a request (always titillating to an author's vanity) for my autograph. I now proceed to give it, in as good a style as this most decrepit and abominable steel pen will allow— assuring the sceptical half of the world that it is my real name, in proof of which I refer, not merely to my own books, but to those of the butcher, the baker, the tailor, the doctor, and the tax-gatherer, all of whom are likely to hold it in everlasting remembrance.

Truly Yours,
Nathl Hawthorne.

Pomroy Jones, Esq.
Lairdsville,
N.Y.

TO EVERT A. DUYCKINCK

Concord, July 1st, 1845.

Dear Sir,

My story makes no good progress.[1] There are many matters that thrust themselves between, and hinder my mind from any close approximation to the subject; and for days and weeks together, sometimes, I forget that there is any story to be forthcoming—and am sorry to remember it at last. I am fit for nothing, at present, higher or finer than such another piece of book-manufacture as the Journal. My health is not so good, this summer, as it always has been hitherto. I feel no physical vigor; and my inner man droops in sympathy. It was my purpose to construct a sort of frame-work, in this new story, for the series of stories already published, and to make the scene an idealization of our old parsonage, and of the river close at hand, with glimmerings of my actual life—yet so transmogrified that the reader should not know what was reality and what fancy.[2] Perhaps such sketches would be more easily written after I have pitched my tent elsewhere. That will be in a few months, now. It grieves me to keep you waiting for this story, if it be important that you should have it; but if I were to attempt writing it now, the result would be most pitiable.

I sounded Emerson on the subject of a contribution to the series of American Books; but he seems to think it preferable to publish on his own account—which has always been his method hitherto.[3] I doubt, moreover, whether he is prepared with any prose, or likely soon to be so. He contemplates collecting his poetry into a volume, including much that is still in manuscript; but I know not whether this idea has taken the consistency of a purpose. I wish he might be induced to publish this volume in New York. His reputation is still, I think, provincial, and almost local, partly owing to the defects of the New England system of publication.[4] As for Thoreau, there is one chance in a thousand that he might write a most excellent and readable book; but I should be sorry to take the responsibility, either towards you or him, of stirring him up to write anything for the series. He is the most unmalleable fellow alive—the most tedious, tiresome, and intolerable—the narrowest and most notional—and yet, true as all this is, he has great qualities of intellect and character. The only way, however, in which he could ever approach the popular mind, would be by writing a book of simple observation of nature, somewhat in the vein of White's History of Selborne.[5]

A good many years ago, turning over a series of volumes called the "Athenaeum"—a selection from the English Magazines, published at Boston—I met with a series of stories called the Legends of Lampidosa.[6] They struck me as very remarkable productions, quite a species by themselves. I do not know that they ever made any impression on the public; nor am I altogether sure that they would impress me, now, with any of the admiration which I felt then. But I wish you would look them over, and see whether they might not be profitably republished as a number of the Library of Choice Reading. It is twelve years, or more, since I saw them; and they were then of old date—published at least a dozen years before. If I recollect rightly, they were credited to the European Magazine.

Truly Yours
Nath. Hawthorne

1. "The Old Manse: The Author Makes the Reader Acquainted with his Abode," not yet given a name. [*CE*]

2. This became *Mosses from an Old Manse*, 2 vols. (1846).

3. Duyckinck had earlier attempted to get Emerson to contribute to Wiley & Putnam's *Library of Choice Reading* without success. In publishing his books, Emerson assumed the costs of production (composition, printing, binding) and allowed booksellers a percentage of the sale price for distributing them, rather than the normal practice of accepting no financial risks in return for a much smaller percentage of the net sales. While this made Emerson more money, it also decreased the incentives for publishers to sell books sold on commission, as opposed to the standard royalty basis, because they themselves made more money on the latter.

4. In addition to the effect on sales occasioned by the commission vs. royalty method mentioned in note 3, New England publishers were poor at establishing national distribution networks for their books.

5. Gilbert White, *The Natural History of Selbourne* (1789), considered the first work of natural history in English to become a classic.

6. "Legends of Lampidosa, collected by a Recluse," appeared first in the April-November 1817 *European Magazine and London Review*, and were reprinted in the August 1817-March 1818 *Athenaeum; or, Spirit of the English Magazines*. Wiley & Putnam did not reprint them.

TO EVERT A. DUYCKINCK

Salem, October 10th. 1845

My dear Sir,

   Your letter reached me here; for our landlord has driven us out of our Paradise at Concord, and means to establish himself there; so that I have been fain to betake myself for the present to my mother's house.[1] Here I am, accordingly, in the old dingy and dusky chamber, where I wasted many good years of my youth, shaping day-dreams and night-dreams into idle stories—scarcely half of which ever saw the light; except it were their own blaze upon the hearth. I wish now that I had not burned them; for perhaps there might have been one among them fit— or capable of being made fit—to lead the new collection of tales. However, my youth comes back to me here; and I find myself, sad to say, pretty much the same sort of fellow as of old—and already, though not a week established here, I take out my quire of paper and prepare to cover it with the accustomed nonsense. Doubtless, there will be a result of some kind or other, in the course of two or three weeks, so soon as my mind has deposited the sediment of recent anxieties and disturbances.

   As to the history of Witchcraft, I had often thought of such a work; but I should not like to throw it off hastily, or to write it for the sole and specific purpose of getting $500. A mere narrative, to be sure, might be prepared easily enough; but such a work, if worthily written, would demand research and study, and as deep thought as any man could bring to it. The more I look at it, the more difficulties do I see—yet difficulties such as I should like to overcome. Perhaps it may be the work of an after time.

   The Cruiser would like to make a few corrections and amendments in the School Library edition of his journal.[2] I suppose it is to be printed from the same stereotype plates as hitherto; in which case, probably, anything more than verbal alterations will be impracticable. If otherwise, please to let me know. He is greatly delighted, and not a little surprised, at his literary success, especially at the commendation from the other side of the water. Setting my trimmings and varnishing out of the question, the innate frankness and good-sense of the book deserves all the favor it has met with; and the whole work forms a very good expression of the author's character. He is an excellent fellow.

   I shall do my best to send you the story soon.

Truly Yours,
Nath Hawthorne.

1. Samuel Ripley had asked them to leave, so that he could move there, and the family left in early October for Salem, where they rented a room from William Manning.
2. Bridge's notes in his copy (now in the Bowdoin Library) are copious, but the changes were never effected in print. [*CE*]

TO EVERT A. DUYCKINCK

Salem, Jany 24th. 1846.

My dear Sir,

I have just received yours. As touching the Dartmoor papers, nearly the whole of them are now in O'Sullivan's hands, and you can decide for yourself whether they will suit the Library.[1] My only editorial care has consisted in here and there a verbal correction, and in marking out many passages that it seemed advisable to omit. My own opinion is, that they have quite sufficient interest and novelty (especially the portions relating to the mode of life and economy of the prison) to entitle them to a place in the series. They are somewhat roughly written—but that is the propriety of an old privateersman's reminiscences, dashed off by himself; and feeling this, I thought it best not to varnish them, after the manner of the Cruiser. O'Sullivan would doubtless be contented with a few passages here and there, for the Magazine; and it would gratify me much, on the author's account, to have you publish the whole. With what remains in my hands, the papers will be more than sufficient for a volume; but you may leave out just as much or as little as you please. I will write a preface or introduction. In looking over the papers, pray be careful not to disarrange them; for the pages are not numbered, and the confusion would be irremediable.

Now for my own matters. I like the plan of publishing two volumes,[2] and will set about collecting my vagrant progeny forthwith; and as I never mean to write any more stories (the one now in embryo excepted) we will offer this collection to the public as the last that they shall ever be troubled with, at my hands. It is rather a sad idea—not that I am to write no more in this kind, but that I cannot better justify myself for having written at all. As the first essays and tentatives of a young author, they would be well enough—but it seems to me absurd to look upon them as conveying any claim to a settled literary reputation. I thank God, I have grace enough to be utterly dissatisfied with them, considered as the productions of a literary life—or in any point of view whatever; not but what I see the degree of merit they possess. If they were merely Spring blossoms, we might look for good fruit hereafter; but I have done nothing but blossom all through the summer. I am ashamed—and there's an end.

I shall draw on Messrs. Wiley & Putnam for the $125. immediately.[3]

Truly Yours,
Nathl Hawthorne.

1. Hawthorne edited Benjamin Frederick Browne's account of his incarceration in the War of 1812 as "Papers of an Old Dartmoor Prisoner" for the January–March, May–June, and August–September 1846 issues of the *United States Magazine and Democratic Review*. The series was not published by Wiley & Putnam in book form. The first book publication was as *The Yarn of a Yankee Privateer* (New York: Funk & Wagnalls, 1946).

2. Wiley & Putnam published *Mosses from an Old Manse* as numbers seventeen and eighteen in its *Library of American Books*.

3. NH received $125, plus a small share of royalties, for editing Bridge's *Journal of an African Cruiser*.

TO EVERT A. DUYCKINCK

Salem, Feby 22d, 1846.

My dear Sir,

At last, I send you the copy for Part second of the proposed collection; it will make, as nearly as I can calculate, just about 175 pages. I hope, and fully believe, that it will very soon be followed by the contents of Part first.

I have bestowed much and solemn consideration upon the title of the book. 'Wall-Flowers from an Old Abbey' occurred to me;—but it is too fine. 'Moss and Lichens from an Old Parsonage';—that does not go off trippingly enough. 'Mosses from an Old Manse' suits me rather better; and if my wife agrees with me, so shall the book be christened. I will tell you in the postscript. All these titles, you perceive, refer to our old Owl's Nest at Concord, where all but three of four of the tales were written, and to which the introductory article will refer.

Have you looked over the Dartmoor papers?—and do you reject them? They certainly have spirit and novelty.

Truly Yours,
Nath. Hawthorne.

(P.S. We decide on 'Mosses from an Old Manse.')

TO EPES SARGENT

Salem, March 3d, 1846.

My dear Sargent,

The leaves of the magazine did not arrive till yesterday.[1] I had been waiting for them, before acknowledging the reception of your letter, with its valuable and unexpected enclosure. As regards the sum which you were pleased to consider due me, I had dismissed it entirely from my mind; for I considered myself as, in some sort, a joint adventurer with you in the Magazine speculation; and as I should have expected to profit by your success, so I was content to suffer some trifling loss by your failure. Nevertheless, the ten dollars have happened to come when there was abundant room for them in my strong-box—as indeed there generally has been, since I have taken upon myself the marital and paternal responsibilities; so I shall pocket the amount without hesitation, but shall consider it as fully cancelling the debt. And you need have no scruple on this score, as my pecuniary difficulties, I trust, will shortly cease—that is, if any faith is to be put in the promises of the present administration, who, in consideration of my eminent political services, are about to give me an office in this city.[2] It is no great affair but suits me well enough, as ensuring me a comfortable living, with a little margin for luxuries, and occupying only a moderate portion of time—so that I shall have as much freedom for literary employment as hitherto. It is to come in the course of April. Meantime, please not to mention it; for these things are never certainties, till we have them fairly in our gripe.

I wish your fate had happened to cast you on the winning side in politics. It is exceedingly convenient for a literary man to be able to ensconce himself in an office, whenever his brain gets weary and his pen blunted. I have had good luck in this respect, and really do not know what so idle and inefficient a fellow could have done without it. But you have made a far better fight with the world, and, I doubt not, will triumph in due season.

Whenever you come to this region, I shall be truly glad to see you.

Your friend,
Nath. Hawthorne.

1. Either "The Old Apple-Dealer" from the January 1843 *Sargent's New Monthly Magazine*, or "The Antique Ring" from the February issue. The magazine ceased publication after June.
2. Later in March NH would be nominated by President James K. Polk for the post of Surveyor of the Salem Custom House, paying $1,000 per year.

TO EDGAR ALLAN POE

Salem, June 17th 1846

My dear Sir,

I presume the publishers will have sent you a copy of 'Mosses from an Old Manse'—the latest (and, probably, the last) collection of my tales and sketches. I have read your occasional notices of my productions with great interest—not so much because your judgment was, upon the whole, favorable, as because it seemed to be given in earnest.[1] I care for nothing but the truth; and shall always much more readily accept a harsh truth, in regard to my writings, than a sugared falsehood.

I confess, however, that I admire you rather as a writer of Tales, than as a critic upon them. I might often—and often do—dissent from your opinions, in the latter capacity, but could never fail to recognize your force and originality, in the former.

Yours very truly,
Nath. Hawthorne.

E. A. Poe, Esq.
New York.

1. Poe reviewed *Twice-Told Tales* in the May-April 1842 *Graham's Magazine* and commented on NH in "Marginalia" in the December 1844 *United States Magazine and Democratic Review* and "Literati of New York City" in the May 1846 *Godey's Magazine and Lady's Book*.

TO HENRY WADSWORTH LONGFELLOW

Surveyor's Office,
Salem, January 23d. 1847

Dear Longfellow,

I shall be in Boston on some uncertain day, next week, and will call on Mr Martin, and arrange a sitting, either here or there.[1] Since you do not shrink from the hazard of a newspaper wood-cut, I shall readily face it in my own person, though I never saw one that did not look like the devil. Full length, too! I am puzzled what costume to adopt. A dressing gown would be the best, for an author;—but I cannot wear mine to Boston. I once possessed a blue woollen frock, which saw much service at Brook Farm and Concord, and in which I once went to Brighton to buy pigs. Gladly would I appear before men and angels in that garment; but, on leaving the Manse, I bequeathed it to Ellery Channing. In a dress-coat, I should look like a tailor's pattern, (which certainly is not characteristic of my actual presence;)—so that I think I shall show myself in a common sack, with my stick in one hand and hat in the other.

I rejoice to hear that the poem is near its completion, and will certainly come to listen to as much of it as you will vouchsafe to read—in no long time.[2] The Estray came safely;—it is a beautiful collection.[3] Common things (or what might be mistaken for such) are seen to possess a rareness, after you have held them in your hand. Is it an innate virtue of the thing, or a magick in the touch?

Your friend,
Nathl Hawthorne,
Surveyor.

1. No portrait of NH by the English painter Charles Martin has been located.
2. *Evangeline: A Tale of Acadie* was published on 1 November 1847.
3. *The Estray: A Collection of Poems,* edited by Longfellow, was published on 22 December 1846.

TO EPES SARGENT

Salem, April 9th. 1847.

My dear Sargent,

Your poems, though dated February 1st. on the fly-leaf, reached me only a few days since.[1] I have been exceedingly gratified by the perusal of them—they are very beautiful, and natural as daylight; which, methinks, cannot truly be said of any other poems that have been published, these ten years past. I am glad to find one poet trusting, in simplicity, to his own feelings, and letting a natural utterance flow out of them. 'Adelaide's Triumph' is perfect.[2] I fully believe you to be the only writer who would have brought out all the charm of that story, without spoiling it by any extravagance of touch. It positively brought tears into my eyes, though I am as hard-hearted as a grindstone.

I know not what popularity the book may meet with; but I should think people would receive it as they do sunshine and raindrops.

Very truly Yours,
Nathl Hawthorne.

P.S. My wife, whose taste is better and severer than my own, agrees with my opinion about the poems.

1. *Songs of the Sea, with Other Poems* (1847).
2. A sentimental ballad concerning an apparent peasant girl's silence about her noble birth until the unkind usurper of her father's affections dies. [*CE*]

TO HENRY WADSWORTH LONGFELLOW

Custom-House,
Salem. Novr 11, '47.

Dear Longfellow,

I have read Evangeline with more pleasure than it would be decorous to express. It cannot fail, I think, to prove the most triumphant of all your successes.

Everybody likes it. I wrote a notice of it for our democratic paper, which Conolly edits; but he has not inserted it—why I know not, unless he considers it unworthy of the subject; as it undoubtedly was.[1] But let him write a better if he can. I have heard the poem—and other of your poems, the Wreck of the Hesperus among them—discussed here in the Custom-House. It was very queer, and would have amused you much.

How seldom we meet! It would do me good to see you occasionally; but my duties, official, marital, and paternal, keep me pretty constantly at home; and when I do happen to have a day of leisure, it might chance to be a day of occupation with you—so I do not come. I live at No. 14, Mall-street now. May I not hope to see you there?

I am trying to resume my pen; but the influences of my situation and customary associates are so anti-literary, that I know not whether I shall succeed. Whenever I sit alone, or walk alone, I find myself dreaming about stories, as of old; but these forenoons in the Custom House undo all that the afternoons and evenings have done. I should be happier if I could write—also, I should like to add something to my income, which, though tolerable, is a tight fit. If you can suggest any work of pure literary drudgery, I am the very man for it.

I have heard nothing of Hillard, since his departure. Cannot you tell me something about him?

Your friend,
Nathl Hawthorne.

1. Horace Lorenzo Conolly had supported NH's candidacy for surveyor in 1845, but later switched parties from the Democrats to the Whigs and participated in the attempt to remove him. NH's review appeared in the 13 November *Salem Advertiser*.

TO SOPHIA HAWTHORNE

Surveyor's Office [Salem], June 19th. 1848

Only Belovedest,

I received thy letter on Saturday evening, and was more refreshed by it than if it had been a draft of ice-water—a rather inapt comparison, by the way. Thou canst have no imagination how lonely our house is. The rooms seem twice as large as before—and so awfully quiet! I wish, sometime or other, thou wouldst let me take the two children and go away for a few days, and thou remain behind. Otherwise, thou canst have no idea of what it is. And then our great, lonesome bed, at night—the scene of so many blissful interviews—and now so solitary. I really am half afraid to be there alone, and feel shy about looking across the dimly moonlighted chamber. I expend a great deal of sentiment as often as I chance to see any garment of thine, in my rambles about the house, or any of the children's playthings. And after all, there is a strange bliss in being made sensible of the happiness of my customary life, by this blank interval.

Tell my little daughter Una that her dolly, since her departure, has been blooming like a rose—such an intense bloom, indeed, that I rather suspected her of making free with my brandy-bottle.[1] On taxing her with it, however, she showed no signs of guilt or confusion; and I trust it was owing merely to the hot weather. Her color has now subsided into quite a moderate tint, and she looks splendidly at a proper distance; though, on too close inspection, her skin appears rather coarse—not altogether unlike that of thy good Aunt P———. She has contracted an unfortunate habit of squinting; and her mouth, I am sorry to say, is somewhat askew. I shall take her to task on these matters, and hope to produce a reformation. Should I fail, thou must take her in hand. Give Una a kiss, and tell her I love her dearly. The same to little Bundlebreech, who has probably forgot 'favor' by this time.[2]

Dora complains terribly of lonesomeness,[3] and so does Aunty Lou[isa Hawthorne]. In short, we are pretty forlorn. Nevertheless, I have much joy in your all being in the country, and hope thou wilt stay as long as thou feelest it to be for the best. How I love the children!—how I love thee, best of wives!—and how I shall make thee feel it, when thou comest home! Dost thou love me?

Thine ownest Husband.

---

1. As explained by Julian Hawthorne, "the splendor of dolly's complexion, and the other modifications in her physiognomy, were the result of Mr. Hawthorne's practices upon her with his wife's palette and brushes. He often used to amuse himself and the children by painting little faces for them; and it was always his way to make the cheeks of these visages as ruddy as vermilion would allow." [*CE*]

2. That is, Julian.

3. Dora Golden was hired by the Hawthornes in 1846, primarily to take care of Julian, and stayed with them for about three years.

TO UNA HAWTHORNE

Salem, July 7th. 1848

My dear little Una,

I have been very much pleased with the letters which you have sent me; and I am glad to find that you do not forget me; for I think of you a great deal. I bring home a great many beautiful flowers—roses, and poppies, and lilies, and blue bells, and pinks, and many more besides—but it makes me feel sad to think that my little Una cannot see them. Your dolly wants to see you very much. She sits up in my study all day long, and has nobody to talk with. I try to make her as comfortable as I can, but she does not seem to be in very good spirits. She has been quite good, and has grown very pretty, since you went away. Aunt Louisa and Dora are going to make her a new gown and a new bonnet.

I hope you are a good little girl, and are kind to your little brother, and Horace, and Georgie, and the baby. You must not trouble Mamma, but must do all you can to help her.

Dora wishes to see you very much. So do Grandmamma, and Aunt Lizzy [Elizabeth Hawthorne], and Aunt Louisa. Aunt Lizzy and I went to walk together, a day or two ago; and the rain came and wet us a little.

Mr. Pike sends his love to you, and wishes you to gather him a bunch of wild flowers.

Do not you wish to come home and see me? I think we shall be very happy when you come; for I am sure, you will be a good little girl.

Good bye.
Your affectionate father.

TO HENRY D. THOREAU

Salem, October 21st. 1848.

My dear Sir,

The Managers of the Salem Lyceum, some time ago, voted that you should be requested to deliver a Lecture before that Institution, during the approaching season.[1]

I know not whether Mr Chever, the late Corresponding Secretary,[2] communicated the vote to you; at all events, no answer has been received; and, as Mr Chever's successor in office, I am instructed to repeat the invitation. Permit me to add my own earnest wishes that you will accept it—and also, laying aside my official dignity, to express my wife's desire and my own that you will be our guest, if you do come.

In case of your compliance, the Managers would be glad to know at what time it will best suit you to deliver the Lecture.

Very truly Yours,
Nathl Hawthorne,
Cor. Secy
Salem Lyceum.

P.S. I live at No 14, Mall-street—where I shall be very happy to see you. The stated fee for Lectures is $20.

1. Thoreau lectured in Salem on "Student Life in New England, Its Economy," on 22 November 1848.
2. George Francis Chever also managed the Lyceum from 1849 to 1851.

TO HENRY WADSWORTH LONGFELLOW

Salem, Novr 21st. 1848

Dear Longfellow,

I will gladly come on Thursday, unless something unexpected should thrust itself into the space between. Thoreau is to be at my house, as he is engaged to lecture here on Wednesday evening; and I shall take the liberty to bring him with me, unless he have scruples about intruding on you.[1] You would find him well worth knowing; he is a man of thought and originality; with a certain iron-poker-ishness, an uncompromising stiffness in his mental character, which is interesting, though it grows rather wearisome on close and frequent acquaintance. I shall be very glad to see Ellery Channing—gladder to see you.

Your friend,
Nathl Hawthorne.

1. In his journal for 16 November, Longfellow described Thoreau, Alcott, and Channing as Emerson's "meek philosophers." [*CE*]

TO CHARLES W. WEBBER

Salem, Decr 14th. 1848.

My dear Sir,[1]

At last, by main strength, I have wrenched and torn an idea out of my miserable brain; or rather, the fragment of an idea, like a tooth ill-drawn, and leaving the roots to torture me.[2] I shall send it to you by express to-day or tomorrow. Perhaps you will not like it; if so, make no ceremony about rejecting it. I am as tractable an author as you ever knew, so far as putting my articles into the fire goes; though I cannot abide alterations or omissions.

I am ashamed, as a Yankee, and Surveyor of the Revenue, to say that I had not paid proper consideration to the terms of payment mentioned in two of your letters. I concluded your first statement to be as liberal as circumstances would allow, and should still think so, if you did not yourself tell me to the contrary.

When shall you want another article? Now that the spell is broken, I hope to get into a regular train of scribbling; perhaps not, however; for I have many impediments to struggle against.

Pray continue to write freely to me. I feel a real interest in the success of your enterprise.[3]

Very truly Yours,
Nathl Hawthorne.

1. Charles Wilkins Webber, an associate editor of the *American Review: A Whig Journal*, had reviewed *Mosses from an Old Manse* there in September 1846.
2. *CE* identifies this as "Ethan Brand," which first appeared as "The Unpardonable Sin. From an Unpublished Work" in the 5 January 1850 *Boston Weekly Museum*.
3. Webber was unsuccessful in his attempt to edit a new monthly magazine with the sons of the naturalist John James Audubon.

TO ROBERT J. WALKER

Surveyor's Office, Salem,
January 1st. 1849.

Sir,

I learn that, by the operation of a recent circular from the Treasury department, Mr. Z. Burchmore, Jr. is likely to be deprived of the principal part of his emoluments as Clerk in this Custom-House.[1] As my position enables me to perceive the importance of his services, I take the liberty to offer a few considerations, which seem to me to render his case worthy of an exception from the general rule. Mr Burchmore has spent about twenty years (comprising his whole active life) in the Collector's office, and has acquired a knowledge of the nature and forms of this particular business, and a facility in transacting it, which it would be in vain to look for elsewhere. The mercantile community repose the highest confidence in him, and, owing to particular circumstances, feel a strong interest in his continuance in office. The infirmities of the Collector have, for a considerable time past, thrown various responsibilities upon Mr. Burchmore, which, in ordinary cases, would not appertain to the situation which he fills. I know not why I should hesitate to say, that his remarkable business-talent, and thorough familiarity with the revenue-laws, have made him (the Collector's health being such as it now is) practically the head of this Custom House, and that he is so regarded by the merchants. They would feel his loss severely, and could not, for a long time to come, bestow a similar degree of confidence on any other person. In the internal economy of the Custom-House, he would be equally regretted; for there is not a department in which Mr. Burchmore's influence is not beneficially felt, nor an officer who has not frequent occasion to avail himself of his knowledge and experience.

I wish to speak of Mr Burchmore exclusively as a man of business, and shall therefore lay no stress upon his merits as an active friend of the Administration; but I may be allowed to say, that, though his political character has always been most decidedly marked, the Whigs, while in power, found it impossible to dispense with his services in the Custom House.

Nathl Hawthorne,
Surveyor[2]

1. Zachariah Burchmore, Jr., worked with NH at the Salem Custom House and was dismissed along with him.
2. This is a draft, apparently never sent to Washington but kept by Burchmore until his death. [*CE*]

TO RALPH WALDO EMERSON

Salem, January 10th. 1849.

My dear Sir,

I hold the honorable office of Secretary of the Board of Managers of the Salem Lyceum; in which capacity I address you, to inquire, whether you can lecture for that institution on Wednesday evening next, the 17th inst.[1] As you have consented to deliver a lecture during the winter, I hope it will be convenient at that time.

I wish, moreover, for myself and wife, to prefer our claim as townspeople of your own, to receive you under our roof. Sophia is particularly desirous of showing you our children; and, for my part, I shall be truly glad to see you on that and many other accounts. We live at No. 14, Mall-street.[2]

Very truly Yours,
Nathl Hawthorne.

P.S. Be kind enough to reply as soon as possible.

1. The subject, "England and the English," reflected Emerson's recent trip to Britain.
2. Emerson replied: "I am a bad guest, but if you will let me run away suddenly next morning, I will come" (*The Letters of Ralph Waldo Emerson*, ed. Ralph L. Rusk and Eleanor M. Tilton, 10 vols. [New York: Columbia University Press, 1939, 1990–95], 8:203).

TO HENRY D. THOREAU

Salem, Feby 19th. 1849

My dear Thoreau,

The managers request that you will lecture before the Salem Lyceum on Wednesday evening after next—that is to say, on the 28th inst. May we depend on you? Please to answer immediately, if convenient.[1]

Mr Alcott delighted my wife and me, the other evening, by announcing that you had a book in press.[2] I rejoice at it, and nothing doubt of such success as will be worth having. Should your manuscripts all be in the printer's hands, I suppose you can reclaim one of them, for a single evening's use, to be returned the next morning;—or perhaps that Indian lecture,[3] which you mentioned to me, is in a state of forwardness. Either that, or a continuation of the Walden experiment (or, indeed, anything else,) will be acceptable.[4]

We shall expect you at 14, Mall-street.

Very truly Yours,
Nathl Hawthorne.

1. Thoreau lectured at Salem on "Student Life, Its Aims and Employments" on 28 February 1849.

2. *A Week on the Concord and Merrimack Rivers* (1849).

3. Thoreau had lectured at Concord, Massachusetts, on "An Excursion to Ktaadn" on 3 January 1848, and published "Ktaadn and the Maine Woods" in the July-November 1848 *Union Magazine.*

4. During this period Thoreau incorporated material about his Walden experiment into at least four lectures: see Bradley P. Dean and Ronald Wesley Hoag, "Thoreau's Lectures Before *Walden:* An Annotated Calendar," *Studies in the American Renaissance 1995,* ed. Joel Myerson (Charlottesville: University Press of Virginia, 1995), 127–228.

TO GEORGE S. HILLARD

Salem, March 5th. 1849.

Dear Hillard,

It is a very long time since I have held converse with you by tongue or pen; but I have thought of you none the less, and have enjoyed Europe with you, and rejoiced at your safe return.[1] My present object in writing is one with which you would hardly imagine yourself to have anything to do.

I am informed that there is to be a strong effort among the politicians here to remove me from office, and that my successor is already marked out.[2] I do not think that this ought to be done; for I was not appointed to office as a reward for political services, nor have I acted as a politician since. A large portion of the local Democratic party look coldly on me, for not having used the influence of my position to obtain the removal of whigs—which I might have done, but which I in no case did. Neither was my own appointment made at the expense of a Whig; for my predecessor was appointed by [President John] Tyler, in his latter days, and called himself a Democrat. Nor can any charge of inattention to duty, or other official misconduct, be brought against me; or, if so, I could easily refute it. There is therefore no ground for disturbing me, except on the most truculent party system. All this, however, will be of little avail with the slang-whangers[3]—the vote-distributors—the Jack Cades[4]—who assume to decide upon these matters, after a political triumph; and as to any literary claims of mine, they would not weigh a feather, nor be thought worth weighing at all.

But it seems to me that an inoffensive man of letters—having obtained a pitiful little office on no other plea than his pitiful little literature—ought not to be left to the mercy of these thick-skulled and no-hearted ruffians. It is for this that I now write to you. There are men in Boston—Mr Rufus Choate,[5] for instance—whose favorable influence with the administration would make it impossible to remove me, and whose support and sympathy might fairly be claimed in my behalf—not on the ground that I am a very good writer, but because I gained my position, such as it is, by my literary character, and have done nothing to forfeit that tenure. I do not think that you can have any objection to bringing this matter under the consideration of such men; but if you do so object, I am sure it will be for some good reason, and therefore beg you not to stir in it. I do not want any great fuss to be made; the whole thing is not worth it; but I should like to have the Administration enlightened by a few such testimonials as would take my name out of the list of ordinary officeholders, and at least prevent any hasty action. I think, too, that the letters (if you obtain any) had better contain no allusion to the proposed attack on me, as it may possibly fall through of itself. Certainly, the general feeling here in Salem would be in my favor; but I have seen too much of the modes of political action to lay any great stress on that.

Be pleased on no account to mention this matter to any Salem man, however friendly to me he may profess himself. If any movement on my part were heard of, it would precipitate their assault.

So much for business. I do not let myself be disturbed by these things, but employ my leisure hours in writing, and go on as quietly as ever. I see that Longfellow has written a prose-tale.[6] How indefatigable he is!—and how adventurous! Well he may be, for he never fails.

Remember me to Mrs. Hillard. Sophia is well, and our children continue to flourish famously. Why do you not come to see us?

Your friend,
Nathl Hawthorne.

1. Hillard sent letters home from his European trip to his wife, who shared them with friends. They were published as *Six Months in Italy* (1853).

2. NH was removed from his role at the Salem Custom House because a different political party had won the election and wished to appoint its own people. In addition, NH was accused (falsely) of being too political in what was supposed to be a non-political job.

3. Slang-whangers, noisy or abusive talkers or writers. [*CE*]

4. Cade was the leader of a rebellion in southern England in 1450. As dramatized in Shakespeare's *II Henry VI*, Act IV, he is a ranting, anti-intellectual demagogue who orders the beheading of a learned and loyal nobleman. [*CE*]

5. Rufus Choate, a well-known lawyer who had organized the Whig party in Massachusetts.

6. *Kavanagh: A Tale* was published on 21 May.

TO SOPHIA HAWTHORNE

14 Mall-street [Salem]. Monday 16th. April, 1849.

Ownest wife,

I suppose thou wilt not expect (nor wish for) a letter from me; but it is so desolate and lonesome here that I needs must write. This is a miserable time. Thy and the children's absence; and this dreary bluster of the wind, which at once exasperates and depresses me to the very last degree; and, finally, a breakfast (the repetition of yesterday's) of pease and Indian pudding!!¹ It is a strange miscellany of grievances; but it does my business—it makes me curse my day. This matter of the breakfast is the most intolerable, just at this moment; because the taste of it is still in my mouth, and the nausea and disgust overwhelm me like the conscious- ness of sin. Hell is nothing else but eating pease and baked Indian pudding! If thou lovest me, never let me see either of them again. Keep such things for thy and my worst enemies. Give thy husband bread, or cold potatoes; and he never will complain—but pease and Indian pudding! God forgive me for ever having bur- thened my conscience with such abominations. They are the Unpardonable Sin and the Intolerable Punishment, in one and the same accursed spoonfull!

I think I hardly ever had such a dismal time as yesterday. I cannot bear the loneliness of the house. I need the sunshine of the children; even their little quar- rels and naughtinesses would be a blessing to me. I need thee, above all, and find myself, at every absence, so much the less able to endure it. It is misery to go to bed without thee. Come home! Come home!

Where dost thou think I was on Saturday afternoon? Thou wilt never guess. In haste; for it is almost Custom House time.

Thy Husband.

1. Indian pudding, a New England specialty, is made with corn meal and molasses.

TO HENRY WADSWORTH LONGFELLOW

Custom House [Salem], June 5th. 1849

Dear Longfellow,

I meant to have written you before now about Kavanaugh, but have had no quiet time, during my letter-writing hours; and now the freshness of my thoughts has exhaled away. It is a most precious and rare book—as fragrant as a bunch of flowers, and as simple as one flower. A true picture of life, moreover—as true as those reflections of the trees and banks that I used to see in the Concord, but refined to a higher degree than they; as if the reflection were itself reflected. Nobody but yourself would dare to write so quiet a book; nor could any other succeed in it. It is entirely original; a book by itself; a true work of genius, if ever there were one; and yet I should not wonder if many people (God confound them!) were to see no such matter in it. In fact, I doubt whether hardly anybody else has enjoyed it so much as I; although I have heard or seen none but favorable opinions.

I should like to have written a long notice of it, and would have done so for the Salem Advertiser; but, on the strength of my notice of Evangeline and some half-dozen other books, I have been accused of a connection with the editorship of that paper, and of writing political articles—which I never did one single time in my whole life![1] I must confess, it stirs up a little of the devil within me, to find myself hunted by these political bloodhounds. If they succeed in getting me out of office, I will surely immolate one or two of them. Not that poor monster of a Conolly, whom I desire only to bury in oblivion, far out of my own remembrance. Nor any of the common political brawlers, who work on their own level, and can conceive of no higher ground than what they occupy. But if there be among them (as there must be, if they succeed) some men who claim a higher position, and ought to know better, I may perhaps select a victim, and let fall one little drop of venom on his heart, that shall make him writhe before the grin of the multitude for a considerable time to come. This I will do, not as an act of individual vengeance, but in your behalf as well as mine, because he will have violated the sanctity of the priesthood to which we both, in our different degrees, belong. I do not claim to be a poet; and yet I cannot but feel that some of the sacredness of that character adheres to me, and ought to be respected in me, unless I step out of its immunities, or make it a plea for violating any of the rules of ordinary life. When other people concede me this privilege, I never think that I possess it; but when they disregard it, the consciousness makes itself felt. If they will pay no reverence to the imaginative power when it causes herbs of grace and sweet-scented flowers to spring up along their pathway, then they should be taught what it can do in the way of producing nettles, skunk-cabbage, deadly night-shade, wolf's bane, dog-wood. If they will not be grateful for its works of beauty and beneficence, then let them dread it as a pervasive and penetrating mischief, that can reach them at their firesides and in their bedchambers, follow them to far countries, and make their very graves refuse to hide them. I have often thought that there must be a good deal of enjoyment in writing personal satire; but, never having felt the slightest ill-will towards any human being, I have hitherto been debarred from this peculiar source of pleasure. I almost hope I shall be turned out, so as to have an opportunity of trying it. I cannot help smiling in anticipation of the astonishment of some of these local magnates here, who suppose themselves quite out of the reach of any retribution on my part.

I have spent a good deal of time in Boston, within a few weeks; my two children having been ill of the scarlet-fever there; and the little boy was in quite an alarming way. I could not have submitted in the least, had it gone ill with him; but God spared me that trial—and there are no real misfortunes, save such as that. Other troubles may irritate me superficially; nothing else can go near the heart.

I mean to come and dine with you, the next time you invite me; and Hillard said he would come too. Do not let it be within a week, however; for Bridge and his wife expect to be here in the course of that time.

Please to present my regards to Mrs. Longfellow, and believe me

ever your friend,
Nath Hawthorne.

1. Eben N. Walton, editor of the *Advertiser* since 1847, was to write to NH on 30 June to deny this charge, in a letter intended to be forwarded to Washington as evidence. Walton stated that "only two articles from your pen have appeared in its columns, one a notice of a dramatic company, the other a notice of Longfellow's 'Evangeline.'" [*CE*] Eight items by NH, including a review of Melville's *Typee* and notices of two theatrical performances, have been located in the *Advertiser*.

TO GEORGE S. HILLARD

Salem, June 12th. 1849.

Dear Hillard,

I have just received your letter. It makes me sick at heart to think of making any effort to retain this office. I trust that God means to put me into some other position; and I care not how hard or how humble it may be. Nevertheless, I shall answer your questions as well as I can.

I am accused, you tell me, of writing political articles for a democratic paper here—the Salem Advertiser. My contributions to that paper have been two theatrical criticisms, a notice of a ball at Ballard Vale, a notice of Longfellow's Evangeline, and perhaps half a dozen other books.[1] Never one word of politics. Any one of the articles would have been perfectly proper for a Whig paper; and, indeed, most of them were copied into Whig papers elsewhere. You know, and the public know, what my contributions to the Democratic Review have been.[2] They are all published in one or another of my volumes—all, with a single exception. That is a brief sketch of the life of my early and very dear friend, Cilley, written shortly after his death, at the request of the Editor.[3] I have not read it for years; but I am willing to refer to it, as a proof of what sort of a politician I am. Written in the very midst of my grief, and when every other man in the nation, on both sides, was at fever-heat, it is, though very sad, as calm as if it had been written a hundred years after the event; and, so far as I recollect it, it might as well have been written by a Whig as by a Democrat. Look at it, and see. It cannot be called a political article; and, with that single exception, I have never, in all my life, written one word that had reference to politics.

As to my political action, I have voted, since I have been in this office, twice. I have listened to a portion of a political address by Mr. Rantoul, and to a portion of another by Caleb Cushing.[4] I suffer under considerable odium, in the view of my own party, for having taken no part whatever. All my official conduct has been under the supervision and sanction of Colonel Miller, a Whig, the Deputy Collector, and now the Collector, of the port. He is now in Washington. I refer to him. If any definite charges were before me, I would answer them. As it is, I have no more to say—and do not care to have said what I have.

I repeat, that it makes me sick to think of attempting to recover this office. Neither have I any idea that it can be recovered. There is no disposition to do me justice. The Whigs know that the charges are false. But, without intending it, they are doing me a higher justice than my best friends. I have come to feel that it is not good for me to be here. I am in a lower moral state than I have been;—a duller intellectual one. So let me go; and, under God's providence, I shall arrive at something better.

Your friend,
Nath Hawthorne.

1. For NH's contributions to the Salem *Advertiser,* see 5 June 1849, note 1.
2. NH contributed twenty-three works to the *United States Magazine and Democratic Review* between October 1837 and April 1845.
3. For the biography of Cilly in the *Democratic Review,* see 21 March 1838, note 5.
4. Robert Rantoul, Boston lawyer and reformer; Caleb Cushing, Whig congressman and unsuccessful Democratic candidate for governor of Massachusetts from 1847 to 1848.

TO LEWIS W. MANSFIELD

Salem, December 26th. 1849.

My dear Sir,[1]

I have been exceedingly reprehensible in not answering your letter sooner; but the fact is, I did not read the accompanying poem till last evening; for I have been much engaged on a book which I am about to publish.[2] Moreover, your autography (permit me to say) is of a very difficult and delusive character, and might well frighten away a timid reader. It served indeed to light me through the story of the Sexton; but it was as if I had been wandering through the old church which you write about, with only a glimmering taper in my hand, affording very indistinct glimpses of the objects around me. I have gone through it again, this morning, with better success, and have received, I think, from the story the impression which you intended to convey. The incident is certainly striking and picturesque, and you have spiritualized it with good effect.

The idea, on which you have written your longer story, seems to me very beautiful.[3] I should be glad, if you will so far favor me, to see the poem, and will by no means undertake to criticise it, or suggest any improvements or modifications; partly because, for my individual self, I have no talent at criticism, although I can usually enter into the spirit of a work and see it as the author sees it;—and still

more, because I doubt whether any desirable influence is ever exercised by a foreign judgment on works of imagination,—in respect to which the author himself
should be despotic and autocratical. If I were you, I would complete the poem at
once, without caring for anybody's opinion, and publish it, were it only for the
sake of looking at your own work from another point of view. Manuscript is as
delusive as moonshine. Print is like common daylight, and enables an author to
comprehend himself as no *dictum* of another man ever will. I doubt not that you
would meet with sympathy enough, from some minds, to compensate you for the
lack of appreciation in others.

I speak with perfect frankness, because the confidence which you repose in me
(and by which I am gratified) gives you a claim to it. Should you favor me with a
sight of the poem allow me to beg that it may be Mrs. Mansfield's manuscript
rather than your own.

Very truly Yours,
Nathl Hawthorne.

L. W. Mansfield, Esq.
Cohoes

1. Lewis William Mansfield, a businessman from Cohoes, near Troy, New York, had retired in
order to turn his attention to a writing career.

2. A reference to *The Scarlet Letter,* which would be published on 16 March 1850.

3. *The Morning Watch: A Narrative* (1850), a poem of more than two thousand lines, mainly
in pentameter couplets. It is an allegorical account of a journey toward immortality, much
influenced by Samuel Taylor Coleridge's "Rime of the Ancient Mariner." [*CE*]

TO JAMES T. FIELDS

Salem, Jan. 15th 1850.

My dear Fields,

I send you, at last, the manuscript portion of my volume; not quite all of it, however, for there are three chapters still to be written of "The Scarlet Letter."
I have been much delayed by illness in my family and other interruptions. Perhaps
you will not like the book nor think well of its prospects with the public. If so (I

need not say) I shall not consider you under any obligation to publish it. 'The Scarlet Letter' is rather a delicate subject to write upon, but in the way in which I have treated it, it appears to me there can be no objections on that score. The article entitled "Custom House" is introductory to the volume, so please read it first. In the process of writing, all political and official turmoil has subsided within me, so that I have not felt inclined to execute justice on any of my enemies. I have not yet struck out a title, but may possibly hit on one before I close the package. If not, there need be no running title of the book over each page, but only of the individual articles.[1] Calculating the page of the new volume at the size of that of the 'Mosses,' I can supply 400 and probably more. "The Scarlet Letter," I suppose, will make half of that number; otherwise, the calculation may fall a little short, though I think not.

Very truly yours,
Nathl Hawthorne.

P.S. The proof-sheets will need to be revised by the author. I write such an infernal hand that this is absolutely indispensable.

If my wife approves—whom I have made the umpire in the matter—I shall call the book Old-Time Legends; together with *sketches, experimental and ideal.* I believe we must consider the book christened as above. Of course, it will be called simply "Old-Time Legends," and the rest of the title will be printed in small capitals. I wish I could have brought a definition of the whole book within the compass of a single phrase, but it is impossible. If you think it essentially a bad title, I will make further trials.

1. According to Fields, it was at "my suggestion" that NH changed his plan from making the book a novelette and short stories to expanding the novelette and making it the entire work (see *CE,* 1:xx–xxii).

TO JAMES T. FIELDS

Salem, January 20th. 1850.

My dear Fields,

I am truly glad that you like the introduction; for I was rather afraid that it might appear absurd and impertinent to be talking about myself, when nobody, that I know of, has requested any information on that subject.

As regards the size of the book, I have been thinking a good deal about it. Considered merely as a matter of taste and beauty, the form of publication which you recommend seems to me much preferable to that of the 'Mosses.' In the present case, however, I have some doubts of the expediency; because, if the book is made up entirely of 'The Scarlet Letter,' it will be too sombre. I found it impossible to relieve the shadows of the story with so much light as I would gladly have thrown in. Keeping so close to its point as the tale does, and diversified no otherwise than by turning different sides of the same dark idea to the reader's eye, it will weary very many people, and disgust some. Is it safe, then, to stake the fate of the book entirely on this one chance? A hunter loads his gun with a bullet and several buck-shot; and, following his sagacious example, it was my purpose to conjoin the one long story with half a dozen shorter ones; so that, failing to kill the public outright with my biggest and heaviest lump of lead, I might have other chances with the smaller bits, individually and in the aggregate.

However, I am willing to leave these considerations to your judgment, and should not be sorry to have you decide for the separate publication.

In this latter event, it appears to me that the only proper title for the book would be 'The Scarlet Letter'; for 'The Custom House' is merely introductory—an entrance-hall to the magnificent edifice which I throw open to my guests. It would be funny, if, seeing the further passages so dark and dismal, they should all choose to stop there!

If 'The Scarlet Letter' is to be the title, would it not be well to print it on the title-page in red ink? I am not quite sure about the good taste of so doing; but it would certainly be piquant and appropriate—and, I think, attractive to the great gull whom we are endeavoring to circumvent.

Very truly Yours,
Nathl. Hawthorne

J. T. Fields, Esq.[1]

---

1. The following is an undated draft of this letter: "As regards the book, I have been thinking and considering—I was rather afraid that it appears sagacious absurd and impertinent to have some doubts, of the introduction to the book, which you recommend. I have found it impossible to relieve the shadows of the story with so much light as I would gladly stake the fate of the book entirely on the public. However, I am willing to leave these considerations to your judgment, and should not be sorry to have you decide for the separate publication. [¶] If the Judgment Letter is to be the title—print it on the title page in red ink. I think that the only proper title for the book would be the Scarlet Letter. I am quite sure about the taste of so doing. I think it is attractive and appropriate—"

TO GEORGE S. HILLARD

Salem, January 20th. 1850.

My dear Hillard,

I read your letter in the entry of the Post-Office; and it drew—what my troubles never have—the water to my eyes; so that I was glad of the sharply cold west wind that blew into them as I came homeward, and gave them an excuse for being red and bleared.[1]

There was much that was very sweet—and something too that was very bitter—mingled with that same moisture. It is sweet to be remembered and cared for by one's friends—some of whom know me for what I am, while others, perhaps, know me only through a generous faith—sweet to think that they deem me worth upholding in my poor walk through life. And it is bitter, nevertheless, to need their support. It is something else besides pride that teaches me that ill-success in life is really and justly a matter of shame. I am ashamed of it, and I ought to be. The fault of a failure is attributable in a great degree, at least—to the man who fails. I should apply this truth in judging of other men; and it behoves me not to shun its point or edge in taking it home to my own heart. Nobody has a right to live in this world, unless he be strong and able, and applies his ability to good purpose.

The money, dear Hillard, will smooth my path for a long time to come. The only way in which a man can retain his self-respect, while availing himself of the generosity of his friends, is, by making it an incitement to his utmost exertions, so that he may not need their help again. I shall look upon it so—nor will shun any drudgery that my hand shall find to do, if thereby I may win bread.[2]

Your friend,
Nathl Hawthorne.

Hon. Geo. S. Hillard,
Boston.

1. Hillard had collected a considerable sum from "those who admire your genius and respect your character. It is only paying, in a very imperfect measure, the debt we owe you for what you have done for American literature." [CE] This was to help support NH after he lost his sole source of income following his dismissal from the Salem Custom House.

2. NH was able to repay the money after four months as consul in Liverpool, as he announced in a letter to Hillard, 9 December 1853 (CE, 17:154–55). [CE]

TO HORATIO BRIDGE

Salem, April 13th. 1850.

Dear Bridge,

I am glad you like the Scarlet Letter; it would have been a sad matter indeed, if I had missed the favorable award of my oldest and friendliest critic. The other day, I met with your notice of 'Twice-told Tales,' for the Augusta Age; and I really think that nothing better has been said about them since.[1] This book has been highly successful; the first edition having been exhausted in ten days, and the second (5000 copies in all) promising to go off rapidly.[2]

As to the Salem people, I really thought that I had been exceedingly good-natured in my treatment of them. They certainly do not deserve good usage at my hands, after permitting me—(their most distinguished citizen; for they have no other that was ever heard of beyond the limits of the Congressional district)—after permitting me to be deliberately lied down, not merely once, but at two separate attacks, on two false indictments, without hardly a voice being raised in my behalf; and then sending one of the false witnesses to Congress, others to the State legislature, and choosing another as their Mayor. I feel an infinite contempt for them, and probably have expressed more of it than I intended; for my preliminary chapter has caused the greatest uproar that ever happened here since witch-times. If I escape from town without being tarred-and-feathered, I shall consider it good luck. I wish they *would* tar-and-feather me—it would be such an entirely novel kind of distinction for a literary man! And from such judges as my fellow-citizens, I should look upon it as a higher honor than a laurel-crown.

I have taken a cottage in Lenox, and mean to take up my residence there, about the first of May.[3] In the interim, my wife and children are going to stay in Boston, and nothing could be more agreeable to myself than to spend a week or so with you; so that your invitation comes extremely apropos. In fact, I was on the point of writing to propose a visit. We shall remove our household gods from this infernal locality, tomorrow or next day. I will leave my family at Dr. Peabody's,[4] and come to Portsmouth on Friday of this week—or on Saturday at furthest, unless prevented from coming at all. I shall take the train that leaves Boston at 11 oclock; so, if you happen to be in Portsmouth, that afternoon, please to look after me. I am very glad of this opportunity of seeing you; for I am afraid you will never find your way to Lenox.

I thank Mrs. Bridge for her good wishes as respects my future removals from office; but I should be sorry to anticipate such bad fortune as being ever again appointed to one.

Truly Your friend,
Nathl Hawthorne

1. Bridge's review has not been located.
2. The 2,500-copy first printing of *The Scarlet Letter* had been exhausted, and a second edition of 2,500 copies was published on 22 April 1850.
3. The Hawthornes rented the "Red Cottage" in Lenox, western Massachusetts, from the Tappans. They moved on 23 May, stayed with the Tappans for about a week, then moved again into their own home.
4. Nathaniel Peabody, a dentist, was SPH's father.

TO HORATIO BRIDGE

Lenox, August 7th 1850.

Dear Bridge,

Putnam consents to publish a new edition of the African Cruiser, with the proposed additions, and desires that they may be sent *soon*.[1] So, if you will send me the additional matter by express (advising me of the transmission, by letter) it shall be put into shape as soon as possible. As I am busy with my own literary matters, and as you have probably a fair share of leisure, I should be glad if you would leave me very little to do. Do not fear being too prolix; as I shall be pretty sure to expunge whatever may seem superfluous. Above all, be quick.

Your surmise as to Putnam's failure was wholly groundless. He has paid up the balance due me, and appears to be in the full tide of success. He has just got out a new edition of my Mosses[2]—not that I mention that fact as accounting for his success.

Duyckinck, of the Literary World, and Herman Melville are in Berkshire, and I expect them to call here this morning. I shall ask Duyckinck to announce your forthcoming book with the author's name. I met Melville, the other day, and liked him so much that I have asked him to spend a few days with me before leaving these parts.[3]

I have two hens sitting. My wife and children are well. We all have very pleasant recollections of your visit. Julian broke a china cup, a few days ago, and very coolly remarked that "Mr. Bridge could mend it!" We have got some maple paper, and shall soon begin the transmutation of your boxes.

With my best regards to Mrs. Bridge, and remembrances to Mrs. Holbrook, (if with you) I remain

Very truly yours,
Nath. Hawthorne.

P.S. You had better write to Greene of the Post, to announce the African Cruiser.

1. The book was, in fact, reprinted without changes.
2. A fourth printing of *Mosses* was done in July or early August.
3. For a description of the most famous picnic excursion in American literature, see Hershel Parker, *Herman Melville: A Biography, Volume 1, 1819–1851* (Baltimore, Md.: Johns Hopkins University Press, 1996), 744–49.

TO EVERT A. DUYCKINCK [WITH SOPHIA HAWTHORNE]

My dear Sir,

I thank you very much for these admirable outlines. I am such a profound admirer of Flaxman, & the severe beauty of his classic style is so particularly in accord with my love of sculpture, that I thought I could not like any other out-lines.[1] Retzsch never had for me the charm which obtains with so many persons.[2] But I think these are superior to those of Retzsch. I am weary of his consumptive profiles. Rip Van Winkle himself is wonderfully fine, I think. The fathomless goodnature, the patience, gentleness & mild sufferance of his face & figure tran-scend Irving's conception.[3]

But, my dear Mr Duyckinck, I cannot speak or think of any thing now but the extraordinary review of Mr Hawthorne, in the Literary World.[4] The Virginian is the first person who has ever in *print* apprehended Mr Hawthorne. I keep constantly reading over & over the inspired utterances, & marvel more & more that the word has at last been said, which I have so long hoped to hear, & so well said. There is such a generous, noble enthusiasm as I have not before found in any critic of any writer.

While bringing out the glory of his subject, (excuse me, but I am speaking as an indifferent person) he surrounds himself with a glory. The freshness of primeval nature is in that man, & the true Promethean fire is in him.[5] Who can he be, so fearless, so rich in heart, of such fine intuition? Is his name altogether hidden?

We have been very much interested in Mr Melville's books, & we are very much obliged to you for them.[6] Mr Hawthorne has read them all on the new hay in the barn, which is a delightful place for the perusal of worthy books.

Truly yours,
S A. Hawthorne

E. A. Duyckinck Esq.

Aug. 29 1850

Lenox, August 29th. 1850

My dear Sir,

I have read Melville's works with a progressive appreciation of the author. No writer ever put the reality before his reader more unflinchingly than he does in "Redburn," and "White Jacket." "Mardi" is a rich book, with depths here and there that compel a man to swim for his life. It is so good that one scarcely pardons the writer for not having brooded long over it, so as to make it a great deal better.

You will see by my wife's note that I have all along had one staunch admirer; and with her to back me, I really believe I should do very well without any other. Nevertheless, I must own that I have read the articles in the Literary World with very great pleasure. The writer has a truly generous heart; nor do I think it necessary to appropriate the whole magnificence of his encomium, any more than to devour everything on the table, when a host of noble hospitality spreads a banquet before me. But he is no common man; and, next to deserving his praise, it is good to have beguiled or bewitched such a man into praising me more than I deserve.

Sincerely Yours,
Nathl Hawthorne.

E. A. Duyckinck, Esq.
New York

1. John Flaxman, English artist and book illustrator.

2. Friedrich Augustus Moritz Retzsch, German artist known for his outline engravings of the works of Goethe, Schiller, and Shakespeare.

3. Duyckinck had apparently sent NH the designs by F. O. C. Darley for an illustrated edition of *The Sketch Book* (1848) by Washington Irving, essayist, biographer, historian, and one of America's best-known writers.

4. Melville's famous "Hawthorne and His Mosses, by a Virginian spending July in Vermont" had appeared in the 17 and 24 August *Literary World*s. The Hawthornes did not know of Melville's authorship.

5. Prometheus, Greek god who made humankind from clay and stole fire from heaven to animate them. As a penalty, Zeus chained him to a mountain, where an eagle ate his liver daily.

6. To this date, Melville had published *Typee: A Peep at Polynesian Life* (1846), *Omoo: A Narrative of Adventures in the South Seas* (1847), *Mardi and a Voyage Thither* (1849), *Redburn: His First Voyage* (1849), and *White-Jacket; or, The World in a Man-of-War* (1850). Duyckinck sent to Melville "'parcels' for Hawthorne . . . that included copies of *Redburn, White-Jacket,* and *Mardi*"; in turn, Melville "promised to deliver the parcels (presumably without knowing what they contained) to Hawthorne" (Melville, *Correspondence,* ed. Lynn Horth [Evanston, Ill.: Northwestern University Press, 1993], 166n).

TO JAMES T. FIELDS

Lenox. October 1. 1850

My dear Fields,

I shall be glad to have you publish an edition of the Twice-told Tales; and as it seems to be the fashion now-adays for authors to write prefaces to their new editions, I will write a very pretty one—biographical and bibliographical; perhaps half-a dozen pages long, perhaps rather more.[1] You need not wait for it before printing the book, as I suppose the paging of the main text will be independent of that of the preface; or, if you choose, you might print the second volume first. I don't like to turn aside from my new volume just now to write anything else.[2]

I shan't have the new story ready by November, for I am never good for anything in the literary way till after the first autumnal frost which has somewhat such an effect on my imagination that it does on the foliage here about me, multiplying and brightening its hues; though they are likely to be sober and shabby enough after all.

I am beginning to puzzle myself about a title for the book. The scene of it is one of those old projecting-storied houses familiar to my eye in Salem; and the story horrible to say, is little less than two hundred years long; though all but thirty or forty pages of it refers to the present time. I think of such titles as—"The House of the Seven Gables" there being that number of gable ends to the old shanty—or "The Seven Gabled House" or simply "The Seven Gables." Tell me how these strike you. It appears to me that the latter is rather the best; and has the great advantage that it would puzzle the devil to tell what it means.

Yours truly,
Nathl Hawthorne

1. NH wrote a new preface to the 1850 edition of *Twice-Told Tales* at Fields' request (see *CE*, 9:3–7).
2. *The House of the Seven Gables* would be published on 9 April 1851.

TO JAMES T. FIELDS

Lenox, November 3d. 1850
Dear Fields,

"The Old Pyncheon House; a Romance," "The Old Pyncheon Family; or the House of the Seven Gables; a Romance." Choose between them. I have rather a distaste to a double title; otherwise I think I should prefer the second. Is it any matter under which title it is announced? If a better should occur hereafter, we can substitute. Of these two, on the whole, I judge the first to be the better.

I write diligently, but not so rapidly as I had hoped. I find the book requires more care and thought than the "Scarlet Letter";—also, I have to wait oftener for a mood. The Scarlet Letter being all in one tone, I had only to get my pitch, and could then go on interminably. Many passages of this book ought to be finished with the minuteness of a Dutch picture, in order to give them their proper effect. Sometimes, when tired of it, it strikes me that the whole is an absurdity, from beginning to end; but the fact is, in writing a romance, a man is always—or always ought to be—careering on the utmost verge of a precipitous absurdity, and the skill lies in coming as close as possible, without actually tumbling over. My prevailing idea is, that the book ought to succeed better than the Scarlet Letter; though I have no idea that it will.

You probably won't get it out before the first of January. I don't believe it is any great matter.

Yours truly,
Nathl Hawthorne.

The MS. of the Scarlet Letter was burnt long ago.
Will you ask Whipple's advice as to those two titles?[1]

1. Whipple, Fields, and Longfellow all agreed that *The House of the Seven Gables* was the best title for the book.

TO PETER OLIVER

Lenox, May 3d, 1851.

Sir,[1]

It pains me to learn that I have given you what I am content to acknowledge a reasonable ground of offense, by borrowing the name of the Pyncheon family for my fictitious purposes, in the "House of the Seven Gables." It never occurred to me, however, that the name was not as much the property of a romance-writer as that of Smith, for instance; while its unhackneyed singularity, and a certain indescribable fitness to the tone of my work, gave it a value which no other of the many sirnames, which suggested themselves to me, seemed to possess. Writing the book at a distance from Salem, I had no opportunity for consulting ancient records or the recollection of aged persons; and I beg you to believe that I was wholly unaware, until the receipt of your letter, that the Pyncheons, at so recent a period as you mention, if at any former one, had been residents of that place. Had this fact been within my knowledge—and especially had I known that any member of the family had ever borne the title of judge—I should certainly have considered it discourteous and unwarrantable to make free with the name. I would further say, that I intended no allusion to any Pyncheons, now or at any previous period extant—that I never heard anything to the discredit, in the slightest degree, of this old and respectable race—and that I give the fullest credence to your testimony in favor of your grandfather, Judge Pynchon, and greatly regret that I should have seemed to sully his honorable name, by plastering it upon an imaginary villain.

As regards my mention of the Oliver family, in 'Grandfather's Chair,' I believe I have no apology to make. The book is not at hand, and I have no very distinct recollection of the manner or matter of my allusions to your distinguished ancestors; but whatever I may have written, it was with an honest desire to convey true impressions, and in anything but an unkindly or disrespectful temper. You bear a historic name, and cannot reasonably expect (nor do I perceive any reason why you should desire) that the doings and sufferings of your forefathers should be left out of the story of Massachusetts, even as told by so humble an annalist as myself. Few persons, I conceive, unconnected with the Olivers by blood, can entertain a higher respect than I do for the historical and personal characters of the eminent men of the family, who figured before the Revolution. Nothing worse can be said of them, than that it was their misfortune to make an erroneous choice between two deeply seated affections—their attachment to their native land, and their loyalty to the king;—nor, for my part, am I disposed to question that they considered themselves as satisfying both these principles, and as following out the dictates of the purest patriotism by adhering to the royal cause.

You suggest that reparation is due for these injuries of my pen, but point out no mode in which it may be practicable. It is my own opinion that no real harm has been done; inasmuch as I expressly enter a protest, in the preface to 'The House of the Seven Gables,' against the narrative and the personages being considered as other than imaginary.[2] But, since it appears otherwise to you, no better course occurs to me than to put this letter at your disposal, to be used in such manner as a proper regard for your family-honor may be thought to demand.

Respectfully, Sir,
Your obedient Serv't,
Nathl Hawthorne.

Peter Oliver, Esq.
Boston.

1. Peter Oliver, lawyer, historian, and author of *The Puritan Commonwealth* (1856), was later described by NH as "pacified" by this letter (*CE*, 16:433). Oliver's reply is published in Norman Holmes Pearson, "The Pyncheons and Judge Pyncheon," *Essex Institute Historical Collections* 100 (October 1964): 245–46.

2. NH wrote in his preface, "It has been no part of [my] object, however, to describe local manners, nor in any way to meddle with the characteristics of a community" for which he "cherishes a proper respect and a natural regard. . . . The personages of the Tale . . . are really of the Author's own making" (*CE*, 2:3).

TO ELIZABETH PALMER PEABODY

Lenox, May 25th. 1851.

Dear Elizabeth.

This subject of Life Insurance is not new to me. I have thought, read, and conversed about it, long ago, and have a pamphlet, treating of its modes and advantages, here in the house. I know that it is an excellent thing in some circumstances—that is, for persons with a regular income, who have a surplus, and can calculate precisely what it will be. But I have never yet seen the year, since I was married, when I could have spared even a hundred dollars from the necessary expense of living. If I can spare it this year, it is more than I yet know; and if this year, then probably it would be wanted the ensuing year. Then an expenditure must positively increase with the growth of our children and the cost of their education. I say nothing of myself—nothing of Sophia—since it is probably our duty to sacrifice all the green margin of our lives to these children, whom we have seen fit to bring into the world. In short, there is no use in attempting to put the volume of my convictions on paper. I should have insured my life, years since, if I had not seen that it is not the thing for a man, situated like myself, to do, unless I could have a reasonable certainty of dying within a year or two. We must take our chance, or our dispensation of Providence. If I die soon, my copyrights will be worth something, and might—by the exertions of friends, who undoubtedly *would* exert themselves—be made more available than they have yet been. If I live some years, I shall be as industrious as I may, consistently with keeping my faculties in good order; and not impossibly I may thus provide for Sophia and the children.

Sophia and the baby are getting on bravely.[1] She gazes at it all day long, and continually discovers new beauties. As for me, who look at it perhaps half a dozen times a day, I must confess that I have not yet discovered the *first* beauty. But I think I never have had any natural partiality for my children. I love them according to their deserts; they have to prove their claim to all the affection they get; and I believe I could love other people's children better than mine, if I felt that they deserved it more. Perhaps, however, I should not be quite a fair judge on which side the merit lay. It does seem to me, moreover, that I feel a more decided drawing of the heart towards this baby, than either of the other two, at their first appearance. She is my last and latest, my autumnal flower, and will be still in her gayest bloom, when I shall be most decidedly an old man—the daughter of my age, if age and decrepitude are really to be my lot. But, if it were not for the considerations in the first part of my letter, I should wish this scribbling hand to be dust, ere then.

Your father, as I see him here, presents as comfortable an aspect of old age as I can possibly imagine. He does not appear to suffer any disquietude from your mother's precarious condition; what is not present to his perceptions, has no existence for him. The children hang about him continually, and find him an excellent playmate; merely a playmate, however, for he is the most heedless and venturesome of the three, and when left to his guidance, they do things and undertake adventures which they would never dream of, by themselves. Una, I think, discovers a certain pleasant weakness in him. Julian, who has far more natural reverence, thinks him wise, and thinks everything wise that he sanctions. Happily, he finds my surroundings so rough and rugged that he has continually some little job or other to do; and when tired of these, he sits in Sophia's room, quietly exulting in the baby, or talks with me, who have always taken pleasure in his talk, more than in that of shrewder people. At the birth-scene, his imperturbableness was heroic and sublime—and, at the same time, almost laughable. I do not believe he has any uneasy desire to leave us, but rather dreads returning to the anxieties which he has left behind him. He will stay, I trust, as long as he can be contented here, and is not necessary with you; and I doubt whether he has had any more peaceful or really happier season, in his life, than this. I have not the least idea of leaving him in charge here; being well assured that it would be far safer to leave the house and children to take care of themselves.

Yours affectionately
Nathl Hawthorne.

1. Rose had been born on 20 May.

TO CAROLINE STURGIS TAPPAN

[Lenox] Sept. 5th, 1851.

Dear Mrs. Tappan,[1]

As questions of disputed boundary are very ticklish ones, whether between nations or individuals, I think it best to take the diplomatic correspondence, on our part, into my own hands; and I do it the more readily as I am quite an idle man nowadays, and shall find it rather agreeable than otherwise; whereas Sophia is exceedingly busy, and, moreover, is averse to any kind of a dispute.[2] You will be kind enough to give me credit for writing in a spirit of undisturbed good humor and friendly courtesy; and this being the case, I shall feel myself safe in writing with, likewise, the most perfect frankness.

In the first place permit me to notice the question which you put to Sophia, whether she would not prefer to receive kindness rather than assume rights. I do not know what would be her reply; but for myself, in view of the infirmities of human nature in general and my especial infirmities, and how few people are fit ever to receive kindnesses, and how a far fewer are worthy to do them, I infinitely prefer a small right to a great favor. It was this feeling that made me see the necessity of a sum stipulated in the way of rent, between Mr. Tappan and myself. The little difficulty in which we now find ourselves merely serves to confirm me in my principle, and will instruct me in all future cases to have my rights more sharply defined than they are now.

Undoubtedly, by consenting to receive money from me, Mr. Tappan did invest me with certain rights, and among the most evident of them I consider the property in the fruit. What is a garden without its currant-bushes and fruit-trees? Last year no question of this nature was raised; our right seemed to be tacitly conceded, and if you claimed or exercised any manorial privileges, it never came to my knowledge. This season when Mr. Tappan inquired what part of the garden I wanted to cultivate, I supposed he wished to know in order that he might send Cornelius to plough it— as he very kindly did. It never came into my mind that I should lose the most valued part of the demesne by failing to plant it. If the fruit trees have suffered by my neglect, this was reasonable ground for remonstrance on Mr. Tappan's part, but would hardly justify him in so summary a measure as that of taking the property out of my hands at once, and without a word of explanation, or either informing me of the fact. Nor do I conceive that he had any purpose of doing so.

At all events, Sophia and I supposed ourselves to be in full possession of that part of the garden, and in having a right of property over its products more extensive than that of Adam and Eve in Eden, inasmuch as it excluded not a single tree. Such being our view of the matter, you meet Mary Beekman, carrying a basket of fruit. You stop her, look at the contents of the basket, and inquire as to its destination. You ask her (at least so she averred to Mrs. Peters, although she has since qualified her statement) whether it had been given away or sold. You conduct this examination in such a mode as to make it evident to our servant-girl that you consider Sophia and Mrs. Peters as combining in a depredation on your property.

You follow this up with a note of remonstrance to Sophia, in which you take her to task not merely for giving away some of the fruit, but for presuming to choose her own time to gather it for our own use. Now let us suppose the perfectly parallel case, that Mrs. Ward should take upon herself to pursue the same course in regard to the fruit of Highwood.[3] Would Mrs. Tappan have responded to Mrs. Ward by a gentler assertion of right than Sophia's to yourself? I think not. I do not see how you could. And if you did so, it would be purely out of your own abundant grace and good nature, and would by no means be due to any propriety in the supposed behavior of Mrs. Ward.

Finally in your note of last evening, you give us very clearly to understand that you look upon us as having no rights here whatever. Allow me to say that this is precisely the crisis which I contemplated when I felt it essential to be understood that I had *bought* my rights, even from persons so generously disposed as yourself and Mr. Tappan. The right of purchase is the only safe one. This is a world of bargain and sale and no absurdity is more certain to be exposed than the attempt to make it anything else.

As regards the apples of discord (meaning thereby the plums, pears, peaches, and whatever besides), we sincerely hope you will take as many of them as you please, and on such grounds as may cause them to taste most agreeably. If you choose to make a raid, and to seize this fruit with the strong hand, so far from offering any armed resistance, we shall not so much as remonstrate. But would it not be wiser to drop the question of right, and receive it as a free-will offering from us? We have not shrunk from the word "gift," although we happen to be so much the poorer of two parties, that it is rather a suspicious word from you to us. Or, if this do not suit you, you can take the fruit in humble requital of some of the many favors bestowed in times past, and which we may perhaps remember more faithfully than you do.

And then the recollection of this slight acidity of sentiment, between friends of some years' standing, may impart a pleasant and spirited flavor to the preserves and jams when they come upon your table. At any rate, take what you want, and that speedily, or there will be little else than a parcel of rotten plums to dispute about.

With kind regards to Mr. Tappan,

Very truly yours,
N. H.

1. Caroline Sturgis Tappan, friend of Emerson's and a contributor to the *Dial*, and her husband William owned property at Lenox, near the Berkshire Mountains of Massachusetts.

2. This letter ended the dispute over who had rights to the fruit.

3. While the Hawthornes were renting their estate, the Tappans were living at "Highwood," the property of Samuel Gray Ward, a banker and, with his wife Anna Hazard Barker Ward, a friend of Emerson.

TO EVERT A. DUYCKINCK

West-Newton, Decr 1st. 1851

My dear Sir,

I have run away from the Berkshire winter—in fact, given up Lenox for good and all—and am established here for some months to come; and I shall be glad if you will direct the Literary World hitherward.[1] It was one of my regrets in leaving Lenox, that I should no longer be benefitted by your visits to our friend Melville; but then it is not impossible you may come to Boston—in which case (having good store of bedrooms) I shall hope to have you for my own guest. We are less than half an hour's ride (by rail-road) from the city.

What a book Melville has written![2] It gives me an idea of much greater power than his preceding ones. It hardly seemed to me that the review of it, in the Literary World, did justice to its best points.[3]

Truly Yours,
Nathl Hawthorne.

E. A. Duyckinck, Esq.

1. The Hawthornes were renting Horace Mann's house.
2. *Moby-Dick* had been published shortly before 14 November.
3. Duyckinck's review of *Moby-Dick* appeared in the 15 and 22 November *Literary Worlds*.

TO RUFUS W. GRISWOLD

West Newton, Decr 15th. 1851.

Dear Sir,[1]

I greatly regret that circumstances render it impossible for me to be present, on the occasion of Mr Bryant's discourse in honor of James Fenimore Cooper.[2]

No man has a better right to be present than myself, if many years of most sincere and unwavering admiration of Mr. Cooper's writings can establish a claim. It is gratifying to observe the earnestness with which the literary men of our country write in paying honor to the deceased; and it may not be too much to hope that, in the eyes of the public at large, American literature may henceforth acquire a weight and value, which have not heretofore been conceded to it. Time and death have begun to hallow it.

Very Respectfully Yours,
Nathl Hawthorne.

Rev. Rufus W. Griswold,
Secry &c.

1. Rufus Wilmot Griswold, prolific editor and anthologist, edited the *International Monthly Magazine of Literature, Art, and Science* between 1850 and 1852.
2. William Cullen Bryant, poet and editor of the *New York Evening Post*. James Fenimore Cooper, one of America's most popular authors of this period, had died on 14 September. A memorial ceremony was held in New York, and NH's letter was later published in a memorial volume.

TO RUFUS W. GRISWOLD

West Newton, Decr 15th. 1851.

My dear Sir,

As regards the proposition for twelve short tales, I shall not be able to accept it; because experience has taught me that the thought and trouble, expended on that kind of production, is vastly greater, in proportion, than what is required for a long story.

I doubt whether my romances would succeed in the serial mode of publication; lacking, as they certainly do, the variety of interest and character which seem to have made the success of other works, so published. The reader would inevitably be tired to death of the one prominent idea, if presented to him under different aspects for a twelvemonth together. The effect of such a story, it appears to me, depends on its being read continuously. If, on completion of another work, it should seem fairly and naturally divisible into serial portions, I will think further of your proposal.

I have by me a story which I wrote just before leaving Lenox, and which I thought of sending to Dr. Bailey of the National Era, who has offered me $100 for an article.[1] But, being somewhat grotesque in its character, and therefore not quite adapted to the grave and sedate character of that Journal, I hesitate about so doing, and will send it to the International, should you wish it at the price above-mentioned.[2] The story would make between twenty and thirty of such pages as Ticknor's editions of my books—hardly long enough, I think, to be broken into two articles for your magazine; but you might please yourself on that point. I cannot afford it for less than $100, and would not write another for the same price.

Very truly Yours,
Nathl Hawthorne.

1. "The Great Carbuncle" had appeared in the *National Era,* edited by Gamaliel Bailey, in January 1850.
2. "Feathertop" appeared in the 1 February and 1 March 1852 *International Magazines.*

TO EDWIN PERCY WHIPPLE

West Newton, May 2d 1852.

Dear Whipple,

Behold a huge bundle of scribble, which you have thoughtlessly promised to look over![1] If you find it beyond your powers, hand it over to Ticknor at once, and let him send it to the Devil; but before that happens, I should be glad to have it looked over by a keen, yet not unfriendly eye, like yours. Nobody has yet read it, except my wife; and her sympathy, though very gratifying, is a little too unreserved to afford me the advantages of criticism. After all, should you spy ever so many defects, I cannot promise to amend them; the metal hardens very soon after I pour it out of my melting-pot into the mould.

I wish, at least, you would help me to choose a name. I have put 'Hollingsworth,' on the title-page, but that is not irrevocable; although, I think, the best that has occurred to me—as presenting the original figure about which the rest of the book clustered itself.

Here are others—"Blithedale,"—well enough, but with no positive merit or suitability. "Miles Coverdale's Three Friends";—this title comprehends the book, but rather clumsily. "The Veiled Lady"—too melodramatic; and, besides, I do not wish to give prominence to that feature of the Romance. "Priscilla"—she is such a shrinking damsel that it seems hardly fair to thrust her into the vanguard and make her the standard-bearer. "The Blithedale Romance"—that would do, in lack of a better. "The Arcadian Summer"—not a taking title. "Zenobia"—Mr. Ware has anticipated me in this.[2] In short, I can think of nothing that exactly suits the case. Perhaps just the thing will pop into your mind.

Now that the book is off my mind, I feel as if I were out of the body; but (like a great many other translated spirits, I fear) the sense of it does not exactly increase my happiness. I hope to get to Concord soon, and shall there set to work on a Second Wonder Book.[3]

Truly Yours,
Nathl Hawthorne.

P.S. Are you a Kossuthian?[4] I am about as enthusiastic as a lump of frozen mud, but am going to hear him at Charlestown, tomorrow, in hope of warming up a little.

1. *The Blithedale Romance* was published on 14 July 1852. Whipple read the manuscript for NH and gave a "most glowing account of it" to Fields (*CE*, 3:xx).
2. William Ware, *Zenobia: or, The Fall of Palmyra: An Historical Romance* (1837).
3. *Tanglewood Tales* was published on 20 September 1852.
4. Lajos Kossuth (1802–94), Hungarian patriot, was welcomed to Concord by Emerson in May 1852.

TO EVERT A. DUYCKINCK

Concord, June 15th. 1852.

Dear Sir,

Will you be kind enough to direct the Literary World to Concord (Mass.) where I have bought a house, and feel myself, for the first time in my life, at home.[1] It is no very splendid mansion, being originally a farm-house, of moderate size, and ante-revolutionary date; but Mr. Alcott, the Orphic Sayer,[2] of whom I bought it, had wasted a good deal of money in fitting it up to suit his own taste, all which improvements I get for little or nothing. Having been much neglected, the place is the raggedest in the world; but it will make, sooner or later, a comfortable and sufficiently pleasant home. Alcott called it "Hillside," as it stands close at the base of a steep ascent; but as it is also in proximity (too nigh, indeed) to the road leading into the village, I have re-baptized it "The Wayside"—which seems to me to possess a moral as well as descriptive propriety. It might have been called "Woodside"—the hill being covered with a growth of birch, locust-trees, and various sorts of pine.— I hope, some time or other, that you will come and see it for yourself.

I see that the papers announce me as having begun a new work, the day after finishing the Blithedale Romance.[3] My poor intellect is not quite so ready and flexible as that. It is now six weeks since I finished the romance; and I have neither written nor thought of the first sentence of another book.

With much regard,
Yours,
Nathl Hawthorne.

1. Samuel E. Sewell, acting as trustee for Mrs. Alcott, who actually held deed to "Hillside," sold the house and the land it sat on; Emerson sold eight acres across the street. NH bought both for $1,500 on 2 April and the family moved in late May.

2. Alcott's "Orphic Sayings" was the most ridiculed and parodied contribution to the *Dial*.

3. Possibly the facetious comment in the Boston *Transcript* of 15 June about the possibility of a "grand exodus of all literary people" from the Berkshires because of the new prohibition law: "Hawthorne will leave the unfinished sheets of some 'golden legend,' and look out for some nook among the hills, where 'mountain dew' is not proscribed." [*CE*]

TO FRANKLIN PIERCE

Concord, July 5th. 1852

Dear Pierce,

I had some hopes of seeing you to-day; but as there are no signs of your coming, I sit down to write. I have now obtained, I think, as many materials as will serve for your father's share in the biography;[1] but such as relate to yourself come in more slowly, and, in proportion, more scantily. I hope Mr. Ayer will soon be able to send me some matter for the legal part of your life; and Col. Whipple like-wise promised to send me something adapted to the same object. As regards your life at Washington, I saw Atherton on Saturday; but he had not many facts to give me; and, to say the truth, your conduct there was so unlike that of most other political men that your biographer's task becomes the more difficult. Instead of thrusting yourself forward on all good or bad occasions, it always required a case of necessity, to bring you out; and having done the needful with as little noise as possible, you withdrew into the background. Now, I see no impropriety in your-self indicating to me the points, as to this part of your career, which it may be best to illustrate; and I wish you also to supply me with copies of such speeches as may most fitly be quoted or alluded to. Reports of committees, too, of which you may have been the author, would be available matter for this purpose.

I have seen in the Boston Times, two or three numbers, from an "old Soldier," describing your warfare in Mexico. Is this account authentic? If so, I might get some good points from it. I have not been able to obtain all the numbers, and should be glad if you will supply me with the whole, if in your possession, and supposing it to be reliable. Also, anything else of the same nature. There will be ample stuff, I think, for this part of the work—which, though it should be made prominent, ought not to be so much so as to overshadow you as a man of peace-ful pursuits. "Cedant arma togae."[2] A statesman in your proper life—a gallant sol-dier in the hour of your country's need—such, in the circumstances, is the best mode of presenting you.

I am sensible of a very difficult and delicate part of my task, in your connec-tion with the great subject of variance between the North and South.[3] There is no way, however, open to my perception—no course either of true policy, or worthy either of you or your biographer—save to meet the question with perfect candor and frankness, and to state what has been your action, and what your position; not pugnaciously, and, by no manner of means, defensively, but so as to put you on the broadest ground possible, as a man for the whole country. I suppose I shall see my way clearer, when I actually approach these knotty points; but at all events, they are not to be shirked nor blinked.

Mr Atherton spoke of a report on the "Right of Petition," written by Mr. Baker. I should be glad to have a copy.

It will be highly desirable, if not absolutely necessary, that we hold a long and quiet discussion, before I cast the biography into its final shape. No matter how soon; but any time within two or three weeks will probably do. I wish you could at least spend a night here; and I should think the seclusion and repose of this place would be beneficial to you, after the continual disturbances to which your position subjects you.

I sometimes wish the convention had nominated old Cass![4] It would have saved you and me a great deal of trouble; but my share of it will terminate four years sooner than your own.

I sent you a book by Col. Whipple. Be pleased not to let it go abroad, as the publication is kept back in order to let the English edition come out first—my copyright, on that side of the water, being more valuable, in its immediate results, than here.

Your friend,
Nathl Hawthorne.

P.S. You invariably direct your letters to Concord, *N.H.*—but your postmaster has now learned to correct the error. Let him keep his office for that good deed.

1. NH volunteered to prepare a campaign biography of Pierce on 9 June, and Pierce accepted soon after. The book was completed on 27 August and published on 11 September 1852.
2. "Let wars yield to peace," from Cicero, *De Oficiis*, I, xxii, 77.
3. Pierce supported the Compromise of 1850 (which included the Fugitive Slave Law) and the recognition of states' rights.
4. Lewis Cass, senator from Michigan, had been Pierce's main opponent for the presidential nomination of the Democrats.

TO GEORGE WILLIAM CURTIS

Concord, July 14th. 1852.

My dear Howadji,[1]

I think (and am glad to think) that you will find it necessary to come hither in order to write your Concord Sketches;[2] and as for my old house, you will understand it better after spending a day or two in it. Before Mr Alcott took it in hand, it was a mean-looking affair, with two peaked gables; no suggestiveness about it, and no venerableness, although, from the style of its construction, it seems to have survived beyond its first century. He added a porch in front, and a central peak, and a piazza at each end, and painted it of a rusty olive hue, and invested the whole with a modest picturesqueness—all which improvements, together with its

situation at the foot of a wooded hill, make it a place that one notices, and remembers for a few moments after passing it. Mr Alcott expended a good deal of taste,
and some money (to no great purpose) in forming the hill side, behind the house,
into terraces, and building arbors and summer-houses out of rough stems and
branches of trees, on a system of his own. These must have been very pretty in
their day, and are so still, although much decayed, and shattered more and more
by every breeze that blows. The hill-side is covered chiefly with locust-trees, which
come into luxurious blossom in the month of June, and look and smell very
sweetly; intermixed with a few young elms, and some white pines, and infant
oaks—the whole forming rather a thicket than a wood. Nevertheless, there is
some very good shade to be found there. I spend delectable hours there, in the
hottest part of the day, stretched out at my lazy length, with a book in my hand,
or an unwritten book in my thoughts.[3] There is almost always a breeze stirring
along the side or brow of the hill.

From the hill-top there is a good view along the extensive level surfaces, and
gentle hilly outlines, covered with wood, that characterize the scenery of Concord.
We have not so much as a gleam of lake or river in the prospect; if there were, it
would add greatly to the value of the place, in my estimation.

The house stands within ten or fifteen yards of the old Boston road (along
which the British marched and retreated) divided from it by a fence, and some
trees and shrubbery of Mr Alcott's setting out. Whereupon, I have called it "The
Wayside"—which I think a better name, and more morally suggestive than that
which, as Mr Alcott has since told me, he bestowed on it—'The Hillside.' In front
of the house, on the opposite side of the road, I have eight acres of land; the only
valuable portion of the place, in a farmer's eye, and which are capable of being
made very fertile. On the hither side, my territory extends some little distance over
the brow of the hill, and is absolutely good for nothing, in a productive point of
view—though very good for many other purposes.

I know nothing of the history of the house; except Thoreau's telling me that it
was inhabited, a generation or two ago, by a man who believed that he should
never die. I believe, however, he is dead—at least, I hope so; else he may possibly
appear, and disturb my title to his residence.

Of course, you will not understand me to have written the above with the
remotest idea of your putting it into your sketch, but only for you to make out
your sketch from, in case of your not coming to Concord. But you must come—
not only to see the place and its inhabitants—but for the more important end of
our seeing you. We have a guest-chamber, into which we shall gladly instal you,
though with some degree of remorseful reluctance, in view of your probably being
tormented to death by musquitoes. They do plague us most damnably.

I asked Ticknor to send a copy of "The Blithedale Romance" to G. P. Putnam's care, for you. Do not read it as if it had anything to do with Brook Farm (which essentially it has not) but merely for its own story and characters.

Truly Yours
Nathl Hawthorne.

1. A reference to Curtis's *Nile Notes of a Howadji* (1851) and *The Howadji in Syria* (1851). The term, derived from Arabic, means "a traveler."

2. Curtis was preparing the sketches of Emerson and Hawthorne for *Homes of American Authors* (1852). The sketch of NH appears on pp. 291–313.

3. The last two phrases are quoted directly by Curtis in *Homes of American Authors,* 306, and much of the remainder of the description is paraphrased. [*CE*]

TO WASHINGTON IRVING

Concord (Mass) July 16th. 1852

My dear Sir,

Some months ago (in requital of a little book, which was not worth it) I had the pleasure to receive a note from your hand; and almost ever since, I have been daily intending to answer it.[1] But while I waited for some peculiarly genial mood, so much time went by, that at last I deemed it better to put off the epistle until I could accompany it with another work, which has at least cost me more thought, although it may be no better worth your acceptance than 'The Wonder Book.'

I beg you to believe, my dear Sir, that your friendly and approving word was one of the highest gratifications that I could possibly have received, from any literary source. Ever since I began to write, I have kept it among my cherished hopes to obtain such a word; nor did I ever publish a book without debating within myself whether to offer it to your notice. Nevertheless, the idea of introducing myself to you as an author, while unrecognized by the public, was not quite agreeable; and I saw too many faults in each of my books to be altogether willing to obtrude it beneath your eye. At last, I sent you 'The Wonder Book,' because, being meant for children, it seemed to reach a higher point, in its own way, than anything that I had written for grown people.

Pray do not think it necessary to praise my "Blithedale Romance"—or even to acknowledge the receipt of it.² From my own little experience, I can partly judge how dearly purchased are books that come to you on such terms. It affords me— and I ask no more—an opportunity of expressing the affectionate admiration which I have felt so long; a feeling, by the way, common to all our countrymen, in reference to Washington Irving, and which, I think, you can hardly appreciate, because there is no writer with the qualities to awaken in yourself precisely the same intellectual and heartfelt recognition.

With great respect,
Very truly Yours,
Nathl Hawthorne.

1. *A Wonder Book* had been published on 8 November 1851. Irving thanked NH for a copy of the book but made no comments on its contents or quality.

2. Irving recognized in *The Blithedale Romance* "the same power and originality, the same felicity of language and masterly delineations of character that had delighted me in your previous works" (*CE*, 16:571n).

TO HORATIO BRIDGE

Concord, (Mass) October 13th. 1852

Dear Bridge,

I received your letter some time ago, and ought to have answered long since; but you know my habits of epistolary delinquency—so I make no apology. Besides, I have been busy with literary labor of more kinds than one. Perhaps you have seen Blithedale before this time. I doubt whether you will like it very well; but it has met with good success; and has brought me (besides its American circulation) a thousand dollars from England, whence likewise have come many favorable notices. Just at this time, I rather think, your friend stands foremost there, as an American fiction-monger. In a day or two, I intend to begin a new romance, which, if possible, I mean to make more genial than the last.

I did not send you the Life of Pierce, not considering it fairly one of my literary productions; but Sam Bridge tells me he transmitted one of the earliest copies. I was terribly reluctant to undertake this work, and tried to persuade Pierce, both by letter and viva voce, that I could not perform it so well as many others; but he thought differently, and of course, after a friendship of thirty years, it was impossible to refuse my best efforts in his behalf, at the great pinch of his life. It was a hard book to write; for the gist of the matter lay in explaining how it has happened that, with such extraordinary opportunities for eminent distinction, civil and military, as he has enjoyed, this crisis should have found him so obscure as he certainly was, in a national point of view. My heart absolutely sank, at the dearth of available material. However, I have done the business, greatly to Frank's satisfaction; and, though I say it myself, it is judiciously done; and, without any sacrifice of truth, it puts him in as good a light as circumstances would admit. Other writers might have made larger claims for him, and have eulogized him more highly; but I doubt whether any other could have bestowed a better aspect of sincerity and reality on the narrative, and have secured all the credit possible for him, without spoiling all by asserting too much. And though the story is true, yet it took a romancer to do it.

Before undertaking it, I made an inward resolution that I would accept no office from him; but, to say the truth, I doubt whether it would not be rather folly than heroism to adhere to this purpose, in case he should offer me anything particularly good. We shall see. A foreign mission I could not afford to take;—the consulship at Liverpool, I might; and he could not do a better thing, either for me or the credit of his administration, than to make the appointment.[1] I have several invitations from English celebrities to come over there; and this office would make all straight. He certainly owes me something; for the biography has cost me hundreds of friends, here at the north, who had a purer regard for me than Frank Pierce or any other politician ever gained, and who drop off from me like autumn leaves, in consequence of what I say on the slavery question.[2] But they were my real sentiments, and I do not now regret that they are on record.

What luck that fellow has! I have wanted you here, while working up his memoirs, for the sake of talking over his character with you, as I cannot with any other person. I have come seriously to the conclusion that he has in him many of the chief elements of a great ruler, and that if he wins the election, he may run a great career. His talents are administrative; he has a subtle faculty of making affairs roll onward according to his will, and of influencing their course without showing any trace of his action. There are scores of men in the country that seem brighter than he is; but Frank has the directing mind, and will move them about like pawns on a chess-board, and turn all their abilities to better purpose than they themselves could. Such is my idea of him, after many an hour of reflection on his character, while making the best of his poor little biography. He is deep, deep, deep. But what luck withal! Nothing can ruin him.

Nevertheless, I do not feel very sanguine about the result of this election. There is hardly a spark of enthusiasm in either party; but what little there is, so far as I can judge, is on the side of Scott.[3] The prospect is none of the brightest, either in New York, Ohio, or Pennsylvania; and unless he gets one of them he goes to the wall. He himself does not appear to admit the possibility of failure; but I doubt whether in a position like his, a man can ever form a reliable judgment of the prospect before him. Should he fail, what an extinction it will be. He is now in the intensest blaze of celebrity—his portrait is everywhere, in all the shop-windows, and in all sorts of styles—on wood, steel, and copper, on horseback, on foot, in uniform, in citizen's dress, in iron medallions, in little brass medals, and on hand-kerchiefs; and it seems as if the world were full of his not very striking physiog-nomy. If he loses the election, in one little month, he will fade utterly out of sight, and never come up again. He is playing a terrible game, and for a tremendous stake;—on one side, power, the broadest popularity, and a place in history; on the other (for I doubt whether it would not prove a knock-down blow) insanity, or death, and a forgotten grave. He says, however, that he should bear it with equa-nimity. Perhaps he might; but I think he is not himself aware of the intense excite-ment in which he lives. He seems calm; but his hair is whitening, I assure you. Well; three weeks more will tell the story.[4]

By-the-by, he speaks most kindly of you, and his heart seems to warm towards all his old friends, under the influence of his splendid prospects. If he wins, he will undoubtedly seek for some method of making you the better for his success. I love him; and, oddly enough, there is a kind of pitying sentiment mixed up with my affection for him, just now.

I meant to have told you all about my visit to [Bowdoin College at] Brunswick, at the recent semi-centennial celebration; but the letter has already grown to too great length. It was rather a dreary affair. Only eight of our classmates were pres-ent, and they were a set of dismal old fellows, whose heads looked as if they had been out in a pretty copious shower of snow. The whole intermediate quarter of a century vanished, and it seemed to me as if they had undergone this miserable transformation in the course of a single night—especially as I myself felt just about as young as when I graduated. They flattered me with the assurance that time had touched me tenderly; but, alas, they were each a mirror, in which I beheld the reflection of my own age. I did not arrive there till the public exercises were nearly over—and very luckily, too, for my praises had been sounded by ora-tor and poet, and, of course, my blushes would have been quite oppressive.

I have recently spent a fortnight at the Isle of Shoals. In Portsmouth, I had the pleasure of meeting your wife; and I never saw her look so well. The baby flourishes. Your sister Hannah, escorted by your cousin Sam, made us a call here, last week. My wife and children are in excellent health. We like our home, and are quite comfortable in all respects.

Your friend,
Nathl Hawthorne.

1. President Pierce nominated NH to the Senate as consul to Liverpool, which confirmed his appointment on 26 March 1853.

2. In *The Life of Franklin Pierce,* Chapter VI, NH opposes to the view of the abolitionists "another view, and probably as wise a one. It looks upon slavery as one of those evils which divine Providence does not leave to be remedied by human contrivances, but which, in its own good time, by some means impossible to be anticipated, but of the simplest and easiest operation, when all its uses shall have been fulfilled, it causes to vanish like a dream" (*The Complete Works of Nathaniel Hawthorne,* 12 vols. [Boston: Houghton, Mifflin, 1883], 12:417). The Boston *Transcript* quoted this, and the surrounding three paragraphs on slavery, in its review on 8 September. Local comment is perhaps typified by the antislavery minister Theodore Parker's linking NH to the Scottish writer Thomas Carlyle as "the only two men of Genius in this age [who] have appeared on the side of slavery . . . on the side of the enemies of mankind." [*CE*]

3. General Winfield Scott was the Whig candidate.

4. Pierce was elected on 12 November.

TO GEORGE WILLIAM CURTIS

Concord, Octr 28th. 1852

My dear Curtis,

Intelligence of your great event had come to me, two or three weeks ago, through two or three channels[1]—one of them a young Englishman, a "Clerk of Oxenford,"[2] who had bean spending some time at Newport.[3] It must have made a prodigious sensation in society; else the swell and ripple of it would scarcely have been perceptible, here in my quiet harbor. We both congratulate you with all our hearts; and were I privileged to do so, I should quite as earnestly congratulate the lady.

As for this Magazine of yours, I wish it had never been undertaken, and that you had nothing to do with it.[4] I turn a weary and a dreary ear to projects of this kind—having no faith in their succeeding, to any desirable extent, and no sort of alacrity in endeavoring to promote their success. I have wasted far too much of my life, and done myself more than enough of moral and intellectual harm, with scribbling sketches for Magazines. As for a serial, it would be excruciating to me to have a story dragging itself, for six months or a year, before the public, like a half-torpid snake out of its hole, and becoming defunct at one end before the other had seen the light. Then again (an absolutely insurmountable objection,) I should lose the English copyright by prepublication in this country. I received a thousand dollars for Blithedale, and mean to get more (if I can) for the next one; and Mr. Putnam, I rather imagine, would stand aghast at the idea of making good such a deficit.

If I had a short tale or essay, or a dozen of them, I would send them to you; and whenever I have leisure, I will strenuously twist my poor wits towards the concoction of something that may suit this projected Magazine. My name (if that be any object) may be announced among the expected contributors; and at some period during the existence of the work (that is to say, in the course of a twelve-month) I will do my best to redeem the pledge. Meantime, allow me to hope that your own connection with the Magazine will not be very conspicuous—at least, not before it is quite settled that it is to take the top rank among periodicals, a phenomenon which I shall believe when I see it. There can be no great harm in contributing as much as you like, and making other people's articles serve as foils to the glow and brilliancy of your own; but I would not be responsible for alien stupidity and ponderosity.

After all, I may be entirely in the wrong. Heaven grant it, and give all manner of success to the Magazine; but in that case, it must be effected by new talent, and not by such stumpy and rheumatic pens as mine. I counsel you, therefore, to seek the aid of young men, or young women. There is a woman somewhere in the West—I forget her name; but she wrote an article called the "Age of Jonathan," for the gold medal of the Albany Female Academy, in 1850—who is bound to shine in our literature.[5] You had better hunt her up, and engage her.

Very truly,
Nathl Hawthorne.

P.S. Since writing the above, I have found the lady's name—Miss Mary Mather, of Flint, Michigan—and likewise her article, which I send you. It is certainly very clever—not astonishingly so, perhaps—but she would be better for your purpose than twice her weight of old writers.

1. Curtis had become engaged on 11 October to Elizabeth Winthrop.
2. Chaucer, *Canterbury Tales*, "General Prologue," 285.
3. Charles d'Urban Morris had received his B.A. and M.A. degrees from Oxford; he would stay in America as a professor at Johns Hopkins University.
4. Curtis and Charles F. Briggs were the editors of the *Putnam's Monthly Magazine*, which would begin publication in January 1853. NH did not contribute anything to *Putnam's*.
5. Mary Mather had been a student at the Albany Female Academy. Her essay was selected by a committee of Harvard professors and was published in *Exercises of the Alumnae of the Albany Female Academy on Their Ninth Anniversary, July 1st, 1850.* [CE]

TO NATHANIEL J. LORD

Concord, April 4th. 1853

My dear Sir,[1]

Mr. Burchmore has handed me a note from the President to myself, which I take the liberty to enclose. You will perceive from it his kind opinion of Mr. B., although his delicate regard to his own position and that of the Collector of Boston restrains him from requesting an appointment from the latter. I see no way in which I can better comply with the President's suggestion, in the last sentence of the note, than by requesting your own good offices in Mr. B's behalf. As the head of our party in Essex County, his case falls properly under your supervision; and a word from you would be more efficacious in his behalf, than anything that I could say or write. In fact, I do not feel myself entitled to ask a political favor, in this matter, and shall therefore confine myself to offering testimony.

A few years ago, as you are aware, I held the office of Surveyor in the Salem Custom House, and had full opportunities of observing Mr. Burchmore's ability as a man of business, and his intimate acquaintance with every department of Custom House duty. In this respect, I sincerely believe, he has no superior. His whole active life (comprising a quarter of a century) has been spent in that vocation; and there is no branch of it in which he is not perfectly at home. During several years (and up to the period of his removal, solely for political reasons, under President Taylor) though nominally a clerk, he was really the chief-officer of the Custom House, and administered the duties of that position to the entire satisfaction of the whole body of your Salem merchants. I, at least, have never heard a whisper of complaint against him, as a man of business; nor (while often incurring hostility by his political course) have his enemies ever been able to affix a stain on his official integrity. In this particular, the record of his conduct has lain open, during four years, to the criticism of his political antagonists, who have succeeded him in office; and Mr. Burchmore has always been ready to challenge scrutiny.

Such a man, it appears to me, is far too useful to be laid aside; and I can only farther say, that any support, which you may think fit to afford him in his application for a suitable office, would be regarded as a personal favor by myself.

With great respect,
truly Yours,
Nathl Hawthorne.

N. J. Lord, Esq.
Salem.

P.S. I likewise transmit to you a letter from the accounting offices of the Treasury, received this morning, showing Mr. Burchmore's high character at the Department.

N. H.

1. Nathaniel James Lord, lawyer and president of the National Democrats of Salem. [*CE*]

TO WILLIAM D. TICKNOR

U. S. Consulate,
Liverpool,[1] August 6th '53.

Dear Ticknor,

Grace arrived, last evening, and, by this time, is probably getting a little sea-sick.[2] She did not seem to be in very good spirits. I fear she has left her heart in England, but whether in possession of a single individual, or of the whole nation, is more than I can tell.

Before I reached England, a man named Wm. S. Orr, of Amen Corner, Paternoster Row, had directed a letter hither, expressing his intention to publish an illustrated edition of the "Mosses," and offering me £50 for my sanction of the publication.[3] In a subsequent letter to my clerk, he requests that the preceding let-ter should not be delivered to me—thereby indicating that he wishes to back out of his proposal. Of course, he is entirely at liberty to do so; but if he is really going to publish a handsome edition of the "Mosses," I should be glad to correct the proof-sheets; for there are several errors in the American edition. Will you be kind enough to call, and look into this matter? Do not say anything about the £50. It is a matter for him to settle with his own liberality and conscience, and cannot be bargained for on my part.

I thank you for your oratorical efforts in my behalf, and make no doubt that you did a great deal better for me than I could have done for myself.[4] On two occa-sions, already, I have mumbled some d—d nonsense, and shall have to mumble some more, next Friday, when I dine with the Mayor. However, it is one comfort that I cannot cut a much more foolish figure than the Englishmen themselves; for the tongue of man never uttered worse speeches than theirs are. For my part, I charge myself pretty high with champagne and port before I get upon my legs; and whether the business is to make a speech or to be hanged, I come up to it like a man—and I had as lief it should be one as the other.

I am going to carry my family across the river to-day, and establish them at the Rockferry Hotel, about two miles from town. The children have suffered very much from want of air. Mrs. Hawthorne, too, has a continual cold; and I really doubt whether she will be able to bear this abominable climate. It suits me, how-ever, and I have never felt better in my life than since we landed.

I have looked at "Tanglewood," since my last, and find that Chapman has it all.[5] Do write often,

Truly Yours,
Nathl Hawthorne.

1. The Hawthornes had sailed from Boston with Ticknor on 6 July, arriving at Liverpool on the seventeenth.

2. "Grace Greenwood," the pen name of Sara Jane Lippincott, poet, journalist, and travel writer.

3. The English publisher William Somerville Orr did not publish an edition of *Mosses from an Old Manse*.

4. Perhaps at a dinner with the Lord Mayor of London arranged by his friend Francis Bennoch. [CE] Bennoch—a great friend and help to NH during his English stay—was a London politician and businessman.

5. *Tanglewood Tales* was published in England by Chapman and Hall on 13 August 1853.

TO WILLIAM L. MARCY

Consulate of the United States
Liverpool 12 Aug 1853

Sir,[1]

It becomes my duty to acquaint you with a claim that has been made upon me, for compensation for loss sustained in the rescue of a number of American Citizens from the burning wreck of an American vessel at Sea.

The claim is made by Captain Claussen of the Norwegian schooner "Ebenezer" of Stavanger, & is for £30. 1—" sterling.

The circumstances under which the claim is made are these—The Ebenezer was on her voyage from New York to Liverpool on the morning of the 7th of last month (July), when Captain Claussen saw a vessel to leeward with a signal of distress flying, and immediately bore down to her relief. He found her to be the Ship "JZ" of New York Captain Spencer 4 days from New York on her voyage to Liverpool, and was informed that she was on fire and requested to lay by her. He at once hove his vessel to and sent his Boats with proffer of help, but it had been discovered that the fire was so far advanced as to defy any effort to extinguish it, and the ship was soon after a mass of flames. The Captain and Crew, with what provisions & water they could save, were then taken on board the Ebenezer. Captain Claussen however at the request of Captain Spencer continued to lay by the burning vessel while any hope remained of saving anything from her, but by two in the afternoon she was a complete wreck, burnt to the water's edge, and they left her. The "Ebenezer" being but a very small vessel had no accommodation for so large an accession to her people, and the Captain to provide it was obliged to throw overboard 33 Barrels of Tar which were stowed on deck, to enable him to build a temporary house, and that being done the shipwrecked people were made as comfortable as possible under the circumstances, and brought in safety to this Port.

These statements were confirmed in every particular by the Mate and Crew (the declaration of the Mate & three Seamen I enclose herewith) who spoke highly of the kindness with which they had been treated.

The value of the Tar thus thrown overboard, amounting to £30.15.0, as before stated, the Captain has been obliged to pay to the parties it belonged to, and as he cannot recover it from the Insurance he will lose it unless our Government will reimburse him.

I have therefore the honor to submit the matter to you, not being in possession of any Instructions, nor acquainted with any Law, under which I can pay such a claim.

I am requested if you should instruct me to pay it, to pay it to the agent of the vessel in Liverpool.

I may add that Captain Claussen has made no mention of claiming for the subsistence money usually claimed by English vessels in such cases.[2]

With high respect
I have the honor to be
Your obedient Servant
Nathl Hawthorne

To The Hon Wm L Marcy
Secretary of State
Washington

1. William Learned Marcy, a career politician, was secretary of state under Pierce.

2. The treasury auditor who evaluated this case disallowed the costs for the tar but gave the captain a subsistence allowance of fifty cents a day for the seamen. NH was authorized to pay the owners of the *Ebenezer* $180. At this time, one British pound was equal to approximately five American dollars.

TO MRS. WILSON AULD

U. S. Consulate,
Liverpool, August 24th, 1853.

Madam,

It is my painful duty to inform you of the decease of your late husband, Captain Wilson Auld, who died in this city on Sunday last.[1] His disease was erysipelas,[2] combined with some internal complaint. He had been ill nearly three weeks, during the latter part of which time, he was in a state of partial insensibility, and appeared to suffer comparatively little. Every attention was paid to his comfort; and rest assured that he received the kindest treatment from those near him in his last moments.

By the first opportunity, I shall forward the effects he left behind him, together with a statement of the expenditures attending his sickness and funeral. He was buried yesterday, in the Cemetery of Saint James, in this city.

I beg leave to assure you of my heartfelt sympathy in this sad bereavement,

and remain, Madam,
very sincerely Yours
Nathl Hawthorne,
U. S. Consul for the
port of Liverpool.

Mrs. Wilson Auld,
New Orleans.

1. NH's account of Auld's death and funeral is in *English Notebooks, CE,* 21:19–24.
2. Erysipelas, a contagious disease marked by a diffused inflammation of the skin.

TO WILLIAM B. PIKE

[Liverpool, 13 September 1853]

Dear Pike,[1]

I have been intending to write to you this some time, but wished to get some tolerably clear idea of the state of things here before communicating with you.[2] I find that I have three persons in my office—the head clerk, or vice-consul, at £150; the second clerk, at £150; and the messenger, who also does some writing, at £80. They are all honest and capable men, and do their duty to perfection. No American would take either of these places for twice the sums which they receive; and no American without some months' practice would undertake the duty. Of the two, I would rather displace the vice-consul than the second clerk, who does a great amount of labor, and has a remarkable variety of talent, whereas the old gentleman, though perfect in his own track, is nothing outside of it. I will not part with either of these men unless compelled to do so; and I don't think old Lord Massey can compel me.[3]

Now as to the Manchester branch, it brings me in only about £200. There is no consular agent there, all the business being transacted here in Liverpool. The only reason for appointing an agent would be that it might shut off all attempts to get a separate consulate there. There is no danger, I presume, of such an attempt for some time to come, for Pierce made a direct promise that the place should be kept open for my benefit. Nevertheless, efforts will be made to fill it, and very possibly representations may be made from the businessmen of Manchester that there is necessity for a consul there. In a pecuniary point of view, it would make very little difference to me whether the place were filled by an independent consul or by a vice-consul of my own appointment, for the later would, of course, not be satisfied with less than the whole £200. What I should like would be to keep the place vacant and receive the proceeds as long as possible, and at last, when I could do no better, to give the office to you. No great generosity in that, to be sure. Thus I have put the matter fairly before you. Do you tell me as frankly how your own affairs stand, and whether you can live any longer in that cursed old custom-house without hanging yourself. Rather than that you should do so, I would let you have the place to-morrow, although it would pay you about £100 less than your present office. I suppose, as a single man, you might live within your income at Manchester; but, judging from my own experience as a married man, it would be a very tight fit. With all the economy I could use, I have already got rid of $2,000 since landing in England. Hereafter I hope to spend less and save more.

In point of emolument, my office will turn out about what I expected. If I have ordinary luck I shall bag from $5,000 to $7,000 clear per annum; but to effect this I shall have to deny myself many things which I would gladly have. Colonel Crittenden told me that it cost him $4,000 to live with only his wife at a boarding-house, including a journey to London now and then.[4] I am determined not to spend more than this, keeping house with my wife and children. I have hired a good house, furnished, at £160, on the other side of the river Mersey, at Rock Park, where there is good air and playground for the children; and I can come over to the city by steamboat every morning. I like the situation all the better because it will render it impossible for me to go to parties, or to give parties myself, and will keep me out of a good deal of nonsense.

Liverpool is the most detestable place as a residence that ever my lot was cast in—smoky, noisy, dirty, pestilential; and the Consulate is situated in the most detestable part of the city. The streets swarm with beggars by day and by night. You never saw the like and I pray that you may never see it in America. It is worth while coming across the sea in order to feel one's heart warm towards his own country; and I feel it all the more because it is plain to be seen that a great many of the Englishmen whom I meet here dislike us, whatever they may pretend to the contrary.

On the morning when I left America, Mr. William Manning requested me to give him a letter of introduction to Pierce. I promised to send him one, and accordingly enclose it. When you deliver it, I enjoin it upon you to talk to the old man like a father to his son, and tell him the absolute absurdity of his going to Washington in pursuit of office, and the impossibility of his obtaining anything through a personal interview with the President. I expressed all this to him in the strongest terms at the time when he asked me for the letter. It did no good, however; neither will you do any good by your remonstrances; but as a matter of conscience, I beseech you to let him have the naked truth.

My family and myself have suffered very much from the elements. There has not been what we should call a fair day since our arrival, nor a single day when a fire would not be agreeable. It is always threatening to rain, but seldom rains in good earnest. It never does rain, and it never don't rain; but you are pretty sure to get a sprinkling if you go out without an umbrella. I long for one of our sunny days, and one of our good hearty rains. Except by the fireside, I have not once been as warm as I should like to be; but the Englishmen call it a sultry day whenever the thermometer rises above 60°. There has not been heat enough in England this season to ripen an apple.

My wife and children often talk of you. Even the baby has not forgotten you; and I need not say that nothing would give us so much pleasure as to see you here. It must come by and by.

When you write to me send your letter to the care of Ticknor & Co., Boston, and they will get the despatch agent to transmit it to me free of cost. Write often, and say as much as you can about yourself, and as little as you please about A—, N—, and B—, and all the rest of those wretches of whom my soul was weary to death before I made my escape.

Your friend ever,
Nathl Hawthorne.

1. William Baker Pike, a sometime politician and journalist, had worked at the Salem Custom House under NH.
2. NH was trying to get a position for Pike as vice-consul to Manchester.
3. That is, Secretary of State William Marcy.
4. Thomas Leonidas Crittenden from Kentucky, NH's predecessor as the Liverpool consul.

TO JAMES T. FIELDS

Liverpool, Jany 20th 1854

Dear Fields,

I wish your epistolary propensities were rather stronger than they seem to be. All your letters to me, since I left America, might be squeezed into one page of note-paper. However, I quite sympathize with you in hating to write.

I send Ticknor a big cheese, which I long ago promised him. My advice is, that he keep it in the shop, and daily, between eleven and one oclock, distribute slices of it to your half-starved authors, together with crackers and brandy-and-water. At any rate, let him take it from me by way of New Year's gift.

I thank you for Grace's "Haps and Mishaps"—(miserable stuff—nothing genuine in the volume—I don't care a button for it)—and more especially for Mrs. Mowatt's Autobiography, which seems tome an admirable book.[1] Of all things I delight in autobiographies; and I hardly ever read one that interested me so much. She must be a remarkable woman, and I cannot but lament my ill-fortune in never having seen her, on the stage or elsewhere.

I count strongly upon your promise to be with us in May. Can't you bring Whipple with you?

Truly Yours,
Nathl Hawthorne.

P.S. I shall always be glad of any of your new publications you see fit to send me.

1. Grace Greenwood, *Haps and Mishaps of a Tour in Europe* (1852), and Anna Cora Mowatt, *Autobiography of an Actress; or, Eight Years on the Stage* (1854).

TO MRS. ANNA MARIA HEYWOOD

Brunswick Street [Liverpool], Feb 16th 1854

Mr Hawthorne has this morning received a visit from Mr Henry Bright, who tells him that he will be expected, tomorrow evening, at Mrs. Heywood's fancy-ball.[1] Mr. H. begs to assure Mrs. Heywood that he is quite sensible of his own folly and absurdity in declining an invitation which any other man would go down upon his knees to get. He finds himself, indeed, in the position of an owl or a bat, when invited to take a pleasure-trip in the sunshine; he cannot deny that it would be a most delightful affair, but still feels it fitter for himself to stay in his dusky hole than to go blinking about among other people's enjoyments. The truth is, Mr. H. has all his life been under a spell, from which it is now too late to free himself;—or rather, he was *born* a solitary brute; and he can no otherwise account for his now being able to resist Mrs. Heywood's invitation.

Mr. H. trusts that Mrs Heywood will not think him vain enough to suppose it of the slightest consequence to her, whether he comes or stays away. Mr. Henry Bright endeavoured to suggest that view of the matter; but Mr. H. forms too just an estimate of his own social deficiencies to believe one word of what he said. Mr. H. must bear testimony in Mr Bright's behalf, that the latter gentleman left nothing unsaid which could possibly be supposed to have weight in the matter. His arguments were powerful, and indeed irrefragable; but Mr. H. will never henceforth think quite so favorably of his modesty as he has heretofore done. For what is any man's reason and power of argument to the cenobite[2] who does not yield at once to the all but omnipotence of a lady's request? After once saying "No" to Mrs. Heywood, Mr. H. would have been heartily ashamed of himself, if he could have given up his ground on any other consideration or compulsion.

In conclusion, Mr. H. begs Mrs. Heywood's indulgence for this very long note, which he feels to be almost as great a trespass on her good nature, as if he were actually to come it person.

Mrs Heywood,
Norris Green.

1. Anna Maria Heywood, the fashionable daughter of a Liverpool banker and Henry Bright's aunt, later served as NH's hostess on a number of occasions.
2. Cenobite, a member of a religious order who lives in a convent or in a community.

TO HENRY A. BRIGHT

Brunswick-street [Liverpool]
April 4th 1854

My dear Mr. Bright,

I have read the Review, and I cannot say that I find anything to dissent from, either as regards its censure or praise.[1] Also, it is exceedingly well done in a literary point of view.

But you must allow me to clench this laudation of your article with a remark or two about what seem to me its deficiencies. I think, then, that you were not sufficiently carried away by De Quincey to be able to write an adequate review of his works, in the present state of English opinion respecting him. You needed the warm and wide sympathy of the American mind, on this subject. The first reviewer of an unrecognized writer should be drunken with his spirit, like the immediate converts of a new prophet. Your article is calm, wise, well-considered, and, so far as it goes, unquestionably just; but yet you remind me of a connoisseur of wine, sipping a drop or two out a glass, and praising or criticising its flavor, when you ought to swallow it at one gulp, and feel your heat warmed through and through with it. Here comes De Quincey begging at your door, a poor old man of genius, to whom the world is in arrears for half-a-century's revenue of fame! You examine his title-deeds, find them authentic, and send him away with the benefaction of half-a-crown ! If everybody else had given him what he deserves, this might have been your full proportion; but, as the case stood, ought you not to have considered that you had the whole world's debt to pay?

I do not ask you to excuse my frankness; for what is the use of speaking at all (and I am sure such a good Englishman as yourself will agree with me in this) unless one speaks one's mind?

Truly Yours
Nathl Hawthorne.

1. Bright's "Thomas De Quincy and His Works" appeared in the April 1854 *Westminster Review*. Thomas De Quincy, a prolific prose writer best known for *Confessions of an English Opium Eater* (1821), lived in a constant state of financial distress.

TO JAMES T. FIELDS

U. S. Consulate,
Liverpool, April 13th '54

Dear Fields,

I am very glad that the "Mosses" have come into the hands of our firm; and I return the copy sent me, after a careful revision.[1] When I wrote those dreamy sketches, I little thought that I should ever prepare an edition for the press amidst the bustling life of a Liverpool consul. Upon my honor, I am not quite sure that I entirely comprehend my own meaning in some of these blasted allegories; but I remember that I always had a meaning—or, at least, thought I had. I am a good deal changed since those times; and to tell you the truth, my past self is not very much to my taste, as I see myself in this book. Yet certainly there is more in it than the public generally gave me credit for, at the time it was written. But I don't think myself worthy of very much more credit than I got. It as been a very disagreeable task to read the book.

The story of "Rappaccini's Daughter" was published in the Democratic Review about the year 1844; and it was prefaced by some remarks on the celebrated French author (a certain M. de l'Aubepine) from whose works it was translated.[2] I left out this preface, when the story was republished; but I wish you would turn to it in the Democratic, and see whether it is worth while to insert it in the new edition. I leave it altogether to your judgement.

A young poet, named Allingham, has called on me, and has sent me some copies of his works to be transmitted to America.[3] It seems to me there is good in him; and he is recognized by Tennyson, by Carlisle, by Kingsley, and other of the best people here.[4] He writes me that this edition of his poems is nearly exhausted, and that Routledge is going to publish another, enlarged, and in better style. Perhaps it might be well for you to take him up in America. At all events, try to bring him into notice; and some day or other, you may be glad to have helped a famous poet in his obscurity. The poor fellow has left a good post in the customs, in Ireland, to cultivate literature in London!

We shall begin to look for you now by every steamer from Boston. You must make up your mind to spend a good while with us before going to see your London friends.

Did you read the article on your De Quincy in the last Westminster? It was written by Mr. H. A. Bright of this city, who was in America a year or two ago. The article is pretty well, but does nothing like adequate justice to De Quincy; and in fact no Englishman cares a pin for him. We are ten times as good readers and critics as they. By the by, I hear horrible stories about De Quincy's morality, in times past.[5]

Is not Whipple coming here soon?

Truly Yours,
Nathl Hawthorne.

---

1. Ticknor and Fields published a new edition of *Mosses from an Old Manse* on 18 September 1854.

2. "Rappaccini's Daughter" is introduced as a translation from (the fictitious) M. de l'Aubépine, with the intention of "introducing him favorably to the American public" (*CE*, 10:93). The introduction was restored to the story in the 1854 edition.

3. The English poet William Allingham was not published by Ticknor and Fields until 1861.

4. Alfred, Lord Tennyson, had succeeded William Wordsworth as England's Poet Laureate in 1850; Charles Kingsley, a clergyman and novelist. NH means Thomas Carlyle for "Carlisle."

5. Probably a reference to De Quincy's frequenting prostitutes in Liverpool at the age of seventeen, as he had recorded once in his as yet unpublished diary. [*CE*]

TO HORATIO BRIDGE

U. S. Consulate
Liverpool, April 17th '54

Dear Bridge,

I trust you received my letter, written a fortnight or thereabouts ago, and that the business with Ticknor has been arranged to your satisfaction.

As you are now in Washington—and of course in frequent communication with Pierce—I want you to have a talk with him on my affairs. O'Sullivan (who arrived here a day or two ago) tells me that a bill is to be brought forward in relation to diplomatic and consular offices, and that, by some of its provisions, a salary is to be given to certain of the consulates. I trust in Heaven's mercy that no change whatever will be made as regards the emoluments of the Liverpool consulate—unless indeed, a salary is to be given in addition to the fees, in which case I should receive it very thankfully.[1] This, however, is not to be expected; and if Liverpool is touched at all, it will be to limit its emoluments by a fixed salary—which (even should it be larger than any salary now paid by our government, with the exception of the President's own,) will render the office not worth any man's holding. It is impossible (especially for man with a family and keeping any kind of an establishment) not to spend a vast deal of money here. The office, unfortunately, is regarded as one of great dignity, and puts the holder on a level with the highest society, and compels him to associate on equal terms with men who spend more than my whole income on the mere entertainments and other trimming and embroidery of their lives. Then I feel bound to exercise some hospitality towards my own countrymen. I keep out of society as much as I decently can, and really practise as stern an economy as ever I did in my life; but, nevertheless, I have spent many thousands of dollars in the few months of my residence here, and cannot reasonably hope to spend less than six-thousand per annum, even after all the expenditure of setting up an establishment is defrayed. All this is for the merely indispensable part of my living; and unless I make a hermit of myself, and deprive my wife and children of all the pleasures and advantages of an English residence, I must inevitably exceed the sum named above. Every article of living has nearly doubled in cost, within a year. It would be the easiest thing in the world for me to run in debt, even taking my income at $15.000 (out of which all the clerks &c. are to be paid)—the largest sum that it ever reached in Crittenden's time. He had no family but a wife, and lived constantly at a boarding house, and nevertheless went home (as he assured me) with an aggregate of only $25000 derived from his official savings.

Now, the American public can never be made to understand such a statement as the above; and they would grumble awfully, if more than $6000 per annum were allowed for a consul's salary. But with that salary, the office may go to —, as far as I am concerned; nor would it be worth my keeping at $10000. I beg and pray, therefore, that Pierce will look at the reason and common sense of this business; and not let Mr Dudley Mann shave off so much as a half-penny from my official emoluments.[2] Neither do I believe that we have a single consulship, in any part of the world, the net emoluments of which overpay the trouble and responsibility of the office. If these are lessened, the incumbent must be compelled to turn his official position to account by engaging in commerce—a curse which ought not to be permitted, and which no Liverpool consul has ever adopted.

After all, it is very possible that no change is contemplated, as regards the large consulships. If so, I beg Mr. Dudley Mann's pardon, and wish all success to his bill.

Tell the President that I was a guest at a public entertainment, the other day, where his health was drunk standing, immediately after those of the queen and royal family. When the rest of the party sat down, I remained on my legs and returned thanks in a very pretty speech, which was received with more cheering and applause than any other during the dinner. I had missed no opportunity of gulping down champagne, and so had got myself into that state of pot-valor which (as you and he know) is best adapted to bring out my heroic qualities. I think it was altogether the most successful of my oratorical efforts—of which I have made several since arriving here.

I wish you would get some of your Congressional friends to send me whatever statistical documents are published by Congress, and also any others calculated to be of use. I am daily called upon for information respecting America, which I do not always possess the materials to give in a reliable shape.

Your friend,
(in haste)
Nathl Hawthorne.

1. Because of reported abuses of their fee-leveling powers by American consuls, Congress passed a bill on 1 March 1855 which fixed the salary of the consul at Liverpool at $7,500 per year, and required that after charging fees the consul "shall account to the government at the expiration of every three months, and hold the proceeds subject to its drafts." NH was also upset by the statement of Representative John Perkins of Louisiana, who, in introducing the bill, contended "We would have a consul, for instance, at Liverpool, or Rio, or Havre, realizing $20,000 from the commerce of the country in the way of fees, enjoying himself in foreign travel, while the duties were discharged by a foreigner." For more on this, see *CE*, 17:205–6n.

2. The assistant secretary of state, Ambrose Dudley Mann, was the joint author of the new bill concerning consuls' salaries.

TO THOMAS KEOGH

U. S Consulate.
Liverpool May 29. 1854.

Sir[1]

In reply to your favor of the 24th instant containing queries in regard to the sources of my Income, on which a Tax has been assessed, I beg leave to state in the first place that no part of my Income is derived from Trade. It is derived entirely from fees, as prescribed and regulated by the Laws of the United States, with the exception of about £150 which is received directly from the American Government as Salary for a particular Service and as Commission on disbursements. The Greater part of my Fees (but in what proportion I cannot accurately state) accrues from American Citizens; the remainder is derived chiefly from the American transactions of British Subjects.

Having entered upon the Duties of American Consul at this port on the first day of August, I have made only one payment of the Income Tax.

I have the honor to be
Sir,
Your obedient Servant,
Nathl Hawthorne.
U. S. Consul, &c

Thomas Keogh Esq.
Secretary &c
Somerset House.

1. Thomas Keogh, Secretary of the Board of Inland Revenue.

TO JAMES BUCHANAN

Liverpool, May 30th 1854.

My dear Sir,[1]

I sincerely thank you for the steps which you have so kindly taken toward relieving me from the income-tax. I do not yet know what will be the result; but, a few days ago I received a letter from the Secretary of the Commissioners of Inland Revenue, propounding certain queries as to the sources of my official emoluments;—viz. Whether it was derived from salary or from fees; whether any part of it resulted from trade; and what was the proportion derived from American citizens. I rather suspect that the Commissioners are inclined to make a stand on the point that a considerable part of my income comes from British subjects. I responded to these queries as accurately as I could, but was not able to state the proportion of fees derived from American citizens, and from British subjects. The latter, no doubt, amounts to several hundred pounds annually, but is, of course, derived wholly from American transactions. The proportion of fees paid by American citizens is much the larger. The larger part of the fees on Invoice Certificates is paid by British subjects; but, I presume, the fee is reckoned into the price of the article; and ultimately paid by the consumer in America.

With many thanks,
Very sincerely
& Respectfully Yours,
Nathl Hawthorne.

Hon. James Buchanan.

1. James Buchanan had been appointed minister to Britain by Pierce in 1853.

TO HENRY WADSWORTH LONGFELLOW

Liverpool, Aug 30th '54
Dear Longfellow,

Our friend Henry Bright has handed me some autographs for you.
Why don't you come over?—being now a man of leisure, and with nothing to
keep you in America.[1] If I were in your position, I think that I should make my
home on this side of the water—though always with an indefinite and never-to-
be-executed intention to go back and die in my native land. America is a good
land for young people, but not for those who are past their prime. It is impossible
to grow old comfortably there; for nothing keeps one in countenance. For my
part, I have no love for England nor Englishmen, and I do love my own country;
but, for all that, the honest truth is, I care little whether I ever set eyes on it again.
Every thing is so delightfully sluggish here! It is so pleasant to find people holding
on to old ideas, and hardly now beginning to dream of matters that are already
old with us! I have had enough of progress;—now I want to stand stock still; or
rather, to go back twenty years or so;—and that is just what I seem to have done,
in coming to England. Then, too, it is so agreeable to find one's self relieved from
the tyranny of public opinion—or, at any rate, under the jurisdiction of quite a
different public sentiment from what we have left behind us. A man of individuality and refinement can certainly live far more comfortably here (provided he
have the means to live at all) than in New England. Be it owned, however, that I
sometimes feel a tug at my very heart-strings, when I think of my old home and
friends; but this is only for a moment—indeed, I should think all the better of
myself, if I felt the heart-tug oftener and longer.
    Remember me kindly to Mrs Longfellow, and believe me

Most Sincerely Yours
N. H.

---

1. Longfellow had offered his resignation as Smith Professor of Modern Languages at
Harvard on 16 February and attended his last academic function on 19 July. [*CE*]

TO RICHARD MONCKTON MILNES

U. S Consulate,
Liverpool, Novr 18th, '54

My dear Mr Milnes,[1]

The beautiful edition of Keats has arrived, and also several other books, which I rejoice to possess—the more because you sent them. I began to read them to Mrs. Hawthorne, last evening, and they will be very long a pleasure to us.

The author of "Margaret" (about whom you inquire) was the Rev. Sylvester Judd, a country clergyman, who died a little while ago. He wrote several other works, but none so good as this.[2]

I have known Thoreau a good many years; but it would be quite impossible to comprise him within this little sheet of note-paper. He is an excellent scholar, and a man of most various capacity; insomuch that he could make his part good in any way of life, from the most barbarous to the most civilized. But there is more of the Indian in him, I think, than of any other kind of man. He despises the world, and all that it has to offer, and, like other humorists, is an intolerable bore. I shall cause it to be made known to him that you sat up till two oclock, reading his book;[3] and he will pretend that it is of no consequence, but will never forget it. I ought not to forbear saying that he is an upright, conscientious, and courageous man, of whom it is impossible to conceive anything but the highest integrity. Still, he is not an agreeable person; and in his presence one feels ashamed of having any money, or a house to live in, or so much as two coats to wear, or of having written a book that the public will read—his own mode of life being so unsparing a criticism on all other modes, such as the world approves. I wish anything could be done to make his books known to the English public; for certainly they deserve it, being the work of a true man and full of true thought.[4] You must not think that he is a particular friend of mine. I do not speak with quite this freedom of my friends. We have never been intimate; though my home is near his residence.

Very Sincerely
& Respectfully
Nathl Hawthorne.

1. Richard Monckton Milnes, poet and patron of writers.

2. The novelist, poet, and Unitarian minister Sylvester Judd was best known for *Margaret. A Tale of the Real and Ideal, Blight and Bloom; Including Sketches of a Place Not before Described, Called Mons Christi* (1845), regarded as the only novel produced by the Transcendental movement.

3. *Walden* had been published on 9 August 1854.

4. *Walden* first appeared in Britain in 1884, when an Edinburgh publisher excised the title page from copies of the twenty-second American printing and substituted his own; the first British edition was in 1886. No published comments by Milnes on Thoreau have been located.

TO SHERIDAN MUSPRATT

U. S. Consulate,
Liverpool, Jany 10th 1855

My dear Sir,[1]

This Mr. Josephs (who certainly does look like a scoundrel) is one of innumerable countrymen of mine who come here without funds, seeking my consular aid to get them home again. My clerk gave him the addresses of some American houses, but he assures me that he did not give him yours; and I trust you will believe that I myself have had no share in inflicting his visitation upon you. He must have taken this step entirely of his own accord, and on the strength of his intimacy (!!) with our lady and Miss Cushman. I am glad you gave him nothing; and no doubt it will be all the better for America if this estimable citizen never finds his way back.

Very truly
& Respectfully yours,
Nathl Hawthorne.

1. Possibly James Sheridan Muspratt, founder of the Liverpool College of Chemistry. [*CE*]

TO HORATIO BRIDGE

U. S. Consulate
Liverpool, March 23d 1855

Dear Bridge,

I thank you for all your efforts against this Bill; but Providence is wiser than we are, and doubtless it will all turn out for the best. All through my life, I have had occasion to observe that what seemed to be misfortunes have proved, in the end, to be the best things that could possibly have happened to me; and so it will be with this—even though the mode in which it benefits me should never be made clear to my apprehension. It would seem to be a desirable thing enough that I should have had a sufficient income to live comfortably upon, for the rest of my life, without the necessity of labor; but, on the other hand, I might have sunk prematurely into intellectual sluggishness—which now there, will be no danger of my doing; though, with a house and land of my own, and a good little sum at interest besides, I need not be under very great anxiety for the future. When I contrast my present situation with what it was five years ago, I see a vast deal to be thankful for; and I still hope to thrive by my legitimate instrument—the pen. One consideration which goes very far towards reconciling me to quitting the office is my wife's health, with which the English climate does not agree, and which I hope will be greatly benefitted by a winter in Italy.[1] In short, we have wholly ceased to regret the action of Congress, (which, nevertheless, was most unjust and absurd,) and are looking at matters on the bright side.

However, I shall be glad to get whatever advantage I can out of the office; and therefore I hope Pierce will give me as long a line as his conscience will let him. He will meet with no sharp practice on my part. If I pledge myself to the new system by accepting a new commission, of course I shall act accordingly. My present and very decided impression is, that I shall not accept it, but, on the contrary, shall decline it as soon as received. Perhaps, however, it will not be advisable to let him know this, as he might then think himself bound to appoint somebody else in the first instance.

It ought to be considered, on my behalf, that I lost five very valuable months of this office by Pierce's courtesy in permitting my predecessor, at his own request, to resign prospectively, instead of being at once ejected. It was then supposed that my term would run an equal length into that of my successor; but, as matters have turned out, that little bit of Presidential courtesy took at least six thousand dollars out of my pocket. I have no objection to Frank's being as civil as he pleases, but I wish he would do it at his own expense rather than mine.

For some time past, I have done but little more than get a living from the office, business being so very bad. It now promises rather better, but probably will not flourish to any great extent between now and July.[2] Every week after that time will be worth gold, and will contribute towards making my future life easier, and my children's prospects better, than they would otherwise be. I ask no undue favors; but, after all, has an office-holder no rights?—are there no ethical considerations belonging to the case?—was it relying too much upon the good faith and stability of our laws, to suppose that I was sure of my legal income for at least a year to come, unless resigned by my own consent, or forfeited by my own bad behavior? It seems to me that the new law has been left thus at loose ends for the very purpose of allowing officeholders some extremely inadequate compensation for their losses; and I hope the President will consider it in that way. The lease of my home does not expire till some months after the first of July; and all my domestic arrangements are made on the idea that I might prudently expend at least $5000 per annum; and it is impossible to contract my expenditure within what it has hitherto been, without vast mortification and indignity.

I don't see how the next Consul is to get along here, unless he be either a rich man or a rogue. God knows, he will find temptations enough to be the latter.

Give our best regards to Mrs Bridge. How I wish you could spend the next two years with us in Italy!

Truly your friend,
Nathl Hawthorne.

1. NH did not go to Italy until January 1858, after leaving the consulship. The family did, though, visit the Lake Country in July,
2. The Consular Bill, as passed on 1 March, was to go into effect on 1 July.

TO ELIZABETH PALMER PEABODY

U. S. consulate,
Liverpool, April 20th 1855

Dear E.

I have just received yours; and am glad, on the whole, that you take mine just in the way you do; for, after all, it is not my business to present you with your own portrait, true or false.

I shall not let Sophia have your letter to her, because she has had trouble enough about the matter of the Galpin money, and because I fully believe that her first view of it was right.[1] I sometimes feel as if I ought to vindicate her (which would be so easily done) as to all those accusations of neglecting her father and family, which you both hint and express; and also to endeavor to enlighten you as to the relation between husband and wife, and show you that she fully comprehends it in its highest sense. But this conjugal relation is one which God never meant you to share, and which therefore He apparently did not give you the instinct to understand; so there my labor would be lost. And as to the former object, I think I may fairly use Sophia like myself, and say not a word in her defence.

You DID make the suggestion about my borrowing the money to set your brother up in life. What a memory! Perhaps you write in your sleep?

I shall hold office till after next January.[2]

I did not mean to close all correspondence forever, but only on that particular subject. I hope, in whatever years we may have left, to exchange many letters, and see you many times; for there are few people whose society is so pleasant to me. I never in my life was angry with you; and if you will only allow me to think of you just as I please (or, rather, just as I cannot help) I really think we shall find great comfort in one another. Upon my honor, I consider myself the one person in the world who does justice to your character!!—an assertion at which you will probably laugh outright; especially as I do not withdraw one word of my last letter, or any other I ever wrote you, all of which were considerately and conscientiously written.

Truly your friend,

N. H.

1. The dispute involved SPH's father's funeral expenses, with her worrying that he had denied his earlier stated wish to be buried next to his wife because he wished to save expenses.
2. Hawthorne wrote his letter of resignation on 13 February 1857, to take effect on 31 August.

TO JOSEPH GRAHAM

Consulate of the United States
Liverpool 3d May 1855

Sir,

A man named Sam[ue]l Makin alias Graham died of Small Pox in the Fever Hospital of this place in August last. Being 2nd mate of an American vessel the Hospital authorities delivered his clothing to me, and the Captain of the vessel before sailing, previous to Makin's death, paid me £10.0.5 wages due. Yesterday on having the chest opened for the purpose of taking an acct. of the contents, preparatory to having them sold with the view of remitting the proceeds with the wages to the United States, the enclosed Letter was found with your address. From such Letter I judge that the deceased was your Son, & on your sending me satisfactory proof of the fact, (the affidavits of two respectable witnesses) and the guarantee of a responsible person, attested by a magistrate who must state that the witnesses & surety are known to him, I will forward the clothing to you in such way as you may direct & remit the amount of wages. The clothing & effects are worth about £5 or £6—but being old, would not likely bring so much if sold. Part of the effects consist of a silver verge watch & a quadrant worth about £2.10.0 together.

I am
Your obedt Servant
Nathl Hawthorne

Mr Jos Graham
Ardtrea House
Stewardstown

TO CHARLES SUMNER

U. S. Consulate, Liverpool, May 23d 1855.

My dear Sumner,[1]

For some time past I have been thinking of asking you to interest yourself in bringing the condition of our mercantile marine before Congress. Matters are really in a very terrible state between shipmasters and seamen; and having been thrust by Providence (and Pierce) into this consulate, I ought not to leave it without an attempt to do some little good. Every day, some miserable cruelty and wrong is brought under my notice. For instance, a month or two ago, I took the deposition of a free white citizen, a farmer of South Carolina, who had been absolutely kidnapped by a shipping-master at Charleston, and, without ever intending to go to sea, had been sent off to Liverpool as a seaman, and so abused by the Captain and officers, during the voyage, that when I saw him he was half-dead. He has since died in the Hospital.[2] In three instances, which came before me, sailors have been shot dead by their officers; and the most perplexing part of the matter is, that all this bloodshed and cruelty seems to be strangely justifiable, and almost inevitable under the circumstances. It certainly is not the fault, so much as it is the fate, of our shipmasters to do these abominable deeds. They are involved in a wrong system, which renders it impossible for them to do right; and they themselves become morally deteriorated by it, and continually grow worse and worse. As for the seamen, they are no better than pirates. The truth is, we have no seamen of our own, our ships being manned almost entirely by the offscourings of the British merchant-service, and by German and other foreigners whom the shipping-masters entrap. I should like to know what is to become of us, at sea, in case of a war—but that you don't care about.

If you will let slavery alone, for a little while, and attend to this business (where much good may, and no harm can possibly, be done) I think you will be doing our country a vast service. The shipping-masters in the American ports seem to be at the bottom, or near the bottom, of the mischief. You would have to make inquiries into their system, on your side of the water; and I could help you to many atrocities which come to my knowledge through the statements of seamen. These shipping-masters should be annihilated at once;—no slave-drivers are so wicked as they, and there is nothing in slavery so bad as the system with which they are connected.

I see no way to secure a supply of good seamen, unless by establishing a system of apprenticeage, compelling each vessel to take a certain number of apprentices. England, however, has given up this plan, so that it probably has its defects. For my part, I only see what is bad, and do not pretend to any faculty of suggesting what may be better.

Do think seriously of the above.

Truly Yours,
Nathl Hawthorne.

P.S. I had a most agreeable little bit of a visit from your brother George, last Saturday and Sunday.

P.S. 2d You must not suppose that I wish to represent the American shipmasters as worse than the system of manning their ships inevitably makes them. As a body, they are men of admirable qualities, and far superior to the same class of Englishmen; capable, many of them, of acting on high moral considerations, and sincerely desirous (were it only for their own sakes) of finding a remedy for the evils to which I allude. Still, they are human, and therefore apt to become devilish, under evil influences.

N. H.

P.S. 3d A law went into effect on the first of this month, regulating the British merchant-service. I have not seen it; but it may suggest some available ideas.

1. Charles Sumner, Senator from Massachusetts, was very active in the antislavery cause.
2. For NH's comments on Daniel Smith, see *English Notebooks, CE*, 21:165–69.

TO WILLIAM L. MARCY

Consulate of the United States
Liverpool 14th Nov 1855

Sir,

I have the honor to inform you that two prisoners John Woods and John Suze, sent here from Cork, charged with an assault with intent to commit murder on board American ship "Wandering Jew" on the High seas, and delivered up pursuant to the tenth article of the treaty with Great Britain of 1842, together with two Witnesses John F Johnson and John S Jones, were sent in the Ship "America" Captain Barstow which sailed for New York on the 11th Inst. I agreed to pay the master Thirteen pounds sterling for each prisoner, and for the Witnesses, as prescribed by Law, 50 cents a day calculating the passage at 40 days. These were the best terms I could obtain. Having no power of compulsion, I found great difficulty in obtaining a vessel, many masters refusing to carry prisoners on any terms.
I enclose a copy of the certificate given to the master.[1]

I have the honor to be
Your obedt Servant
Nathl Hawthorne.

Hon W L Marcy
Secretary of State
Washington

1. NH's Certificate, given 9 November 1855, engages the *America* to carry the prisoners and witnesses for a total of £30. [*CE*]

TO THE EDITORS OF *PUTNAM'S MONTHLY MAGAZINE*

Liverpool, Novr 19th '55

Gentlemen,

It would give me much pleasure to send you something for Putnam's Monthly, if I had any suitable articles, or could write one. But, for the present, my official occupations so far engross my time and thoughts as to leave me no freedom for literary employment. I might, indeed, throw off a few sketches of English scenery and life; but the English people look with such jealousy upon any American who is suspected of "taking notes," that I should soon find the ill effects, socially, of publishing my impressions and experiences.

I regret that I cannot serve you; for I very much like the Magazine, and wish it all success.

Truly Yours
Nathl Hawthorne.

TO WILLIAM L. MARCY

Consulate of the United States
Liverpool 1 February 1856

Sir,

I have the honor to report the rescue from shipwreck, of the Crew, 15 in number, of the American Bark "Olivia" of New York, George S Span master, by the English Bark "Emperor," Captain Ferguson, of Liverpool, under circumstances reflecting great credit on the latter.

The "Olivia" sailed from Cardiff 18 Decr, bound for New York with a cargo of Iron, & experiencing very boisterous weather, the Cargo broke adrift and the vessel sprung a leak. On the 9th of January she had seven feet of water in the hold, &

the Cargo surged about so that it was dangerous to attempt to secure it, a hard gale blowing with a very high sea, forbade any idea of resorting to the Boats, and the condition of the vessel becoming rapidly worse, the position of the crew was getting critical. In this emergency, they say "An American Ship hove in sight, we hoisted a signal of distress, she passed within three miles of us, hoisted her Ensign and sailed away." About an hour and a half after "A Bark hove in sight standing towards us. She proved to be the Emperor of & for Liverpool, she hove to under our lee and offered us any assistance and to lay by us." She laid by them about four hours, when they abandoned their vessel in their own Life boat & were received on board of her.

She was short of Provisions & her Crew were put on short allowance to provide for the newcomers. On the 15 she put into Crookhaven for Provisions, where the master & mate, to reach Liverpool more speedily overland, left her, as did also eight of the sailors who received the offer of £5 each to work another vessel to Liverpool. The others remained on board and were landed at Liverpool on the 26th Instant. They all speak in the highest terms of the treatment they received. There being no American Consul at Crookhaven they were kindly subsisted on board the vessel while there windbound.

The master of the Emperor is a very old man, & from enquiries I have made, I believe he has been unfortunate, & is very poor, so that I suspect any recognition of his service in this matter, would be most acceptable in money.[1]

I must also report a further statement made by the Crew. That about the same time or soon after the "Emperor" came to their rescue, a Brig, supposed the "Eventua," hove to near them, & laid by them until they were all safely on board the Emperor, when she telegraphed that she was bound to St John N[ew] B[runswick], and would take any on board that chose to come. It was not deemed prudent to venture into the Boat again however, & the offer was declined, but the circumstance reflects so much credit on the Crew of the Brig whoever they were, that it deserves mention.

Respecting the statement of an American vessel recognising the signal of distress, & disregarding its appeal, I trust there is some mistake. I would not believe that any American could commit the act the statement implies. It sometimes occurs that vessels hoist signals of distress for the mere purpose of speaking another vessel. A case recently came under my notice of a vessel hoisting a signal of distress, & on another vessel going to her assistance, hauling it down, & sailing away without speaking. Such wanton acts tend to weaken the effect of the signal and deserve punishment.

I should be glad to be informed respecting the payment of subsistence money to the owners of the Emperor, if they should apply to me.[2]

With high respect
I have the honor to be
Your Obedt Servant
Nathl Hawthorne

To
Hon Wm L Marcy
Secretary of State

1. President Pierce awarded Ferguson £50.
2. NH was instructed to compensate the owners "in the manner provided by the instructions given to your predecessor." [*CE*]

TO SOPHIA PEABODY HAWTHORNE

Liverpool, February 7th 1856.

Thy letter, my own most beloved, (dated Jany 31st) arrived yesterday, and revived me at once out of a state of half-torpor, half-misery just as much of each as could co-exist with the other.[1] Do not think that I am always in that state; but one thing, dearest, I have been most thoroughly taught by this separation that is, the absolute necessity of expression. I must tell thee I love thee. I must be told that thou lovest me. It must be said in words and symbolized with [*obliteration*] caresses; or else, at last, imprisoned Love will go frantic, and tear all to pieces the heart that holds it. And the only other alternative is to be torpid. I just manage to hold out from one letter of thine to another; and then comes life and joy again. Thou canst not conceive what an effect yesterday's letter had on me. It renewed my youth, and made my step lighter; it absolutely gave me an appetite; and I went to bed joyfully to think of it. Oh, my wife, why did God give thee to poor unworthy me? Art thou sure that He made thee for me? Ah, thy intuition must have been well-founded on this point; because, otherwise, all through eternity, thou wouldst carry my stain upon thee; and how could thine own angel ever wed thee then? Thou art mine!—Thou shalt be mine! Thou hast given thyself to me irredeemably. Thou hast grown to me. Thou canst never get away.

Oh, my love, it is a desperate thing that I cannot embrace thee this very instant. Dost thou ever feel, at one and the same moment, the impossibility of doing without me, and also the impossibility of having me? I know not how it is that my strong wishes do not bring thee here bodily, while I am writing these words. One of the two impossibilities must needs be overcome; and it seems the strongest impossibility that thou shouldst be anywhere else, when I need thee so insufferably.

Well, my own wife, I have a little wreaked myself now, and will go on more quietly with what I have further to say. As regards O'Sullivan—(how funny that thou shouldst put quotation marks to this name, as if astonished at my calling him so! Did we not entirely agree in thinking "John" an undue and undesirable familiarity? But thou mayst call him "John," or "Jack" either, as best suits thee.)— as regards O'Sullivan, then, my present opinion of him is precisely what thou thyself didst leave upon my mind, in our discussions of his character.[2] I have often had a similar experience before, resulting from thy criticism upon any views of mine. Thou insensibly convertest me to thy own opinion, and art afterwards surprised to find it so; in fact, I seldom am aware of the change in my own mind, until the subject chances to come up for further discussion, and I find myself on what was thy side.

But I will try to give my true idea of his character. I know that he has most vivid affections—a quick, womanly sensibility—a light and tender grace, which, in happy circumstances, would make all his deeds and demonstrations beautiful. In respect to companionship, beyond all doubt, he has never been in such fortunate circumstances as during his present intercourse with thee; and I am willing to allow that thou bringest out his angelic part, and therefore canst not be expected to see anything but an angel in him. It has sometimes seemed to me that the lustre of his angel-plumage has been a little dimmed—his heavenly garments a little soiled and bedraggled—by the foul ways through which it has been his fate to tread, and the foul companions with whom necessity and politics have brought him acquainted. But I had rather thou shouldst take him for a friend than any other man I ever knew (unless, perhaps, George Bradford, who can hardly be reckoned a man at all,) because I think the Devil has a smaller share in O'Sullivan than in other bipeds who wear breeches. To do him justice, he is miraculously pure and true, considering what his outward life has been. Now, dearest, I have a genuine affection for him, and a confidence in his honor; and as respects his defects in everything that concerns pecuniary matters, I believe him to have kept his integrity intact to a degree that is really wonderful, in spite of the embarrassments of a lifetime. If we had his whole life mapped out before us, I should probably forgive him some things which thy severer sense of right would condemn. Thou talkest of his high principle; but that does not appear to me to be his kind of moral endowment. Perhaps he may have the material that principles are manufactured from.

My beloved, he is not the man in whom I see my ideal of a friend; not for his lack of principle, not for any ill-deeds or practical short-comings which I know of or suspect, not but what he is amicable, loveable, fully capable of self-sacrifice, utterly incapable of selfishness. The only reason, that I can put into words, is, that he never stirs me to any depth beneath my surface; I like him, and enjoy his society, and he calls up, I think, whatever small part of me is elegant and agreeable; but neither of my best nor of my worst has he ever, or could he ever, have a glimpse. I should wish my friend of friends to be a sterner and grimmer man than he; and it is my opinion, sweetest wife, that the truest manly delicacy is to be found in these stern, grim natures—a little alpine flower, of tenderest texture, and loveliest hue, and delicious fragrance, springing out of rocky soil, in a high, breezy, mountain atmosphere. O'Sullivan's quick, genial soil produces an abundant growth of flowers, but not just this precious little flower. He is too much like a woman, without being a woman; and between the two characters, he misses the quintessential delicacy of both. There are some tests of thorough refinement which, perhaps, he could not stand. And yet I shall not dispute that for refinement and delicacy he is one out of a thousand; and we might spend a lifetime together without putting him to a test too severe. As for his sympathies, he would be always ready to pour them out (not exactly like Niagara, but like a copious garden-fountain) for those he loved.

If thou thinkest I have done him great injustice in the foregoing sketch, it is very probable that thou wilt bring me over to thy way of thinking, and perhaps balance matters by passing over to mine.

Dearest, I do hope I shall next hear of thee from Madeira; for this suspense is hard to bear. Thou must not mind what I say to thee, in my impatient agonies, about coming back. Whatever can be bore, I shall find myself able to bear, for the sake of restoring thee to health. I have now groped so far through the thick darkness, that a little glimmer of light begins to appear at the other end of the passage; it will grow clearer and brighter continually, and at last it will show me my dearest wife. I do hope thou wilt find thy husband wiser and better than he has been hitherto; wiser, in knowing the more adequately what a treasure he has in thee, and better, because I feel it such a shame to be loved by thee without deserving it. Dost thou love me?

Give my love to Una, to whom I cannot write now, without doubling the postage. Do not let little Rosebud forget me.[3] Remember me to Fanny, and present my regards to Madam O'Sullivan, and Mrs. Susan, and Miss Rodgers. So all is said very properly.

Thou toldest me not to write to Madeira before hearing from thee there; but I shall send this to the care of the American Consul, to whom I wrote by the last Lisbon steamer, sending the letter to O'Sullivan's care.

Thine own-ownest.

Julian is perfectly well.

1. SPH left with Una and Rosa on 8 October 1855 for Lisbon, then went on to Madeira on 6 February, arriving the tenth. In his diary, 6 February, NH wrote: "Letters from Sophia at Lisbon. Thank God!" On the previous Sunday, the third, he had written: "Not well, and much dispirited." [*CE*] NH's comments on his "desolate, bachelor condition" are in *English Notebooks, CE,* 21:406–7.

2. In a letter to Mary Peabody Mann, SPH characterized O'Sullivan's staying in Lisbon when his family accompanied the Hawthornes to Madeira as "a more serious loss to us all than I had imagined. He is the light & light of his family, & in the absence of our sun, he was a light & joy for us, & took such tender care of us, that we each felt like a very precious thing. Here his wife & mother drooped without his shine & warmth, & so did we." [*CE*]

3. The Hawthornes' daughter Rose.

TO MRS. ANNA M. HEYWOOD

Liverpool, April 17th '56

Dear Mrs. Heywood,

I thank you for those beautiful slippers, on which I shall place a soul-felt value—not sole-felt; for I think I shall never have the heart to desecrate them by putting them on. Your gifts ought not to be trodden under foot. If I do put them on, I am afraid I shall be tempted to practise the American fashion of elevating the feet higher than the head, in order to contemplate your handiwork the better.

Believe me,
dear Mrs. Heywood,
very gratefully yours,
Nathl Hawthorne.

Mrs. J. P. Heywood.

TO DELIA BACON

Liverpool, May 12th 1856.

Dear Miss Bacon,[1]

It was quite unnecessary to send me these introductory letters (which I re-enclose) for I have long entertained a high respect for your character, and an interest in your object, so far as I understood it. To be sure, I know very little about it,—not having seen the articles in Putnam,[2] nor heard anything but some vague talk from Miss [Elizabeth Palmer] Peabody, three years ago. Neither do I think myself a very fit person to comprehend the matter, nor to advise you in it; especially now, when I am bothered and bored, and harassed and torn in pieces, by a thousand items of daily business, and benumbed as to that part of my mind to which your work would appeal, and depressed by domestic anxieties. I say this, however, by no means to excuse myself from the endeavor to be of service to you in any and every manner, but only to suggest reasons why I shall probably be useless as a critic and a judge. If you really think that I can promote your object, tell me definitely how, and try me; and if I can say a true word to yourself about the work, it shall certainly be said; or if I can aid, personally, or through any connections in London, in bringing the book before the public, it shall be done.

I would not be understood, my dear Miss Bacon, as professing to have faith in the correctness of your views. In fact, I know far too little of them to have any right to form an opinion; and as to the case of the "old Player" (whom you grieve my heart by speaking of so contemptuously) you will have to rend him out of me by the roots, and by main force, if at all. But I feel that you have done a thing that ought to be reverenced, in devoting yourself so entirely to this object, whatever it be, and whether right or wrong; and that, by so doing, you have acquired some of the privileges of an inspired person and a prophetess—and that the world is bound to hear you, if for nothing else, yet because you are so sure of your own mission.

I gather from your note to Mr. Emerson that you are apprehensive of being anticipated by a work announced for publication in London.[3] I have not seen this announcement; but I would stake my life that you will not find your views trenched upon in the least; although (having made your idea so obvious to yourself) it is natural that you should suppose it as clear as sunshine to any other mind.

I know that you will not take any offense from the frankness with which I write. It is impossible for me to pay any compliments, or to speak anything but

the plainest truth, (according to my own views) in dealing with the noble earnestness of your character.

Believe me,
very sincerely,
& Most Respectfully Yours,
Nathl Hawthorne.

P.S. If I had known that you were still in England, I should have tried to meet
you before now; but I thought you had long ago returned to America. I shall probably be in London in the course of next month, when Mrs. Hawthorne (whose
health is very delicate) will be on her return from Madeira. If your affairs make it
desirable, you can bid me come to you then.

N. H.

Your letter to Mr. Emerson was in season for the steamer, and has gone by it.

N. H.

1. Delia Salter Bacon believed that Shakespeare's plays were written by Francis Bacon, Walter
Raleigh, and Edmund Spenser, and that there were messages to this effect in Bacon's letters.
Encouraged by Emerson and Elizabeth Palmer Peabody, Bacon also enlisted NH in her cause,
and he helped pay for the publication of her *The Philosophy of the Plays of Shakspere Unfolded*
(1857), and wrote a nine-page preface for it. She was institutionalized in December 1857.
2. Bacon published "William Shakspere and his Plays; an Inquiry Concerning Them" in the
January 1856 *Putnam's Monthly Magazine,* in which she referred to Shakespeare as "the old
Player," among other disparaging terms.
3. Presumably William Henry Smith, *Was Lord Bacon the Author of Shakspere's Plays? A letter to Lord Elsmere* (1856). [CE]

TO DELIA BACON

Liverpool, June 21st '56

Dear Miss Bacon,

You will have thought me inexcusably dilatory for not sooner writing to you;
but I have been absent from Liverpool a great part of the time—Mrs. Hawthorne

having recently arrived at Southampton. I shall establish her near London early in July, and will then hope to meet you personally.

Meanwhile, though I have not had time to read the whole of your manuscript, I cannot refrain from saying that I think the work an admirable one. You seem to me to have read Bacon and Montaigne more profoundly than anybody else has read them.[1] It is very long (it was in my early youth, indeed) since I used to read and re-read Montaigne; and in order to do any justice, to your views I ought to re-peruse him now—and Bacon, also—and Shakspeare too. I cannot say, at present, that I adopt your theory, if I rightly comprehend it, as partially developed in this portion of your work. We find thoughts in all great writers (and even in small ones) that strike their roots far beneath the surface, and intertwine themselves with the roots of other writers' thoughts; so that when we pull up one, we stir the whole, and yet those writers have had no conscious society with one another. I express this very shabbily; but you will think it for me better than I can say it.

But this has nothing to do with the depth and excellence of your work and its worthiness to come before the world. If I can contribute in any way to this good end, I shall esteem myself happy. I am not particularly well off pecuniarily, but can do somewhat in that way, and perhaps in other ways. When I see you (or sooner, if you like) we can talk of this.

In haste,
Sincerely Yours
Nathl Hawthorne.

1. Michel Eyquem Montaigné, French essayist and philosopher.

TO LEONARD BACON

U. S. Consulate,
Liverpool, Aug 14th '56

My dear Sir,[1]

I have recently held some communication with your sister, Miss Delia Bacon, at present residing in London; and, as I believe she has no other friend in England, you will not think me impertinent in addressing you with reference to her affairs.

I understand from her (and can readily suppose it to be the case) that you are very urgent that she should return to America; nor can I deny that I should give her similar advice, if her mind were differently circumstanced from what I find it. But Miss Bacon has become possessed by an idea, that there are discoveries within her reach, in reference to the authorship of Shakspeare, and that, by quitting England, she should forfeit all chance of following up these discoveries, and making them manifest to the public. I say nothing as to the correctness of this idea (as respects the existence of direct, material, and documentary evidence) as she has not imparted to me the grounds of her belief. But, at all events, she is so fully and firmly possessed by it, that she will never leave England, voluntarily, until she shall have done everything in her power to obtain these proofs; nor would any argument nor, I think, any amount of poverty and hardship avail with her to the contrary. And I will say to you in confidence, my dear Sir, that I should dread the effect, on her mind, of any compulsory measures on the part of her friends, towards a removal. If I might presume to advise, my counsel would be that you should acquiesce, for the present, in her remaining here and do what may be in your power towards making her comfortable.

However mistaken your sister may be, she has produced a most remarkable work written with wonderful earnestness and ability, and full of very profound criticism. Its merits are entirely independent of the truth of her theory about the authorship of the plays. I am in hopes to find a publisher for the work, here in England; and I should judge that there was a fair chance of its meeting with such success as would render her independent of her friends. But this, of course, must be an affair of time.

At the only interview which I have had with Miss Bacon, I found her tolerably well, in bodily health, perfectly cheerful, and conversing with great power and intelligence. She lodges in the house of some excellent people, who seem to be attached to her, and who treat her as few London lodging-house keepers would treat their inmates, if suspected of poverty. She is very fortunate in having found such a home; and I submit it to your judgment, on a view of the whole case, whether it will not be more for her well-being to remain here, than (against such strong convictions as actuate her) to return to America. And, as I have already said, it seems to me quite certain that she will not return, (with her purpose unfulfilled) while she continues to be a free agent.

I write this note of my own motion, being greatly interested by what I have seen of your sister, and feeling, indeed, an anxious responsibility in putting her situation fairly before you.[2]

Pardon me if I have used an undue freedom, and believe me,

Very Sincerely,
& Respectfully
Nathl Hawthorne.

Rev. Dr. Bacon

1. Leonard Bacon was minister to a Calvinist church in New Haven, Connecticut.
2. For Bacon's friendly reply to NH, see *CE*, 17:530n.

TO JULIAN HAWTHORNE

Liverpool, Aug. 16, 1856.

Old Boy,

We have very good dinners at Mrs. Blodget's, and I think you would like very much to be there.[1] There are so many people, that Charley sits at a side-table, and he lives upon the fat of the land; and so would you, if you sat at the side-table with him. Yesterday, he ate roast-beef and Yorkshire pudding; but if he had preferred it, he might have had some chicken-pie, with nice paste; or some roast duck, which looked very good; or some tripe fried in batter; or some boiled chicken,—or a great many other delectable things. And we had two kinds of fish—boiled salmon and fried soles. I myself ate salmon, but the soles seemed to be very nice too. And we had so many green peas that they were not half eaten, and string-beans besides—oh, how nice! When the puddings, and tarts, and custards, and Banbury cakes, and cheese-cakes, and green gages, and that kind of stuff, was put on the table, I had hardly any appetite left; but I did manage to eat some currant pudding, and a Banbury cake, and a Victoria cake, and a slice of a beautiful Spanish musk-melon, and some plums. If you had been there, I think you would have had a very good dinner, and there would not have been nearly so many nice things left on the table.

Tell mamma that, if she pleases, I have no objection to your taking riding-lessons along with Una. Mamma says you have been a very good boy. I am glad to hear it, and hope you will keep good till I come back.

Your loving father,
Nathl Hawthorne.

I shall write to Una, next week.

1. SPH, Una, Rose, and Julian left to summer at Blackheath on 27 June.

TO RALPH WALDO EMERSON

Liverpool, Septr 10th 1856.

My dear Emerson,

I thank you for your book, which reached me a week or two ago, just as I was about starting on a journey to London; so I made it my travelling companion, and compared it all the way with the England actually before my eyes.[1]

Undoubtedly, these are the truest pages that have yet been written, about this country. Some of them seem to me absolutely true; as regards others, the truth has not been made apparent to me by my own observations. If I had time—and a higher opinion of my own fitness—I should be glad to write notes on the book.

I am afraid it will please the English only too well; for you give them credit for the possession, in very large measure, of all the qualities that they value, or pride themselves upon; and they never will comprehend that what you deny is far greater and higher than what you concede. In fact, you deny them only what they would be ashamed of, if they possessed it.

But perhaps I am no fair judge of Englishmen, just now. Individually, they suit me well; it is very comfortable to live among them. But yet I am not unconscious of a certain malevolence and hostility in my own breast, such as a man must necessarily feel, who lives in England without melting entirely into the mass of Englishmen. I must confess to have sympathized with Russia more than England, in the late war;[2] and nothing has given me quite so much pleasure, since I left home, as the stoop which I saw in every Englishman's shoulders, after the settlement of the Enlistment question.[3]

Sincerely Yours,
Nathl Hawthorne.

1. *English Traits* had been published on 6 August 1856 in America, and in early September in England; NH may have had a copy of the English edition.

2. That is, the Crimean War.

3. John Fiennes Twistleton Crampton was dismissed as British minister to the United States after he refused to stop illegally recruiting American volunteers to serve in the British army.

TO WILLIAM L. MARCY

Consulate of the United States
Liverpool 13th February 1857

Sir,

I have the honor to forward herewith a special report of a Society established in Liverpool, for the relief of Foreigners in distress.[1] The Society is composed of the most influential, & intelligent Foreigners residing in Liverpool, & their opinions are entitled to great consideration.

I also enclose a copy of Resolutions adopted at a meeting of American Shipmasters, lately held in Liverpool.[2]

I have on several previous occasions, called your attention to the system of shipping seamen for our merchant service, and the evils resulting; & am constrained to do so again, by the enclosed papers having been forwarded to me—the first mentioned having been also published in the London Times, & the Local newspapers—& by the frequent occurrence of late, of cases of gross cruelty occurring on board our vessels, during the voyage from the United States. Scarcely a vessel arrives from New York, or any of the Southern ports of the US, the Crew of which does not almost entirely consist of persons totally ignorant of the duties for which they shipped—or rather were shipped—mere landsmen. And these persons are subjected to the most revolting treatment at the hands of the officers, and, in very many cases, at the hands of their irritated shipmates. They arrive here almost naked, & in a state of great debility, the result of exposure & illtreatment combined.

Latterly I have been almost daily called upon to investigate complaints made by such persons, of assaults committed upon them by the inferior officers or their shipmates, or of their being plundered of the little clothing they brought on board. A Despatch which accompanies this, will inform you of a recent case of a man (by trade a grocer, never before at sea but once as passenger to America) dying in the Liverpool Hospital, from the effect of ill usage from the 2nd & 3rd mates & Boatswain of his vessel. And unless this fatal result occurs, & in Liverpool, the perpetrators go unpunished, the authorities having no jurisdiction; & the Treaty giving me none, unless I can make out a case of murder, assault with intent to commit murder, or Robbery.

It is not easy to remedy the evil of inefficient manning of our vessels, of which all the other evils are but branches—& when I speak of inefficient manning I include the entire [*left blank*] for I am sorry to say the officers need improvement, almost as much as seamen, & are becoming rapidly worse; but if what I have before suggested were done—a competent commission of enquiry instituted—I am sure a remedy would be found. The abolition of the pernicious advance system, & of the Law requiring two thirds Americans; the adoption of a better mode of shipping seamen; & an apprentice system—seem to be obvious.

Something must be done, as our National character & commerce are suffering great damage. I have had it from good authority that the rates of Insurance by American vessels have been materially increased, because of the inefficient crews they are known to have.

To carry out an apprentice system, an International arrangement would be necessary to reclaim deserters; For this no Treaty would be needed, as the merchant shipping act, which I had the honor to forward at the time of its passage, contains a provision similar to our own Reciprocity Act—that on satisfactory evidence being given of facilities being granted for the arrest of deserters from British ships in any foreign country, Her Majesty may issue proclamation for like facilities being granted in England in favor of that country.

To put a stop to the violence & thieving on board ships on the high seas; and to remedy the mode of shipping seamen on this side, a Treaty would be necessary. In the first case to give the magistrates jurisdiction in all offences below those provided for in the Treaty. In the other to compel the seaman when shipped, to fulfil his contract, which would enable captains to dispense with shipping masters. And I submit whether there can be any national objection to giving the English local courts jurisdiction in minor offences, on the written application of the National Representative, & with the proviso that the accused should have the right of being tried by a jury of his own countrymen. It would certainly be vastly beneficial to our Commerce.

With high respect
I have the honor to be
Your obedt Servant
Nathl Hawthorne.

Hon Wm L Marcy
Secretary of State[3]

1. See *CE*, 20:108–110n, for this document.
2. See *CE*, 20:110–11n, for this document.
3. Another version of this document, showing minor variations from that printed here, is in *CE*, 20:106–8.

TO RICHARD BENTLEY

U. S. Consulate,
Liverpool, Febr 16th 1857.

My dear Sir:[1]

I beg you to excuse me for not more promptly replying to your kind note of the 4th inst. In the pressure of official business, it was overlooked.

My time has been so entirely occupied, during my residence in England, that I have been compelled to relinquish all literary pursuits;[2] and I have no hope of being able to return to them, while I continue in Office. I have, however, recently taken measures to resign my post; but, as I shall then leave England for the Continent, I fear that we shall not be able to make such an arrangement as you kindly propose. Were it practicable, nothing could be more gratifying to me than to publish a work under such distinguished auspices as your own.

When next in London, I shall make it a point to call on you, if it be only for the pleasure and honor of meeting a gentleman whose name is so familiar to all who take an interest in literature.

Very sincerely
& Respectfully,
Nathl Hawthorne

Richard Bentley, Esq.

1. Richard Bentley, one of England's premier publishers, had earlier turned down *The Scarlet Letter* because unauthorized cheap reprintings had previously appeared. He did not publish anything by NH.

2. NH's only publication while in England was a short descriptive sketch of "Uttoxeter" in *The Keepsake* for 1857 (reprinted as "Lichfield and Uttoxeter" in the April 1857 *Harper's New Monthly Magazine*).

☙

TO LEWIS CASS

Consulate of the United States,
Liverpool, June 17th 1857.

Sir,[1]

There has recently appeared, in most of the English newspapers, what purports to be a letter from the Secretary of State of the United States to Lord Napier,
British minister at Washington, in response to a communication from his
Lordship on the treatment of American seamen.[2] In making some remarks upon
that letter, it is hardly necessary to say that I do not presume to interfere in a discussion between the Head of the Department, in which I am a subordinate officer, and the Minister of a foreign power. But, as the above mentioned letter has
been made public property, there is as much propriety in my referring to it as to
any other matter of public importance, bearing especial reference to my own official duties. I therefore take the liberty to address you, on the supposition that this
document expresses the opinion and intimates the policy of our government
respecting a subject, on which I have bestowed much thought, and with which I
have had opportunities to become practically acquainted.

The sentiment is very decidedly expressed in the letter, that, the "laws now in
force on the subject of seamen, employed on board the mercantile vessels of the
United States, are quite sufficient for their protection."

I believe that no man, practically connected with our commercial navy,
whether as owner, officer, or seaman, would affirm that the present marine laws of
the United States are such as the present condition of our nautical affairs impera-
tively demands. Those laws may have been wise, and effectual for the welfare of all
concerned, at the period of their enactment. But they had in view a state of things
which has entirely passed away; for they are based upon the supposition that the
United States really possess a body of native-born seamen, and that our ships are
chiefly manned by crews whose home is on our own shores. It is unfortunately the
fact, however, that not one in ten of the seamen, employed on board our vessels, is
a native-born or even a naturalized citizen, or has any connection with our country beyond his engagement for the voyage. So far as my observation extends, there
is not even a class of seamen who ship exclusively in American vessels, or who
habitually give them the preference to others. While the present voyage lasts, the
sailor is an American; in the next, he is as likely to be sailing under any other flag
as our own. And there is still another element of the subject, causing a yet wider

discrepancy between the state of things contemplated by the law, and that actually existing. This lies in the fact, that many of the men shipped on board our vessels—comprising much the larger proportion of those who suffer ill-usage—are not seamen at all. Almost every ship, on her trip from New York to Liverpool, brings a number of returning emigrants, wholly unacquainted with the sea, and incapable of performing the duties of seamen, but who have shipped for the purpose merely of accomplishing their homeward passage.

On this latter class of men falls most of the cruelty and severity, which have drawn public notice and reprobation on our mercantile marine. It is the result—not, as one would naturally suppose, of systematic tyranny on the part of the constituted authorities of the ship—but of a state of war between two classes who find themselves, for a period, inextricably opposed on shipboard. One of these classes is composed of the mates and actual seamen, who are adequate to the performance of their own duty, and demand a similar efficiency in others; the second class consists of men who know nothing of the sea, but who have imposed themselves, or been imposed upon the ship, as capable of a seaman's duty. This deception, as it increases the toil and hardship of the real sailor, draws his vengeance upon the unfortunate impostor. In the worst case investigated by me, it appeared that there was not one of the sailor-class, from the second-mate down to the youngest boy, who had not more or less maltreated the landsmen. In another case, the chief and second-mate, during the illness of the master, so maltreated a landsman, who had shipped as sailor, that he afterwards died in a fit. In scarcely a single instance has it been possible to implicate the master as taking a share in these unjustifiable proceedings.

In both the cases, above alluded to, the guilty escaped punishment; and in many similar ones, it has been found that the sufferers are practically without protection or redress. A few remarks will make this fact obvious.

A consul, as I need not inform the Department, has no power (nor could he have, unless by treaty with the government in whose territory he resides) to inflict condign[3] punishment for assaults and other outrages which may come under his official cognizance. The extent of his power (except in a contingency hereafter to be noticed) is, to enable the complainant to seek justice in our own courts of law. If the United States really possessed any native seamen, this might be effectual so far as they were concerned; for such seamen would naturally gravitate homeward, and would there meet the persons who had outraged them, under circumstances which would ensure redress. But the foreigner can very seldom be prevailed upon to return for the mere purpose of prosecuting his officers; and with the returning emigrant, who has suffered so much for the sake of obtaining a homeward passage, it is out of the question. In such cases, what is the Consul to do? Before the complainants make their appeal to him, they have ceased to be under the jurisdiction of his country; and they refuse to return to it in quest of a revenge, which they cannot be secure of obtaining, and which would benefit them little, if obtained. The perpetrators of these outrages are not men who can be made pecuniarily responsible, being almost invariably, as I have said, the lower officers and able seamen of the ship.

In cases of unjustifiably severe usage, if the master of the vessel be found implicated in the offence, the Consul has it at his option to order the discharge of the sufferer, with the payment of three months extra wages. But the instances of cruel treatment, which have come under my notice, are not of the kind contemplated by the act of 1840; not being the effect of the tyranny or bad passions of the master, or of officers acting under his authority, but, as already stated, of the hostile interests of two classes of the crew. To prevent these disorders would require the authority and influence of abler men, and of a higher stamp, than American shipmasters are now usually found to be. In very difficult circumstances, and having a vast responsibility of life and property upon their hands, they appear to me to do their best, with such materials as are at their command. So far as they lay themselves open to the law, I have been ready to inflict it, but have found few opportunities.

Thus, a great mass of petty outrage, unjustifiable assaults, shameful indignities, and nameless cruelty, demoralizing alike to those who perpetrate and those who suffer, falls into the ocean between the two countries, and can be punished in neither. Such a state of things, as it can be met by no law now in existence, would seem to require new legislation.

I have not failed to draw attention of the government to this subject, on several former occasions. Nor has it been denied, by the last Administration,[4] that our laws in this regard were defective and required revision; but the extent of those acknowledged defects, and of that necessary revision, was alleged as a reason why no partial measures should be adopted. The importance of the matter, as embracing the whole condition of our mercantile marine, cannot be over-estimated. It is not an exaggeration to say, that the United States have no seamen. Even the officers, from the mate downward, are usually foreigners, and of a very poor class; being the rejected mates and other subordinates of the British commercial navy. Men who have failed to pass their examination, or have been deprived of their certificates by reason of drunkenness or other ill-conduct, attain, on board of our noble ships, the posts for which they are deemed unworthy in their own. On the deterioration of this class of men necessarily follows that of the masters, who are promoted from it. I deeply regret to say, that the character of American shipmasters has already descended, many degrees, from the high standard which it has held in years past; an effect partly due, as I have just hinted, to the constantly narrowing field of selection, and likewise, in a great degree, to the terrible life which a shipmaster is now forced to lead. Respectable men are anxious to quit a service which links them with such comrades, loads them with such responsibility, and necessitates such modes of meeting it.

In making this communication to the Department, I have deemed it my duty to speak with all possible plainness, believing that you will agree with me that official ceremony is of little importance in view of such a national emergency as is here presented. If there be an interest which requires the intervention of Government, with all its wisdom and all its power—and with more promptitude than governments usually display—it is this. The only efficient remedy, it appears to me, must be found in the creation of a class of native seamen; but, in the years that must elapse before that can be effected, it is most desirable that Government should at least recognize the evils that exist, and do its utmost to alleviate them. No American statesman, being in the position which makes it his especial duty to comprehend and to deal with this matter, can neglect it without peril to his fame. It is a subject which requires only to be adequately represented in order to attract the deepest interest on the part of the public; and the now wasted or destructive energy of our philanthropists might here be most beneficially employed.

In conclusion, I beg leave to say a few words on the personal bearing which the Secretary's supposed letter has upon my own official character. The letter expresses the opinion that the laws of the United States are adequate to the protection of our seamen, and adds that the execution of those laws devolves mostly on Consuls; some of whom, it suggests, in British ports, may have been "delinquent in the discharge of their duty." Now it is undeniable that outrages on board of our ships have actually occurred; and it is equally well-known, and I myself hereby certify, that the majority of these outrages pass without any punishment whatever. Most of them, moreover, in the trade between America and England, have come under my own Consular supervision and been fully investigated by me. If I have possessed the power to punish those offences, and, whether through sluggishness, or fear, or favor, have failed to exercise it, then I am guilty of a great crime, which ought to be visited with a severity and an ignominy commensurate with its evil consequences; and these, surely, would be nothing less than national. If I am innocent—if I have done my utmost, as an executive officer, under a defective law, to the defects of which I have repeatedly called the attention of my superiors—then, unquestionably, the Secretary has wronged me by a suggestion pointing so directly at myself. It trenches upon one of the few rights, as a citizen and as a man, which an office-holder might imagine himself to retain. I leave the matter with the Department. It is peculiarly unfortunate for me that my resignation is already in the hands of the President;[5] for, going out of office under this stigma, I foresee that I shall be supposed to have committed official suicide, as the only mode of escaping some worse fate. Whether it is right that an honorable and conscientious discharge of duty should be rewarded by loss of character, I leave to the wisdom and justice of the Department to decide.

I am, Sir,

Most Respectfully,

Your obedient servant,

Nathl Hawthorne.

General Lewis Cass,

Secretary of State,

Washington,

D. C.

1. Cass was now Secretary of State.
2. See *CE*, 20:149–50n, for this document.
3. Condign, deserved or suitable.
4. James Buchanan had succeeded Pierce as president on 4 March.
5. NH's resignation was formally accepted by Cass on 24 September.

TO RALPH WALDO EMERSON

Liverpool, Septr 24th 1857.

My dear Emerson,

I have not often (if indeed ever) sent anybody to you with a letter of introduction; so that you would pardon me even for introducing a common man; and I know you will thank me for being the medium of making Dr. Mackay known to you.[1] Will you be kind enough to show him Thoreau, and Ellery Channing, and any other queer and notable people who may, by this time, have taken up their abode in Concord?

I have resigned my Consulate, but instead of drawing homeward, am going farther than ever from my old cottage and sand-hill. In fact, I have continually seen so many of my countrymen (more than ever before in my life) that I feel as if I were now only on the point of first coming abroad.

Truly Yours,
Nathl Hawthorne.

R. W. Emerson.

1. Charles Mackay, poet and editor of the *Illustrated London News*.

TO ROSE HAWTHORNE

Liverpool
October 2d 1857

My dear little Pessima,[1]

I am very glad that Mamma is going to take you to see "Tom Thump";[2] and I think it is much better to call him Thump than Thumb, and I always mean to call him so from this time forward. It's a very nice name, is Tom T H U M P. I hope you will call him Tom Thump to his face, when you see him, and thump him well if he finds fault with it. Do you still thump Mamma, and Fanny, and Una and Julian, as you did when I saw you last? If you do, I shall call you little Rose Thump; and then people will think that you are Tom Thump's wife. And now I shall stop thumping on this subject.

Your friend little Frank Hallet is at Mrs. Blodget's. Do you remember how you used to play with him at Southport, and how he sometimes beat you? He seems to be a better little boy than he was then, but still he is not so good as he might be. This morning, he had some very nice breakfast in his plate, but he would not eat it because his mamma refused to give him something that was not good for him; and so, all breakfast-time, this foolish little boy refused to taste a mouthful, though I could see that he was very hungry, and would have eaten it all up, if he could have got it into his mouth without anybody seeing. Was not he a silly child? Little Pessima never behaved so—Oh, no!

There are two or three very nice little girls at Mrs. Blodget's; and also a nice large dog, who is very kind and gentle, and never bites anybody; and also a tabby cat, who very often comes to me and mews for something to eat. So you see we have a very pleasant family; but, for all that, I would rather be at home.

I sent somebody over to see how Mr. Wilding does, this morning; and he has just come back and says that Mr. Wilding is a great deal better. He has kept his bed for a long time, but yesterday he sat up a little while, and he is sitting up to-day. He has sent me a great bundle of papers that I wanted; and I shall go to see him next week, when, I hope, he will be able to tell me some things that I wish to know.

I want you to ask Mamma if she does not think that my old frock-coat could be made into a sack or jacket for Julian. It is a very good and strong cloth, and is not nearly worn out, and I think it would be a great pity to leave it here, when it costs so much to buy clothes for that great boy. I should like to have it made up for him before we leave Leamington.

And now I have written you such a long letter that my head is quite tired out; and so I shall leave off and amuse myself with looking at some pages of figures.

Be a good little girl, and do not tease Mamma, nor trouble Fanny, nor quarrel with Una and Julian; and when I come home, I shall call you little Pessima (because, I am very sure you will deserve that name) and shall kiss you more than once.

Your affectionate father.

1. NH's nicknames for Rose were Rosebud and Pessima.
2. A reference to the fairy story "Tom Thumb" by Jacob and Wilhelm Grimm about a couple who give birth to a child no larger than a thumb.

TO ELIZABETH PALMER PEABODY [FRAGMENT]

Liverpool, October 8th, '57

Dear E.

I read your manuscript abolition pamphlet, supposing it to be a new production, and only discovered afterwards that it was the one I had sent back.[1] Upon my word, it is not very good; not worthy of being sent three times across the ocean; not so good as I supposed you would always write, on a subject in which your mind and heart were interested. However, since you make a point of it, I will give it to Sophia, and will tell her about its rejection and return. Can [*excision*] tating always on one spot, and that the wrong one. You agitate her nerves, without in the least affecting her mind.

As you have suggested dropping your correspondence with Sophia, I hope you will take in good part some remarks which I have often thought of making on that subject. I entirely differ from you in the idea that such correspondence is essential to her peace of mind; not but what she loves you deeply and sincerely, and truly enjoys all modes of healthy intercourse with you. But it is a solemn truth, that I never in my life knew her to receive a letter from you, without turning pale and [*excision*]

And the very fact of my speaking so implies all the love and respect which, because I speak so, you are ready to disbelieve. As for Miss Parsons, I have long ago taken her measure, though she has failed to take mine.[2] What you tell me about the letter is very curious, and it goes to confirm my previous idea of such revelations. A seeress of this kind will not afford you any miraculous insight into a person's character and mind; she will merely discover, through the medium of the letter, what another person, of just the same natural scope and penetration of the seeress, would discover normally by personal intercourse and observation of the person described. Thus her revelations (like all our conceptions of other person's characters) have some truth and much error.

I do not know what Sophia may have said about my conduct in the Consulate. I only know that I have done no good; none whatever. Vengeance and Beneficence are things that God claims for Himself. His instruments have no consciousness of his purpose; if they imagine they have, it is a pretty sure token that they are not his instruments. The good of others, like our own happiness, is not to be attained by direct effort, but incidentally.—All history and observation confirm this. I am really too humble to think of doing good; if I have been impertinent enough to aim at it, I am ashamed. What wretched things are perpetuated under the notion of doing good! Now, I presume you think the abolition of flogging was a vast boon to sea-men. I see, on the contrary, with perfect distinctness, that many murders and an immense mass of unpunishable cruelty—a thousand blows, at least, for every one that the cat-of-nine tails would have inflicted—have resulted from that very thing.[3] There is a moral in this fact, which I leave you to deduce. God's ways are in nothing more mysterious than in this matter of trying to do good.

This is the last letter I shall write you from the Consulate. My successor is in town, and will take his office upon him next Monday. Thank Heaven; for I am weary, and, if it were not for Sophia and the children, would like to lie down on one spot for about a hundred years.

We shall be in England, however, some weeks longer. Good bye.

---

1. For NH's earlier comment on the "manuscript abolition pamphlet," see *CE*, 18:89.

2. Anna Quincy Thaxter Parsons, a clairvoyant of sorts at Brook Farm.

3. On 16 November 1855, NH argued that the legalization of flogging on shipboard is "the best practicable step for the present," for it would eliminate the "miscellaneous assaults and batteries . . . which the inferior officers continually perpetuate, as the only mode of keeping up anything like discipline" (*English Notebooks, CE,* 21:399–400).

TO JAMES T. FIELDS

Villa Montauto, near Florence,[1]
Septr 3d 1858.

Dear Fields,

I wrote to Ticknor from Rome, months ago, and have had no answer; and now I am going to try whether you have any more conscience than he. I am afraid I have staid away too long, and am forgotten by everybody. You have piled up the dusty remnants of my editions, I suppose, in that chamber over the shop, where you once took me to smoke a cigar, and have crossed my name out of your list of authors without so much as asking whether I am dead or alive. But I like it well enough, nevertheless. It is pleasant to feel, at last, that I am really away from America—a satisfaction that I never enjoyed as long as I staid in Liverpool, where it seemed to me that the quintessence of nasal and handshaking Yankeedom was continually filtered and sublimated through my Consulate, on the way outward and homeward. I first got acquainted with my own countrymen there. At Rome, too, it was not much better. But here in Florence and in the summer time, and in this secluded villa, I have escaped out of all my old tracks, and am really remote.

I like my present residence immensely. The house stands on a hill overlooking Florence and is big enough to quarter a regiment; insomuch that each member of the family, including servants, has a separate suite of apartments, and there are vast wildernesses of upper rooms into which we have never yet sent exploring expeditions. At one end of the house there is a moss-grown tower, haunted by owls and by the ghost of a monk, who was confined there in the thirteenth century, previous to being burnt at the stake in the principal square of Florence.[2] I hire this villa, tower and all, at twenty-eight dollars a month; but I mean to take it away bodily and clap it into a Romance, which I have in my head ready to be written out.[3]

Speaking of Romances, I have planned two, one or both of which I could have ready for the press in a few months, if I were either in England or America. But I find this Italian atmosphere not favorable to the close toil of composition, although it is a very good air to dream in. I must breathe the fogs of old England or the east winds of Massachusetts in order to put me into working trim. Nevertheless, I shall endeavor to be busy during the coming winter at Rome; but there will be so much to distract my thoughts that I have little hope of seriously accomplishing anything. It is a pity; for I have really a plethora of ideas, and should feel relieved by discharging some of them upon the public. What an unseemly simile is this!—but I am speaking of brains, not of bowels.

We shall continue here till the end of this month, and shall then return to Rome, where I have already taken a house for six months. In the middle of April, we intend to start for home by way of Geneva and Paris; and, after spending a few weeks in England, shall embark for Boston in July or the beginning of August. After so long an absence (more than five years already, which will be six before you see me at the old 'Corner,')[4] it is not altogether delightful to think of returning. Everybody will be changed, and I myself, no doubt, as much as anybody. Ticknor and you, I suppose, were both upset in the late religious earthquake, and when I enquire for you, the clerks will direct me to the "Business Men's Conference."[5] It won't do. I shall be forced to come back again and take refuge in a London lodging. London is like the grave in one respect—and man can make himself at home there; and whenever a man finds himself homeless elsewhere, he had better either die or go to London.

Speaking of the grave reminds me of old age and other disagreeable matters; and I would remark that one grows old in Italy twice or three times as fast as in other countries. I have three gray hairs now, for one that I brought from England, and I shall look venerable indeed by next summer, when I return.

I want you to tell Ticknor that I have exhausted all but about £100 of my letter of credit, and shall have to send to Baring's for a new one immediately after my arrival in Rome.[6] He must do the needful without delay.

Remember me affectionately to all my friends. Whoever has a kindness for me may be assured that I have twice as much for him. Pray answer this letter, so that I may find one from you when I reach Rome, by the middle of October. Care of Pakenham and Hooker Bankers.

Your friend,
Nathl Hawthorne.

If you put something *black* under this page, it will be more legible.[7]

1. The Hawthornes moved to Villa Montauto on 1 August.

2. Girolama Savonarola, Italian cleric and reformer.

3. Villa Mantauto appeared as Monte Beni in NH's next novel, *The Marble Faun*, published on 7 March 1860 in America.

4. The famous "Old Corner" bookstore of and headquarters for Ticknor and Fields was at the corner of Washington and School streets in Boston.

5. The Great Awakening of 1857–58 in America was spurred by a feeling that wealth had replaced religion as the goal of the people, and was marked by numerous prayer meetings and conversions.

6. Baring Brothers and Company acted as a maildrop and bank for Americans living in England. NH went to Rome on 13 October; he had previously been there on 20 January–24 May.

7. The postscript, written vertically up the left margin of the first manuscript page, refers to the illegibility of the letter because of ink seeping through the paper. In an attempt to compensate for the seepage, NH wrote horizontally and vertically on alternate pages. [*CE*]

TO LOUISA LANDER AND ELIZABETH LANDER

Mr Hawthorne begs to thank the Misses Lander for the letters which they have kindly forwarded.[1] Mr H was not aware that Miss E. Lander called on Thursday evening.

Mr Hawthorne is glad to be informed that some (he hopes many) of Miss Louisa Lander's friends are convinced of the purity of her life and character. He is himself open to conviction on that subject; but as guardian of the sanctity of his domestic circle, he is compelled to be more cautious than if he were acting merely for himself. Before calling at Mr Hawthorne's residence, Miss Louisa Lander had been made fully aware that reports were in circulation, most detrimental to her character; and he cannot but think that any attempt at social intercourse with her former friends, (especially where young people and children are included in the number) should have been preceded by a full explanation and refutation of those reports.

As far as her own conscience is concerned, Miss Lander's life (as she truly observes) lies between her Maker and herself, but in her relations with society, the treatment she receives must depend upon her ability to make a good and reasonable defence against the charges imputed to her. If Mr Hawthorne were one of those friends who have faith in Miss Lander's innocence, his first and last advice to her would be to sift those charges thoroughly, to meet them fully, and to throw her life open to the world. This should be done at once, and nothing short of this will enable Miss Lander to retain her position. Should Miss Lander decide to take this course, no one will be more rejoiced at the triumphant vindication of her character than the present writer. In any case Miss Lander may be assured of Mr

Hawthorne's silence on this painful subject. He has no wish to say a word that may injure her, and would most gladly be enabled again to think and speak as highly of her as he has done hitherto.

Nov. 13 [1858].
68, Piazza Poli [Rome]

1. The local artists had asked Maria Louisa Lander to swear that rumors about her being involved in a scandal were false; and when she failed to do so, they ostracized her. Another explanation for NH's attitude is said to be his dislike of the bust of him that Lander had sculpted (see Gollin, *Portraits of Nathaniel Hawthorne*, 48).

TO CEPHAS THOMPSON

[Rome, ca. 12 March 1859]

Dear Mr Thompson,[1]

I should really take great delight (and so would my wife) in doing anything and everything that you wish; but my wife's health quite precludes the possibility of her going out in the evening, and, as for myself, I suffer under a native and inherent incapacity for making visits. If she could go out, I should accompany her, like a dutiful husband; but I never go "on my own hook"—at least, never, where I can take the friendly liberty of declining. I sometimes go to see strangers and enemies; but I always rely upon my friends to excuse me from making evening visits. Besides, just at present, I have a bad cold.

It will be quite proper for you to call on Genl Pierce, and I am sure he will be very glad to see you; but, if you prefer it, I will call with him at your studio—where, indeed, I had already spoken to him of going. I want you to know him; because I am sure you will like him.

Pray remember Mrs. Hawthorne and myself kindly to Mrs. Thompson, and believe me,

Very sincerely,
Nathl Hawthorne

1. Cephas Giovanni Thompson, Massachusetts-born painter who worked in Rome from 1852 to 1859. His oil portrait of NH is reproduced in color in Gollin, *Portraits of Nathaniel Hawthorne*, 30, and is now at the Grolier Club in New York.

TO JAMES T. FIELDS

21, Bath-street,
Leamington, Octr 10th '59

Dear Fields,

The above is my present address, and probably will continue so for three months to come.[1]

As regards the Romance, it is almost finished, a great heap of manuscript being already accumulated, and only a few concluding chapters remaining behind. If hard pushed, I could have it ready for the press in a fortnight; but unless the publishers are in a hurry, I shall be somewhat longer about it. I have found far more work to do upon it than I anticipated.

Mrs. Hawthorne has read it, and speaks of it very rapturously. If she liked the author less, I should feel much encouraged by her liking the Romance so much. I, likewise, (to confess the truth,) admire it exceedingly, at intervals, but am liable to cold fits, during which I think it the most infernal nonsense. This happens to be the case just at the present moment.[2]

You ask for the title. I have not yet fixed upon one. Here are some that have occurred to me; but neither of them exactly meets my idea. "Monte Beni; or the Faun. A Romance." "The Romance of a Faun." "The Faun of Monte Beni[.]" "Monte Beni; a Romance." "Miriam; a Romance." "Hilda; a Romance." "Donatello; a Romance." "The Faun; a Romance." "Marble and Life / Man; a Romance." When you have read the work (which I especially wish you to do, before it goes to press) you will be able to select one of them, or imagine something better. There is an objection in my mind to an Italian name, though perhaps Monte Beni might do. Neither do I wish, if I can help it, to make the fantastic aspect of the book too prominent by putting the Faun into the title page.

I presume you are going to stay on this side of the water till next spring or summer. We had better all go home together. I had a letter from poor old Ticknor, the other day, and answered it immediately. I long to see him, and shall be a little comforted in going home, by the prospect of it.

Do not stay a great while in Paris.

We are all very well, except that the Romance has worn me down a little. It is not wholesome for me to write; but the bracing air of the German Ocean a little counteracted the bad effect, in the present instance.

With kindest regards to Mrs. Fields,

Your friend ever,
Nathl Hawthorne.

1. The Hawthornes left Italy for England on 25 May; they settled in Leamington on 5 October.

2. SPH wrote to Elizabeth Palmer Peabody at about this time: "As usual, he thinks the book good for nothing, and based upon a very foolish idea which nobody will like or accept. But I am used to such opinions, and understand why he feels oppressed with disgust of what has so long occupied him. The true judgment of the work was his *first* idea of it, when it seemed to him worth the doing. He has regularly despised each one of his books immediately upon finishing it. *My* enthusiasm is too much his own music, as it were. It needs the reverberation of the impartial mind to reassure him that he has not been guilty of a *bêtise*." [CE] *Bêtise*, folly or foolishness.

TO HENRY A. BRIGHT

21 Bath-street,
Leamington, March 10th '60

Dear Mr. Bright,

I thank you very much for your letter, and am glad you like the Romance so far, and so well. I shall really be gratified if you will review it. Very likely you are right about Donatello;[1] for though the idea in my mind was an agreeable and beautiful one, it was not easy so to present it to the reader.

Smith & Elder certainly do take strange liberties with the titles of books.[2] I wanted to call it "The Marble Faun"; but they insisted upon "Transformation," which will lead the reader to anticipate a sort of pantomime. They wrote me, some days ago, that the edition was nearly all sold, and that they are going to print another; to which I mean to append a few pages, in the shape of a conversation between Kenyon, Hilda, and the author, throwing some further light on matters which seem to have been left too much in the dark.[3] For my own part, however, I should prefer the book as it now stands.

It so happened, that, at the very time you were writing, Una was making up a parcel of the manuscript, to send to you. There is a further portion now in the hands of Smith & Elder, which I will procure when I go to London; that is, if you do not consider this immense mass more than enough.

I begin to be restless (and so do we all) with the anticipation of our approaching departure, and, almost for the first time, I long to be at home.[4] Nothing more can be done or enjoyed, till we have breathed our native air again. I do not even care for London now; though I mean to spend a few weeks there before taking a final leave; not that I mean to think it a last leave-taking, either. In three or four years, or less, my longings will no doubt be transferred from that side of the water to this; and perhaps I shall write another book, and come over to get it published.

We are rather at a loss for a suitable place to stay at during the interval between this and the middle of June, when we mean to sail. Liverpool is to be avoided, on Mrs. Hawthorne's account, till the last moment; and I am afraid there is no air in England fit for her to breathe. We have some idea of going to Bath, but more probably we may establish ourselves for a month or two in the neighborhood of London. But, as I said before, we shall enjoy little or nothing, wherever we may be. Our roots are pulled up, and we cannot really live till we stick them into the ground again. There will be pleasure, indeed, in greeting you at Liverpool (the most disagreeable city in England, nevertheless) but a sharp pain, soon afterwards, in bidding you farewell. The sooner it is all over, the better. What an uneasy kind of world we live in!

With this very original remark, I remain

Most sincerely your friend
Nathl Hawthorne.

1. Donatello is a character in *The Marble Faun*.

2. NH forgot that "The Transformation" had been one of his suggestions (see *CE*, 18:200).

3. The first printing of *The Transformation* was published on 28 February 1860, the second, after 16 March. NH's postscript, clarifying the ending in response to the confusion of many readers, first appeared in the second British and fourth American printings (see *CE*, 4:463–67).

4. The Hawthornes left England for America, traveling with James T. and Annie Adams Fields, on 16 June.

TO JOHN LOTHROP MOTLEY

13, Charles-street,
Bath,[1] April 1st, 1860

My dear Motley,[2]

You are certainly that Gentle Reader for whom all my books were exclusively written. Nobody else (my wife excepted, who speaks so near me that I cannot tell her voice from my own) has ever said exactly what I loved to hear. It is most satisfactory to be hit upon the raw; to be shot straight through the heart.[3] It is not the quantity of your praise that I care so much about (though I gather it all up most carefully, lavish as you are of it,) but the kind; for you take the book precisely as I meant it; and if your note had come a few days sooner, I believe I should have printed it in a Postscript which I have added to the second edition, because it explains, better than I found it possible to do myself, the way in which my Romance ought to be taken. These beer-sodden English beefeaters do not know how to read a Romance; neither can they praise it rightly, if ever so well disposed.

Now, don't suppose that I fancy the book to be a tenth part so good as you say it is. You work out my imperfect efforts, and half make the book with your own imagination, and see what I myself saw, but could only hint at.

Well; the Romance is a success, even if it never finds another reader.

We spent the winter in Leamington, whither we had come from the sea-coast in October. I am sorry to say that it was another winter of shadow and anxiety; not on Una's account, however, but my wife's. She had an attack of acute bronchitis, which reduced her very low; and (except for an enduring faith in the energy and elasticity of her constitution,) I should have been almost in despair. After a long confinement to her bed, she at last recovered so far as to enable us to remove from Leamington to Bath; and the change of air seems to have been very beneficial. The physician feels confident that she will be quite restored by our return to the United States. I have engaged our passages for June 16th, and, patriotic as you know me to be, you can conceive the rapture with which I shall embrace my native soil.

Mrs. Hawthorne and the children will probably remain in Bath till the eve of our departure; but I intend to pay one more visit of a week or two to London, and I shall certainly come and see you. I wonder at your lack of recognition of my social propensities. I take so much delight in my friends that a little intercourse goes a great way, and illuminates my life before and after.

Are you never coming back to America? It is dreary to stay away, though not very delightful to go back. I should be most happy, and so would my wife, to think that Mrs Motley, and yourself, and your daughters, were within our reach; and really you ought to devote yourself in the cause of your country. It is the worst sort of treason for enjoyable people to expatriate themselves.

Your friend
Nathl Hawthorne.

1. The Hawthornes were in Bath from 22 March through 14 May.

2. The historian John Lothrop Motley had been appointed ambassador to Austria, a post he took up in 1861.

3. Writing to NH on 29 March, Motley praises "those shadowy, weird, fantastic, Hawthornesque shapes flitting through the golden gloom which is the atmosphere of the book—I like the misty way in which the story is indicated instead of revealed. The outlines are quite definite enough from the beginning to the end, to those who have imagination enough to follow you in your airy flights—and to those who complain, I suppose nothing less than an illustrated edition, with a large gallows on the last page, with Donatello in the most pensile of attitudes,—his ears revealed at last thro' a white nightcap—would be satisfactory. I beg your pardon for such profanation, but it really moves my spleen that people should wish to bring down the volatile figures of your romance, to the level of an everyday novel." More of Motley's letter is printed in *CE,* 18:257–58.

TO HENRY A. BRIGHT

13, Charles-street,
Bath, April 4th '60

Dear Mr. Bright,

I thank you for the notice, and all the kind things you say in it.[1] It must have been originally very excellent, since it remains so good after all the censorship of the press that has been exercised upon it.

As for what you say of the plot, I do not agree that it has been left in an imperfect state. The characters of the story come out of an obscurity and vanish into it again, like the figures on the slide of a magic-lanthern; but, in their transit, they have served my purpose, and shown all that it was essential for them to reveal.

Anything further, if you consider it rightly, would be an impertinence on the author's part towards his reader. I mean to review somebody's Romance ("LATE IN THE AUTUMN," whenever you write it,) and will take that opportunity to develope my ideas about plottish proprieties.

However, the second edition is published, I believe, and my Postscript along with it. You will see, if it comes in your way, how easy it is to explain mysteries, when the author does not more wisely choose to keep a veil over them.

Your friend,
Nathl Hawthorne.

1. Bright reviewed *The Marble Faun* in the 31 March *Examiner.*

TO JAMES RUSSELL LOWELL

The Wayside, Concord,[1]
July 24th. 1860.

My dear Lowell,[2]

I ought to have thanked you for that tobacco days ago; but to tell the honest truth, I am so lazy, as it is so much pleasanter to lie on my hillside smoking the tobacco than to write notes about it—that I left you to think me ungrateful or inappreciative of your gift. But I like it exceedingly.[3]

I sent an article for the Atlantic, this morning.[4] Of course, if you don't think it worth printing, you will tell me so.

Sincerely Yours,
Nathl Hawthorne

1. The Hawthornes returned to Concord on 28 June.

2. The poet and critic James Russell Lowell edited the *Atlantic Monthly* from its beginning in November 1857 until Fields assumed the position in June 1861.

3. On 5 August Lowell wrote an introduction to NH for William Dean Howells: "I have no masonic claim upon you except community of tobacco, & the young man who brings this does not smoke. But he wants to look at you, which will do you no harm & him a great deal of good."

Howells describes his visit to the Wayside in *Literary Friends and Acquaintance; A Personal Retrospect of American Authorship,* ed. David F. Hiatt and Edwin H. Cady (Bloomington: Indiana University Press, 1968), 47–53. [CE] Howells would later become one of America's most influential novelists, editors, and critics.
   4. "Some of the Haunts of Burns; by a Tourist without Imagination or Enthusiasm" appeared in the October 1860 *Atlantic Monthly.*

TO JAMES T. FIELDS

Concord, Septr 21st '60

Dear Fields,

   I have given Mr. Wetherbe, my carpenter, an order on your firm, payable at one day's sight, for $200. If you happen to have the money by you, I wish you would pay it on presentation; as he wants it.
   We are in great trouble on account of our poor Una, in whom the bitter dregs of that Roman fever are still rankling, and have now developed themselves in a way which the physicians foreboded, and forewarned us of.[1] I do not like to write about it, but will tell you when we meet. Say nothing. I am continually reminded, now-a-days, of a response which I once heard a drunken sailor make to a pious gentleman who asked him how he felt:—"Pretty d—d miserable, thank God!" It very well expresses my thorough discomfort and forced acquiescence.

Yours truly,
Nathl Hawthorne

   1. Rose had come down with Roman fever or malaria on 24 October 1858 and was confined to bed for some months. On 5 April, she was given twenty-four hours to live, but the fever soon broke. Her biographer feels that in Concord, "Una apparently suffered from some type of emotional or nervous disorder, which may or may not have had its origin in the Roman fever or the medication used to fight it" (Patricia Dunlavy Valenti, *To Myself a Stranger: A Biography of Rose Hawthorne Lathrop* [Baton Rouge: Louisiana State University Press, 1991], 27).

TO FRANKLIN PIERCE

Concord, October 9th 1860

My dear Pierce,

I am most happy to give you good news of Una. All the violent symptoms were allayed by the first application of electricity, and within two days she was in such a condition as to require no further restraint. Since then, there has been no relapse, and now, for many days, she has seemed entirely well, in mind, and better as to her bodily health than since we left Rome. The lady (Mrs. Rollins) who applied the electricity, tells us that her derangement was the result of a liver-complaint and a slight affection of the heart, probably produced or strengthened by the Roman fever; and these maladies, she says, are perfectly within the control of medical electricity, and proper diet and exercise—the two latter being the most important remedies. She assures us that we need have no apprehension of future mental disturbance, and that we may entertain the most confident hopes of her complete restoration in all respects—her constitution being remarkably good.

I know that you will rejoice with me at these good prospects.

Your friend,
Nathl Hawthorne.

TO LOUIS A. SURETTE

Concord, October 10th '60

My dear Sir,[1]

I should consider it my duty, as a good townsman, to lecture before the inhabitants of Concord, if it were in my power to do so.[2] But I am quite unaccustomed to appear before the public, and feel it to be too late to begin.

Very truly
& Respectfully Yours,
Nathl Hawthorne.

L. A. Surette, Esq.
Curator &c.,
Concord Lyceum.

1. Louis Athanese Surette was president of the Concord Lyceum.
2. NH did not lecture in Concord.

TO MARY OTIS BAILEY

Concord, Decr 11th 1860.

Dear Miss Bailey,

I owe you many apologies for not having immediately replied to your letter; but I have delayed, in the hope of being able to look over some records made in England, and see whether there were anything that would interest you relative to the Hawthorne family. My papers, however, are in such confusion that I know not where to lay my hand upon anything; for I am making an addition to my house, and have deferred the arrangement of my goods and chattels till it is finished.

I met with very little success in my inquiries about the family in England.[1] There was a place called Hawthorne Hall, in the county of Chester, and a Hawthorne chapel in the adjoining church; but there was no record of any family of the name ever having lived or died there. I visited the State paper office, in the hope of discovering the name of the town whence our ancestors emigrated to America; a record having sometimes been kept of such particulars. But I did not succeed. I found reason to believe that there was a connection by marriage between the first emigrant and the family of Sir Gewayse Elwes; but I could not trace this matter out for lack of knowing the name of our ancestor's first wife, whom he married in England. In short, I was much disappointed in my researches, and was only consoled by the hope of returning to England, at some future time, in a better condition to follow up the investigation. Very probably, you could have supplied me with just the information that was needed to make my search successful.

Nothing would give Mrs. Hawthorne and myself greater pleasure than to see you here, whenever our house shall be fit to receive a guest. At this dreary season, we should not venture to solicit such a favor; but I hope that, a few months hence, you will allow the claims of kindred to prevail upon you to make us a visit.

Very sincerely,
Your kinsman,
Nathl Hawthorne

Miss Mary Otis Bailey,
Boston.

P.S. The name of Hathorne or Hawthorne is not very unusual in England; but they all seem to have originated in the South of Scotland. I think our ancestor could not have been of that stock.

1. See Vernon Loggins, *The Hawthornes: The Story of Seven Generations of an American Family* (New York: Columbia University Press, 1951), for more on NH's English ancestors.

TO HENRY A. BRIGHT

The Wayside,
Concord, Decr 17th 1860

Dear Henry Bright,

I ought to have written to you long ago, and I suppose that is one among a hundred reasons why I have never done it. But, heretofore, I have had no place to write in, no table, no inkstand; no epistolary conveniences of any kind. Almost the first use I make of my sky-parlour, in the tower,[1] is to congratulate you on your engagement—and so much the more heartily, as I make no doubt that your matrimonial jaunt will transport you from our cold and meagre Unitarianism into the warmth and glory of the Establishment.[2] I always told you that a loyal and true-hearted Englishman ought to belong to the established Church; and you have certainly taken one very decided step towards that good end. Take care, by all means, that the inevitable conversion of either husband or wife be not in the wrong direction.

Before I quit this subject, will you allow me to congratulate the lady of your choice? I do not believe that any woman in the world has a better prospect of happiness than she; for no woman can have won a truer, kinder, happier-natured man.

Why should not you spend the honeymoon, and a month or two more, in a trip to America? If you come soon enough, you will have the pleasure (and I know it would be a great one, to your wicked English heart) of seeing the Union in its death-throes,[3] and of triumphing over me in revenge for all the uncivil things I used to say about England and her institutions. How queer, that the rotten old patchwork of your Constitution should be so likely to outlast all our bran-new contrivances! Well; I am ashamed to say how little I care about the matter. New England will still have her rocks and ice, and I should not wonder if we become a better and a nobler people than ever heretofore. As to the South, I never loved it. We do not belong together; the Union is unnatural, a scheme of man, not an ordinance of God; and as long as it continues, no American of either section will ever feel a genuine thrill of patriotism, such as you Englishmen feel at every breath you draw.

Don't you think England (if we petition her humbly enough) might be induced to receive the New England States back again, in our old Provincial capacity? What a triumph that would be! Or perhaps it would be a better scheme to arrange a kingdom for Prince Alfred by lumping together Canada, New England, and Nova Scotia.[4] Those regions are almost homogeneous as regards manners and character, and cannot long to be kept apart, after we lose the counterbalance of our Southern States. For my part, I should be very glad to exchange the South for Canada, though I have not quite made up my mind as to the expediency of coming either under the Queen's sceptre or Prince Alfred's. But if any such arrangement takes place, I shall claim to be made a peer for having been the first to suggest it.

Meanwhile (unless you wish me to be indicted for high treason, or tarred and feathered by lynch law) it will be as well to keep these speculations secret.

I met your friend Charles Norton at a dinner, not long ago, and he promised to come and see me at the Wayside, but has not yet made his appearance.[5] I meet Longfellow and all the other prominent literary people at the monthly dinner of the Saturday Club, of which I found myself a member, on my return.[6] It is an excellent institution, with the privilege of first-rate society, and no duties but to eat one's dinner; and it is one of its great advantages, that you can take a guest there, and make him acquainted with all our northern notabilities at one fell swoop.

Longfellow has grown younger in appearance, but seems not to dress quite so smartly as of yore. Emerson is unchanged in aspect—at least, he looks so, at a distance, but, on close inspection, you perceive that a little hoar-frost has gathered on him. He has become earthlier during these past seven years; for he puffs cigars like a true Yankee, and drinks wine like an Englishman.

As for me, I spend a monotonous life, seldom quitting my own hill-side, and trying earnestly to take root here. I find, however, that I staid abroad a little too long, and as a consequence, have lost my home-feelings for the present, if not forever.

Already, I begin to think of paying another visit to England; though whether this idle notion is ever executed will depend, in the first place, on my writing a new Romance, and, secondly, on the contingency of my being able to get a good price for the London copyright.

I should be sorry to think that I am never to see you at your own fireside.

Mrs. Hawthorne, I think, means to enclose a note, if she can find time to write it; at all events, she sends her kindest regards. Write again soon.

Your friend
Nathl Hawthorne

1. NH set aside an attic room, with a stand-up writing desk, for his use.

2. Bright, a Unitarian, was engaged to Mary Elizabeth Thompson, daughter of an Anglican banker.

3. South Carolina would secede from the union on 20 December, as America moved toward the Civil War.

4. Prince Alfred, the sixteen-year-old son of the reigning Queen Victoria.

5. Charles Eliot Norton was professor of art at Harvard University and translator of Dante.

6. NH had been made a member of the Saturday Club of Boston, a group of literary, social, and political figures that met for good conversation and food, in 1859.

TO JAMES T. FIELDS

Concord, Feby 27th, 1861.

Dear Fields,

I am exceedingly gratified by the dedication.[1] I do not deserve so high an honor; but if you think me worthy, it is enough to make the compliments in the highest degree acceptable, no matter who may dispute my title to it. I care more for your good opinion than for that of a host of critics, and have excellent reason for so doing; inasmuch as my literary sucess, whatever it has been or may be, is the result of my connection with you. Somehow or other, you smote the rock of public sympathy on my behalf; and a stream gushed forth in sufficient quantity to quench my thirst, though not to drown me. I think no author can ever have had publishers that he valued so much as I do mine.

Julian will have a vacation in two or three weeks, and nothing would delight the old fellow so much as to spend a few days with Mrs. Fields and yourself; but I have great scruples (on your account) about letting him come to you in this periodical fashion, like a fit of the ague. Unless he is a quieter member of society, with you, than we find him at home, he must be a great deal of trouble.

We have been expecting Ticknor and General Pierce, this week;—that is to say, they promised to come; but I know the General too well not to have anticipated that other engagements would shove him aside from this one.

Your friend,
Nathl Hawthorne.

1. The dedication to NH is in Ticknor and Fields's edition of John Gibson Lockhart's *Memoirs of the Life of Sir Walter Scott.*

TO CHARLES SUMNER

Concord, April 11th 1861

My dear Sumner,

I venture to ask your aid (which I hope it will give you no great trouble to afford) in the following case:—

When I gave up the Liverpool Consulate, the final settlement of my accounts was delayed by the illness of my principal clerk; and I had left Liverpool a month or two before the last documents were forwarded to me. Thus it happened that a sum (shown by the enclosed paper) remained in my hands, which did not belong to me, but ought either to have been paid over to the new Consul or to the Treasury of the United States. The amount accrued chiefly from the unclaimed wages of seamen; that is from sums deposited with me, as Consul, by masters of vessels, at various times, according to law, as wages of seamen discharged from their ships in Liverpool, and which, from one cause or another, were never called for by the seamen, and in all probability never will be.

The fund thus accruing is not subject to the drafts of the Treasury Department, but is wholly under the control of the Consul; and if he chooses to appropriate it to his own use, on retiring, I see nothing to prevent him. It seems to me, however, that the Department ought to make the Consul accountable for this fund, and require him to pay it over on giving up the office; thereby precluding a defalcation which, as the case now stands, would never come to its knowledge.

My wandering life in Europe, and literary occupation, after leaving the Consulate, have heretofore prevented my looking into this matter; and I discovered the enclosed paper only a few days since. It is a great pity I found it at all; for it makes me two hundred dollars the poorer. However, it is full time to rectify the mistake; for the probabilities seem to be, that the government to which, if anywhere, I am responsible, will soon crumble away, leaving me to burn my fingers forever with money not my own. I therefore make haste to do the right thing.

What I ask of your kindness is, that you will explain this affair, on my behalf, to the Secretary of the Treasury, or his proper subordinate, and inform him that the amount ($205,86) is held payable to the order of the Treasury Department by Messrs. Ticknor & Fields, Boston.[1]

Sincerely yours,
Nathl Hawthorne.

P.S. What are we coming to?[2]

1. Sumner replied that NH had to repay the money to the government.
2. The Confederate government had been formed on 8 February, and on 12 April the first gun of the Civil War was fired on Fort Sumter, South Carolina. [*CE*]

TO FREDERICK GODDARD TUCKERMAN

Concord, April 14th 1861.

My dear Sir,[1]

I have read the volume of poems, and think it a remarkable one;[2] not that I am the least in the world of a critic, nor have any rule for judging of poetry or prose, except the impression which it makes on me. I question whether the poems will obtain a very early or wide recognition from the public, either in England or

America, because their merit does not lie upon the surface, but must be looked for with faith and sympathy, and a kind of insight as when you look into a carbuncle to discover its hidden fire. The second reading does more for them than the first; and I have no doubt many of them will glow brighter and brighter on repeated perusal. "The Stranger" impressed me a good deal; so did "Picomegen"; and "Margites"; and the whole series of Sonnets; although I might have liked other pieces as well, if I had made myself equally familiar with them. The great difficulty with you will be, to get yourself read at all; if you could be read twice, the book might be a success; but who reads (in a way that deserves to be called reading) so much as once, in these days?

Pray pardon the frankness with which I write, and believe me

Sincerely Yours,
Nathl Hawthorne.[3]

1. The poet Frederick Goddard Tuckerman, relatively unnoticed in his lifetime, is highly regarded today.

2. Tuckerman privately published *Poems* (1860).

3. Tuckerman replied to NH that his book was "not written to please anybody, and is addressed to those only who understand it." More of his letter is in *CE,* 18:375n.

TO JOSEPH EMERSON WORCESTER

Concord, April 14th 1861

My dear Sir,[1]

I beg to thank you most sincerely for the gift of you noble Dictionary. So much was I impressed with the necessity of possessing it, that I had just ordered a copy from my book-sellers when your kind present arrived. I can hardly deem myself entitled to pass an opinion upon so learned and elaborate a work; but I may venture to say, that, of all Lexicographers, you seem to me best to combine a sense of the *sacredness* of language with a recognition of the changes which time and human vicissitude inevitably work upon it. It will be ominous of anarchy in matters moral and political, when our Dictionaries cease to be mainly conservative; and, for my own part, I would not adopt a single new spelling, unless it were forced upon me by the general practice of the age and country;—nor willingly admit a new word, unless it brought a new meaning along with it.

I well remember your kindness, my dear Sir, in my early days;[2] and I have seen with the greatest pleasure the growth of that solid and indestructible reputation which you have since built up. With the hope that you may live long to enjoy it, and, if possible, to add to it, I remain,

Most Respectfully
& Sincerely Yours,
Nathl Hawthorne.

J. E. Worcester, Esq.
Cambridge.

1. The lexicographer Joseph Emerson Worcester published his first dictionary in 1830, and thereafter was in constant competition with Noah Webster. Worcester was the more conservative of the two, and the one more likely to retain British usages.
2. NH had been a pupil in Worcester's school in Salem.

TO HORATIO BRIDGE

Concord, May 26th 1861.

Dear Bridge,

The two cheques or drafts for $548 came duly to hand, and not inopportunely; for I am about making the final disbursements on account of my house—which, of course, has cost me three times the sum calculated upon. I suppose every man, on summing up the cost of a house, feels considerably like a fool; but it is the first time, and will be the last, that I make a fool of myself in this particular way. At any rate, the result is a pretty and convenient house enough, no larger than was necessary for my family and an occasional friend, and no finer than a modest position in life demands. The worst of it is, that I must give up all thoughts of drifting about the world any more, and try to make myself at home in one dull spot. It is rather odd, that, with all my tendency to stick in one place, I yet find great delight in frequent change; so that, in this point of view, I had better not have burdened myself with taking a house upon my back. Such change of quarters as makes up the life of you naval men might have suited me.

The war, strange to say, has had a beneficial effect upon my spirits, which were flagging woefully before it broke out. But it was delightful to share in the heroic sentiment of the time, and to feel that I had a country—a consciousness which seemed to make me young again. One thing, as regards this matter, I regret, and one thing I am glad of;—the regrettable thing is, that I am too old to shoulder a musket myself; and the joyful thing is, that Julian is too young. He drills constantly with a company of lads, and means to enlist soon as he reaches the minimum age; but I trust we shall either be victorious or vanquished before that time. Meantime (though I approve the war as much as any man) I don't quite understand what we are fighting for, or what definite result can be expected. If we pummel the South ever so hard, they will love us none the better for it; and even if we subjugate them, our next step should be to cut them adrift. If we are fighting for the annihilation of slavery, to be sure, it may be a wise object, and offers a tangible result, and the only one which is consistent with a future Union between North and South. A continuance of the war would soon make this plain to us; and we should see the expediency of preparing our black brethren for future citizenship by allowing them to fight for their own liberties, and educating them through heroic influences.

What ever happens next, I must say that I rejoice that the old Union is smashed. We never were one people, and never really had a country since the Constitution was formed.

I trust you mean to come, and bring Mrs. Bridge, to see us, this summer. I shall like my house twice as well when you have looked at it.

Your friend,
Nathl Hawthorne.

We are all well. Write again.

TO FRANCIS BENNOCH

Concord, Mass. [ca. July 1861]

My dear Bennoch,

I owe you much in many ways, but there is one way in which I ought not to be your debtor, and that is in friendly correspondence. The truth is that, at present, I have little heart for anything. We are, as you know, at the beginning of a great war—a war, the issue of which no man can predicate; and I, for one, have no inclination to attempt prophecy. It is not long since the acute ruler of France—the epigrammatic speech-maker—announced to a startled Europe and a delighted country that he had gone to war for an idea—a very NICE, if not an absolutely true idea.[1] But we Yankees have cast him entirely into the shade. We, also, have gone to war, and we seem to have little, or, at least, a very misty idea of what we are fighting for. It depends upon the speaker, and that, again, depends upon the section of the country in which his sympathies are enlisted. The Southern man will say, We fight for state rights, liberty, and independence. The middle and Western states-man will avow that he fights for the Union; whilst our Northern and Eastern man will swear that, from the beginning, his only idea was liberty to the Blacks, and the annihilation of slavery. All are thoroughly in earnest, and all pray for the blessing of Heaven to rest upon the enterprise. The appeals are so numerous, fervent, and yet so contradictory, that the Great Arbiter to whom they so piously and solemnly appeal, must be sorely puzzled how to decide. One thing is indisputable; the spirit of our young men is thoroughly aroused. Their enthusiasm is boundless; and the smiles of our fragile and delicate women cheer them on. When I hear their drums beating, and see their banners flying, and witness their steady marching, I declare, were it not for certain silvery monitors hanging by my temples, suggesting prudence, I feel as if I could catch the infection, shoulder a musket, and be off to the war myself!

Meditating on these matters, I begin to think our custom as to war is a mistake. Why draw from our young men, in the bloom and hey-day of their youth, the soldiers who are to fight our battles? Had I my way, no man should go to war under fifty years of age, such men having already had their natural share of worldly pleasures and life's enjoyments. And I don't see how they could make a more creditable or more honourable exit from the world's stage than by becoming food for powder, and gloriously dying in defence of their home and country. Then, I would add a premium in favour of recruits of three score years and upwards; as, virtually, with one foot in the grave, they would not be likely to run away. I apprehend that no people ever built up the skeleton of a warlike history so rapidly as we are doing. What a fine theme for the poet! If you were not a born Britisher, from whose country we expect no help and little sympathy, I would ask you for a martial strain—a song to be sung by our camp-fires, to soothe the feelings, and rouse the energies of our troops; inspiring them to meet like men the great conflict that awaits them, resolved to conquer or to die—if dying, still to conquer. Ten thousand poetasters have tried and tried in vain to give us a rousing
"Scots wha hae wi' Wallace bled."[2]
If we fight no better than we sing, may the Lord have mercy upon us and upon the nation!

In the excitement raging everywhere, don't you feel as if you could come and see America in time of war? The room bearing your name is ready; the fire is laid; and here we are prepared to give you welcome. Come and occupy the apartment dedicated to you; come and let us talk over the many pleasant evenings we spent together in dear old England. Come, and I promise that all distracting thoughts and disturbing circumstances shall be banished from us; and although our children are no longer children, I am sure they would unite with the elder folk, and enjoy the opportunity of showing that Yankee hearts never forget kindnesses, and long for the chance to repay them;—not as a cancelling of debt, but to prove how deeply kindly deeds are appreciated by them. We have national foibles;—what nation has not?—we have national peculiarities and whimsical caprices; but we are none the worse for them. We have many sins to answer for, and many short-comings, but ingratitude cannot be reckoned among them. So come, and let us prove that we are, one and all, affectionately your friends.

Always, &c., &c.,

Nathl Hawthorne.

1. Napoleon III had sent French troops to Beirut to stop the massacre of Christians by the Turks. [CE]

2. See the Scottish poet Robert Burns's *Scots, Wha Hae* (1793); the reference in this line is to William Wallace, Scottish patriot and martyr.

TO JAMES T. FIELDS

Concord, Novr 6th 1861.

Dear Fields,

When the story is finished, you may have it for the Magazine if you think best.[1] My hesitation is not so much on the score of comparative profit, as because I think my chapters have not the characteristics that produce success in serial publications; and, moreover, a monotony results from my harping on one string through the whole book, and when prolonged from month to month, it will be likely to tire the reader out. If published in a volume, he may finish the infliction as briefly as he likes.

The story certainly will not be ready for the first months of the year, and I don't know precisely how soon it will be. Judging from appearances, it will be a pretty long story, though I cannot answer for two volumes. Unless I can get something for it from an English magazine, it would be better for me to go to England to secure the copyright there. Do you think Smith & Elder would like it for the Cornhill?[2]

Can't you announce it conditionally, or hypothetically?

If you want me to write a good book, send me a good pen;—not a gold one, for they seldom suit me; but a pen flexible, and capacious of ink, and that will not grow stiff and rheumatic the moment I begin to get attached to it. I never met with a good pen in my life; so I don't suppose you can find one. The one I write with was made in H—and it is d—tion to write with it.

Truly yours
Nathl Hawthorne

1. The unfinished "Septimius Felton" was published in the January-August 1872 *Atlantic Monthly* and also in book form that year.

2. Nothing by NH appeared in the *Cornhill Magazine*.

TO HORATIO BRIDGE

Concord, Feby 13th, 1862.

Dear Bridge

Your proposition that I should pay a visit to Washington is very tempting, and I should accept it if it were not for several 'ifs'—neither of them, perhaps, a sufficient obstacle in itself, but, united, pretty difficult to overcome.[1] For instance, I am not very well, being mentally and physically languid; but, I suppose, there is about an even chance that the trip and change of scene might supply the energy which I lack. Also, I am pretending to write a book, and though I am nowise diligent about it, still each week finds it a little more advanced; and I am now at a point where I do not like to leave it entirely.[2] Moreover, I ought not to spend money needlessly, in these hard times; for it is my opinion that the book-trade, and everybody connected with it, is bound to fall below zero, before this war, and the subsequent embarrassments, come to an end.

I might go on multiplying 'ifs'; but the above are enough. Nevertheless, as I said, I am greatly tempted by your invitation; and it is not impossible but that, in the course of a few weeks, I may write to ask you if it still holds good. Meanwhile, I send you, enclosed, a respectable old gentleman who, my friends say, is very like me, and may serve as my representative.[3] If you will send me a similar one of yourself, I shall be truly obliged.

Frank Pierce came here and spent a night, a week or two since; and we drank a bottle of arrack[4] together, and mingled our tears and condolements for the state of the country. Pierce is truly patriotic, and thinks there is nothing left for us but to fight it out; but I should be sorry to take his opinion implicitly as regards our chances in the future. He is bigoted to the Union, and sees nothing but ruin without it; whereas, I, (if we can only put the boundary far enough south) should not much regret an ultimate separation. A few weeks will decide how this is to be; for, unless a powerful Union feeling shall be developed by the military successes that seem to be setting in, we ought to turn our attention to the best mode of resolving ourselves into two nations. It would be too great an absurdity, to spend all our Northern strength, for the next generation, in holding on to a people who insist upon being let loose. If we do hold them, I should think Sumner's territorial plan the best way.[5]

I trust your health has not suffered by the immense occupation which the war must have brought upon you. The country was fortunate in having a man like yourself in so responsible a situation—"faithful found among the faithless."[6]

My wife and family are quite well, and send their kindest regards to Mrs. Bridge and yourself.

Your friend,
Nathl Hawthorne.

P.S. I ought to thank you for a shaded map of Negrodom, which you sent me a little while ago. What a terrible amount of trouble and expense, in washing that sheet white!—and, after all, I am afraid we shall only variegate it with blood and dirt.

---

1. NH left for Washington with Ticknor on 6 March; during his short stay there, he met Abraham Lincoln on the thirteenth.
2. *Our Old Home*, NH's account of his time in England, was published on 19 September 1863.
3. For NH's photograph of himself, see Gollin, *Portraits of Nathaniel Hawthorne*, 82.
4. Arrack, a liquor often distilled from a fermented mixture of rice, molasses, and coconuts.

5. Charles Sumner had introduced resolutions in the Senate on 11 February intending to reduce the Confederate states to territorial status by ruling that their secession was legally commission of suicide. Their consequent absence from Congress would permit the passage of a constitutional amendment establishing representation in the House on the basis of actual votes cast rather than on population. Slavery would not exist in the new territories because not positively sanctioned by act of Congress. [*CE*]

6. See John Milton, *Paradise Lost*, V, 896–97: "So spake the Seraph Abdiel faithful found, / Among the faithless, faithful only he."

TO GEORGE WILLIAM CURTIS

Concord, October 8th 1862.

My dear friend,

I like Bayard Taylor and his books, and, at your request, have painfully hammered out the enclosed letter to Uncle Abe.[1] I have done such things under one or two former Presidents, but hardly expected to address the present administration in this way. I don't think my letter will have any great effect; for when I was introduced to the President, a few months ago, I could perceive that he had never heard of me before.

Sincerely Yours,
Nathl Hawthorne.

You inquire after our "young men." We have but one boy, and two girls. All well.

1. NH's letter to President Abraham Lincoln (printed below) for the traveler and man of letters Bayard Taylor was never used.

TO ABRAHAM LINCOLN

Concord, October 8th, 1862.

Sir,

I believe that the name of Mr Bayard Taylor has been brought under your notice for the appointment of Minister to Russia; and as one of the brotherhood of literature, I would bear testimony to the respect in which he is held among us, and express my belief that his appointment would be received as gratifying and complimentary to us all. With the public at large, there are very few if any American writers more widely and more favorably known than Mr. Taylor; and I feel assured that the entire country would be glad to see an office of importance filled by a man whose claims, while fully satisfying the demands of party policy, rest mainly on the broad ground of literary excellence, which has won him friends at thousands of firesides.

With great respect,
Your obedient serv't,
Nathl Hawthorne.

To the President of
the United States.

TO FRANCIS BENNOCH

The Wayside,
Concord, (Mass) Octr 12th '62

Dear Bennoch,

You will not think that I forget you, whatever length of time there may be between letter and letter. In the miserable condition of my own country, I remember England and my friends there, and you most of all, more regretfully than ever. But there is not much comfort to be had from you Englishmen in respect to our war, or our prospects generally, and therefore it is the more difficult to keep up a correspondence. But I must say, I wonder that you do not see that the war, disastrous as it has been and is likely to be, was the most inevitable event that ever happened. And it still depends entirely on ourselves whether it shall finally turn out a blessing or a curse. Not being a very sanguine man, my fears are greater than my hopes. And so let us drop the subject.

It gladdens me exceedingly to hear of your returning prosperity. I always felt as if it would be only a passing cloud that hung over you—not a settled gloom. You ought to be prosperous, not so much for your own sake as for that of everybody who comes within your sphere and is sure to be benefitted by the sunshine and warmth that radiates out of you.

We, too (my own family, I mean) are about as prosperous as it is desirable to be in such a world as we live in, where Providence seems to keep a debtor and creditor account with us poor mortals, and is apt to balance every great good with a corresponding evil. In view of this, I content myself with not being very rich, and am even glad of a great many unsatisfied desires, because they encourage me to hope that I have not overdrawn my account.

I wish you could come and see us; for I don't expect ever to see England again. I did think that I might come over with a new Romance, the English copyright of which would pay Mrs. Hawthorne's and my own expences for a year; but it is impossible to possess one's mind in the midst of a civil war to such a degree as to make thoughts assume life. I hear the cannon and smell the gunpowder through everything. Besides, I feel as if this great convulsion were going to make an epoch in our literature as in everything else (if it does not annihilate all,) and that when we emerge from the war-cloud, there will be another and better (at least, a more national and seasonable) class of writers than the one I belong to. So be it. I do not reckon literary reputation as a heavy item on the debtor side of my account with Providence;—indeed, I never realized that I had any at all, and am in doubt about it now.

I send you a photograph of myself, taken four or five months ago. The sun has a grudge against me, and insists upon making my hair whiter than I see it in the glass, but that's of no consequence. I am glad to see so little change in your own face, and likewise in Mrs. Bennoch's, to whom my wife and I send our kindest remembrances.

Don't insist upon a regular exchange of letters, but think kindly of me, and let me know it often.

Your friend,
Nathl Hawthorne.

TO SAMUEL M. CLEVELAND

Concord (Mass) Jany 8th '63

Dear Sir[1]

The first tales that I wrote (having kept them in manuscript, for lack of a pub-lisher, till I was able to see some of their demerits) I burnt. Of those that finally came before the public, I believe that "The Gentle Boy," and "Roger Malvin's Burial," were the earliest written. "Twice-told Tales" was my first collective publi-cation, and comprised the productions of at least ten years, excluding a few which I afterwards inserted in other volumes. The first volume appeared in 1837.

My next publication was "Mosses from an Old Manse," in 1845 or 46. I had been idle (as regards literature) most of the intervening time since the "Twice-told Tales"; and the Mosses had been written during the first three years of my mar-ried life at Concord. In the spring of 1850 (I think) I published the "Scarlet Letter." It had occasionally occupied my thoughts for as much as a year before; but I had no time to write it till after being turned out of the Custom House in Salem, when, after recovering the practice of the pen by writing two or three shorter tales, I sat down seriously to it.

I removed from Salem to Lenox, and wrote "The House of the Seven Gables," published, I believe, in 1851. From Lenox, I came to West Newton and afterwards to Concord, in one or other of which places I wrote the "Blithedale Romance," published in 1852. During the same time, I wrote and published two volumes (The Wonder Book and Tanglewood Tales) of Classical Myths adapted for child-ish readers.

In the spring of 1860, I published the "Marble Faun," written during the pre-vious year, in England, after an absence of six or seven years from home, during which I had written nothing for the press.

I should not have thought it worth while, my dear Sir, to remember these par-ticulars, except at your request.

Very Respectfully
Nathl Hawthorne.

Saml M. Cleveland, Esq.

P.S. It may not be amiss to add that I have never applied myself to writing when I have had anything else to do—not having the faculty of literary composition except with a mind wholly unoccupied by other labor.

N. H.

1. Charles D. Cleveland was probably writing for his cousin, Henry Russell Cleveland, who had included a section on NH in his *A Compendium of American Literature; Chronologically Arranged with Biographical Sketches of the Authors, and Selections from Their Works* (1858). NH's letter may have been solicited for a revised edition of the work that was never published. For NH's inaccuracies in this letter, see *CE*, 18:522n.

TO ELIZABETH B. STODDARD

Concord, Jany 26th 1863

My dear Mrs. Stoddard,[1]

I am very glad to hear that you are writing another novel, and do not doubt that something good and true will come of it.[2] I was particularly impressed with the childhood of the heroine, in the Morgessons, and the whole of the first part of the book. It seemed to me as genuine and lifelike as anything that pen and ink can do. The latter part showed much power, but struck me as neither so new nor so true. Pray pardon the frankness of my crude criticism; for what is the use of saying anything, unless we say what we think? There are very few books of which I take the trouble to have any opinion at all, or of which I could retain any memory so long after reading them, as I do of the Morgessons. I hope you will not trouble yourself too much about the morals of your next work;—they may be safely left to take care of themselves.

I thank Heaven I am not a Forrester; the family is connected with mine by old Simon Forrester having married into it. He drank terribly through life, as I have been informed, and transmitted the tendency, I believe, to all his sons, several of whom killed themselves by it. I know of no descendent in the male line who can be said to have turned out well, but some of his grandchildren by his daughters are irreproachable so far as I know.

I recognized the Dunlaps in your book, and should much have enjoyed a finished portrait of old Mrs. Dunlap, but you can scarcely have known much of her from your own observation. It would not have been altogether a lovely picture.

I thank Mr. Stoddard for the German translation of the Wonder Book, and shall give it to one of my daughters to aid her in her German studies. So far as I can judge, it seems to be very faithfully done.

Very Sincerely
& Respectfully Yours
Nathl Hawthorne.

1. Elizabeth Barstow Stoddard, novelist wife of the poet and critic Richard Henry Stoddard, had published *The Morgessons* (1862), which NH thought "a remarkable and powerful book, though not without a painful element mixed up in it" (*CE*, 18:524).
2. Stoddard would publish *Two Men: A Novel* in 1865.

TO JAMES RUSSELL LOWELL

Concord, Febr 22d 1863.

Dear Lowell,

I want Julian, my only boy, to enter at Cambridge at the next commencement, and he has been studying with that view since our return to America, besides some previous instruction in Latin by myself.[1] But as the time approaches, I begin to feel rather nervous about his success; for I doubt whether Mr. Sanborn, his present instructor, has the faculty of putting a young fellow upon his mettle, and, at all events, Julian does not seem to be thoroughly alive to the emergency of the crisis. Do you think that there would be any advantage in his spending the intervening time under some instructor who would give special attention to filling up the gaps of his knowledge, and giving the precise kind of preparation that he needs? Are there not persons resident at Cambridge who devote themselves to such purposes? And would you recommend one?

Of course, I do not propose to take a private tutor into my family, nor that Julian should occupy his whole time, but merely that he should take up his residence at Cambridge for the present and recite to him.

Truly Your friend,
Nathl Hawthorne

1. Julian entered Harvard in 1863, left, returned in 1865, and then left for good in 1867 without receiving a degree.

TO THOMAS BAILEY ALDRICH

Concord, (Mass) April 30th '63

My dear Sir,[1]

I thank you most sincerely for your volume of Poems,[2] which I had not time to read as true poetry ought to be read, when it first arrived, and therefore handed them over to my domestic circle, (my wife, a daughter of nineteen, and a boy of seventeen) who unanimously awarded higher praise than ever I knew them to bestow on any other native poetry. They admire them greatly; and I myself have been reading some of them this morning, and find them rich, sweet, and imaginative, in such a degree that I am sorry not to have fresher sympathies in order to taste all the delight that every reader ought to draw from them. I was conscious, here and there, of a delicacy that I hardly dared to breathe upon.

I cannot doubt of your acquiring a high name in American literature, and believe me, I very earnestly wish it.

Very sincerely Yours
Nathl Hawthorne

1. Thomas Bailey Aldrich, poet and novelist.
2. *Poems* (1863).

TO JAMES T. FIELDS

Concord, April 30th '63

Dear Fields,

I send the article with which the volume is to commence, and you can begin printing it whenever you like. I can think of no better title than this—"OUR OLD HOME; a series of English Sketches by &c."

I submit to your judgment whether it would not be well to print these 'Consular Experiences' in the volume without depriving them of any freshness they may have, by previous publication in the Magazine?[1] The article has some of the features that attract the curiosity of the foolish public, being made up of personal narrative and gossip, with a few pungencies of personal satire, which will not be the less effective because the reader can scarcely find out who was the individual meant. I am not without hope of drawing down upon myself a good deal of critical severity on this score, and would gladly incur more of it if I could do so without seriously deserving censure. The story of the Doctor of Divinity, I think, will prove a good card in this way.[2] It is every bit true (like the other anecdotes) only not told so darkly as it might have been for the reverend gentleman. I do not believe there is any danger of his identity being ascertained, and do not care whether it is or no—as it could only be done by the impertinent researches of other people. It seems to me quite essential to have some novelty in the collected volume, and, if possible, something that may excite a little discussion and remark. But decide for yourself and me; and if you conclude not to publish it in the Magazine, I think I can concoct another article in season for the August No, if you wish.[3] After the publication of the volume, it seems to me the public had better have no more of them.

I send two letters, on which please to put the proper addresses, as I do not know them.

Julian has been telling us a mythical story of your intending to walk with him from Cambridge. We should be delighted to see you, though more for our own sakes than yours; for our aspect here is still a little winterish. When you come, let it be on Saturday, and stay till Monday. I am hungry to talk with you.

With kindest regards to Mrs. Fields,

Yours affectionately
Nathl Hawthorne

P.S. I think you will see Mrs. H. early next week.

1. There was no magazine publication of "Consular Experiences."
2. See *Our Old Home, CE*, 5:25–30.
3. "Civic Banquets" appeared in the August 1863 *Atlantic Monthly*.

TO WILLIAM D. TICKNOR

Concord, April 30th '63

Dear Ticknor,

I thank you for that excellent lot of cigars, and expect to have as much enjoyment as a man can reasonably hope for in this troublesome world, while smoking
them after breakfast and dinner. Their fragrance would be much improved if you
would come and smoke in company.

Your friend
Nathl Hawthorne

TO JAMES T. FIELDS

The Wayside [Concord], July 18th '63.

Dear Fields,

I thank you for your note of 15th inst., and have delayed my reply thus long in
order to ponder deeply on your advice, smoke cigars over it, and see what it might
be possible for me to do towards taking it.[1] I find that it would be a piece of
poltroonery in me to withdraw either the dedication or the dedicatory letter. My
long and intimate personal relations with Pierce render the dedication altogether
proper, especially as regards this book, which would have had no existence without his kindness; and if he is so exceedingly unpopular that his name is enough to

sink the volume, there is so much the more need that an old friend should stand by him. I cannot, merely on account of pecuniary profit or literary reputation, go back from what I have deliberately felt and thought it right to do; and if I were to tear out the dedication, I should never look at the volume again without remorse and shame. As for the literary public, it must accept my book precisely as I think fit to give it, or let it alone.

Nevertheless, I have no fancy for making myself a martyr when it is honorably and conscientiously possible to avoid it; and I always measure out my heroism very accurately according to the exigencies of the occasion, and should be the last man in the world to throw away a bit of it needlessly. So I have looked over the concluding paragraph, and have amended it in such a way that, while doing what I know to be justice to my friend, it contains not a word that ought to be objectionable to any set of readers. If the public of the north see fit to ostracize me for this, I can only say that I would gladly sacrifice a thousand or two of dollars rather than retain the good will of such a herd of dolts and mean-spirited scoundrels. I enclose the re-written paragraph, and shall wish to see a proof of that and the whole dedication. I send the proof-sheet in another enclosure.

I had a call from an Englishman yesterday, and kept him to dinner—not the threatened Stephen, but a Mr. Thompson, introduced by Henry Bright.[2] He says he knows you, and he seems to be a very good fellow. I have strong hopes that he will never come back here again, for Julian took him on a walk of several miles, whereby they both caught a most tremendous ducking, and the poor Englishman was frightened half to death by the thunder.

Mrs. Hawthorne, I am sorry to say, is unwell and confined to her room.

With kindest regards to Mrs. Fields,

Your friend
Nathl Hawthorne.

P.S. We had a delightful letter from Gail Hamilton, the other day.[3] From what she says about "Civic Banquets," I am afraid that that production is a little funnier than befits the gravity and dignity of a man of consular rank. If Mrs. H. had read it, she would not have let me print it.

1. Pierce, seen as friendly to slaveholders, opposed the Civil War and attacked Lincoln's administration. Fields had warned NH that the dedication would upset many and hurt the book's sales. For the dedication and the brief notice "To a Friend," see *Our Old Home, CE,* 5:2–5.

2. Henry Yates Thompson, Bright's brother-in-law, would become a noted book and manuscript collector.
3. Gail Hamilton, the pen name of Mary Abigail Dodge, essayist and journalist.

TO ELIZABETH PALMER PEABODY

The Wayside [Concord], July 20th '63

Dear E.

I do not think that the Dedication to Genl Pierce can have the momentous political consequences which you apprehend. I determined upon it long since, as a proper memorial of our life-long intimacy, and as especially suitable in the case of this book, which could not have been in existence without him. I expressly say that I dedicate the book to the friend, and decline any present colloquy with the statesman, to whom I address merely a few lines expressing my confidence in his loyalty and unalterable devotion to the Union—which I am glad to have the opportunity of saying, at this moment, when all the administration and abolition papers are calling him a traitor. A traitor? Why, he is the only loyal man in the country, North or South! Every body else has outgrown the old faith in the Union, or got outside of it in one way or another; but Pierce retains it in all the simplicity with which he inherited it from his father. It has been the principle and is the explanation (and the apology, if any is needed) of his whole public life, and if you look generously at him, you cannot but see that it would ruin a noble character (though one of limited scope) for him to admit any ideas that were not entertained by the fathers of the constitution and the republic. Knowing that he is eternally true to them, I say so, and that is all I say of his political character. The dedication was written before the New Hampshire Convention, and when I had not seen him for months; but I speak of his faith with the same certainty as if I had just come from a talk with him. Though I differ from him in many respects, I would fain rather that he should die than change. There is a certain steadfastness and integrity with regard to a man's own nature (when it is such a peculiar nature as that of Pierce) which seems to me more sacred and valuable than the faculty of adapting one's self to new ideas, however true they may turn out to be.

The Dedication can hurt nobody but my book and myself. I know that it will do that, but am content to take the consequences, rather than go back from what I deliberately judge it right to do. As for Posterity, it will have formed a truer opinion of General Pierce than you can do; and yet I should suppose that you have breadth and insight enough (however disturbed by the potent elixir of political opinions) to appreciate the sterling merits of this kind of man.

You do not in the least shake me by telling me that I shall be supposed to disapprove of the war; for I always thought that it should have been avoided, although, since it has broken out, I have longed for military success as much as any man or woman of the North. I agree with your friend Genl Hitchcock,[1] who thinks (as I gather from a letter to Mary or yourself) that the war will only effect by a horrible convulsion the self-same end that might and would have been brought about by a gradual and peaceful change. Nor am I at all certain that it will effect that end. Even these recent successes have not an indubitable tendency in that direction. They will suggest to the rebels that their best hope lies in the succor of the Peace Democrats of the North, whom they have heretofore scorned, and by amalgamation with whom I really think that the old Union might be restored, and slavery prolonged for another hundred years, with new bulwarks; while the people of the North would fancy that they had got the victory, and never know that they had shed their blood in vain, and so would become peace Democrats to a man. In that case, woe to the Abolitionists! I offer you in advance the shelter of the nook in our garret, which Mary contrived as a hiding-place for Mr. Sanborn.[2]

The best thing possible, as far as I can see, would be to effect a separation of the Union, giving us the West bank of the Mississipi, and a boundary line affording as much Southern soil as we can hope to digest into freedom in another century. Such a settlement looks impossible, to be sure, and so does every other imaginable settlement, except through the medium of the peace Democrats, who (as I have just said) would speedily comprise the whole population, in view of such a result. You cannot possibly conceive (looking through spectacles of the tint which yours have acquired) how little the North really cares for the negro-question, and how eagerly it would grasp at peace if recommended by a delusive show of victory. Free soil was never in so great danger as now. If the Southern statesmen manage their matters sagaciously, there may come a revulsion of feeling that would give them more than they ever asked. Do you suppose that the pendulum is not to swing back again?

I have written the foregoing not in a controversial way, (and I beg you will not so consider it,) but because I am willing that you should know that I entertain certain ideas of my own; and also because I admire the valor and generous pertinacity with which you come again to the scratch, offering me the same kind of advice as when I was going to write the Life of Cilley, and the Life of Pierce, and which availed nothing, then as now, because I trusted to my own instinct to guide me into my own right way. I do not write (if you will please to observe) for my letter to be read to others; for this is the first time that I have written down ideas which exist in a gaseous state in my mind, and perhaps they might define themselves rather differently on another attempt to condense them. My views about Dis-Union, for example, though long crudely entertained, are not such as I should choose to put forth at present; and I am very often sensible of an affectionate regard for the dead old Union, which leads me to say a kind thing or two about it, though I had as lief see my grandfather's ghost as have it revive.

Mr. Whiting himself sent me his pamphlet.[3] It has no bearing on my position. I do not care a fig what powers the President assumes, at such a crisis as this, if he only used them effectually; but I must say that I despise the present administration with all my heart, and should think that you would do the same.

I don't know how Ellery Channing gets his literary intelligence. I supposed that this affair of the Dedication was an entire secret between me and the publisher. Even Sophia did not know it and I have never whispered it to General Pierce, nor meant that it should be known till the publication of the book, which will not be sooner than September. It is a pity that it should be bruited about so untimely.

The older I grow, the more I hate to write notes, and I trust I have here written nothing now that may make it necessary for me to write another.

Truly Yours,

N. H.

1. Ethan Allen Hitchcock, after serving for thirty years in the military, began writing books on such subjects as Swedenborg and Shakespeare. He had become great friends with the Peabody sisters.

2. In April 1860, Mary Peabody Mann had found a hiding place for Sanborn in the Wayside when it was feared that he would be taken by Federal officers for his knowledge of John Brown's plans for the Harper's Ferry attack. [*CE*]

3. William Whiting, *The War Powers of the President and the Legislative Powers of Congress on Relation to Rebellion, Treason, and Slavery* (1862).

TO SAMUEL H. EMERY, JR.

Concord (Mass) Novr 6th '63

Dear Sir,[1]

In reply to your note of 31st ult., I beg leave to state that the sketch of the Doctor of Divinity is entirely true and neither overdrawn nor overcolored.

Though a professed man of fiction, I am scrupulous in whatever purports to be matter of fact; and I should consider myself severely reprehensible, if, under the guise of truth, I had made a false statement that might be construed as reflecting upon the moral character of the reverend clergy. I trust that your friend the minister will not suppose that I had any such malignant purpose as this last. I narrated the fact because it was in itself so striking, and because it illustrated the liability of those who stand highest among us to fall into the depths of error and iniquity, whenever they throw aside the external safeguards which surround them at home. The true moral is, that no man is safe from sin and disgrace till by divine assistance he has thoroughly cleansed his heart—which few of us take the pains to do, though many satisfy themselves with a shallow and imperfect performance of that duty.

I hope the minister will not consider that I am infringing upon his office by this bit of a sermon.

Respectfully Yours,
N. Hawthorne

1. Samuel H. Emery, Jr., the son of a minister, appeared in the "Consular Experiences" chapter of *Our Old Home*. Here he writes NH on behalf of a local minister who doubts the veracity of NH's depiction of the Doctor of Divinity in *Our Old Home*.

TO HENRY WADSWORTH LONGFELLOW

Concord. Jany 2d 1864.

Dear Longfellow,

It seems idle to tell you that I have read the "Wayside Inn" with great comfort and delight.[1] I take vast satisfaction in your poetry, and take very little in most other men's, except it be the grand old strains that have been sounding all through my life. Nothing can be better done than these tales of yours, one and all. I was especially charmed with the description of an old Scandinavian ship of war, with her officers and crew, in which, by some inscrutable magic, you contrive to suggest a parallel picture of a modern frigate.

It gratified me much to find my own name shining in your verse—even as if I had been gazing up at the moon, and detected my own features in its profile.[2]

I have been much out of sorts of late, and do not well know what is the matter with me, but am inclined to draw the conclusion that I shall have little more to do with pen and ink. One more book I should like well enough to write, and have indeed begun it, but with no assurance of ever bringing it to an end. As is always the case, I have a notion that this last book would be my best; and full of wisdom about matters of life and death—and yet it will be no deadly disappointment if I am compelled to drop it. You can tell, far better than I, whether there is ever anything worth having a literary reputation, and whether the best achievements seem to have any substance after they grow cold.

Your friend,
Nathl Hawthorne.

1. Longfellow's *Tales of a Wayside Inn* had been published on 25 November 1863.
2. In the "Prelude" to Part First, "The Wayside Inn," Longfellow described "Flashing on the window-pane, / Emblazoned with its light and shade / The jovial rhymes, that still remain, / Writ near a century ago, / By the great Major Molineaux [*sic*], / Whom Hawthorne has immortal made." [*CE*]

TO DONALD GRANT MITCHELL

The Wayside,
Concord, Jany 16th, '64.

My dear Mr. Mitchell,[1]

I am full of delight and wonder at your book.[2] I remember long ago, at Liverpool, your speaking prospectively of a farm, but I never dreamed of your being really much more of a farmer than myself, whose efforts in this line may only make me the father of a progeny of weeds in a garden patch. I have about twenty-five acres of land, seventeen of which are a hill of sand and gravel, covered with birches, locusts, & pitch-pines, and apparently incapable of any other growth; so that I have great comfort in that part of my territory. The other eight acres are said to be the best land in Concord, and they have made me miserable and would soon have ruined me, if I had not determined never more to attempt raising anything from them. So there they lie along the road-side within their broken fence—an eyesore to me, and a laughing-stock to all the neighbors. If it were not for the difficulty of transportation by express or otherwise, I would thankfully give you those eight acres in exchange for your beautiful book.

I have been equally unsuccessful in my architectural projects; and have transformed a simple and small old farm-house into the absurdest anomaly you ever saw; but I really was not so much to blame here as the village-carpenter, who took the matter into his own hands, and produced an unimaginable sort of thing instead of what I asked for. If it would only burn down! But I have no such luck.

Your praise of "Our Old Home," (though I know that I ought to set down a great part of it as a friendly exaggeration) gives me inexpressible pleasure, because I have fallen into a quagmire of disgust and despondency with respect to literary matters.³ I am tired of my own thoughts and fancies, and my own mode of expressing them—a misfortune which I am sure will never befal you, partly because you will never deserve it, and partly because you keep yourself healthful by grappling with the wholesome earth so strenuously.

I will send you my book, as you so kindly ask, when I next go to Boston; but as that is a very rare event (especially in winter) you must not expect it promptly.

I trust Mrs. Mitchell has not forgotten that I can claim the privilege of offering her my regards, as an old acquaintance.

Most Sincerely Yours,
Nathl Hawthorne

1. The essayist Donald Grant Mitchell became famous under his pen name "Ik Marvel."
2. *My Farm of Edgewood: A Country Book* (1863).
3. Mitchell had written NH on 12 April 1863 that he thought *Our Old Home* "thoroughly artistic," and that he liked it "because it has striven for such a marrowy depth, the British phlegm, & taught our good cousins that insensitiveness was not altogether an American quality." For more, see *CE*, 18:632–33n.

TO JAMES T. FIELDS

Concord, Febry 25th, 1864

Dear Fields,

I hardly know what to say to the Public about this abortive Romance, though I know pretty well what the case will be. I shall never finish it. Yet it is not quite pleasant for an author to announce himself, or to be announced, as finally broken down as to his literary faculty. It is a pity that I let you put this work in your pro-gramme for the year, for I had alway a presentiment that it would fail us at the pinch. Say to the Public what you think best, and as little as possible;—for exam-ple—"We regret that Mr. Hawthorne's Romance, announced for this Magazine some months ago, still lies upon its author's writing-table; he having been inter-rupted in his labor upon it by an impaired state of health"—or—"We are sorry to hear (but know not whether the Public will share our grief) that Mr. Hawthorne is out of health, and is thereby prevented, for the present, from proceeding with another of his promised (or threatened) Romances, intended for this Magazine"—or—"Mr. Hawthorne's brain is addled at last, and, much to our sat-isfaction, he tells us that he cannot possibly go on with the Romance announced on the cover of the Jany Magazine. We consider him finally shelved, and shall take early occasion to bury him under a heavy article, carefully summing up his mer-its (such as they were,) and his demerits, what few of them can be touched upon in our limited space."—or—"We shall commence the publication of Mr Hawthorne's Romance as soon as that gentleman chooses to forward it. We are quite at a loss how to account for this delay in the fulfilment of his contract; espe-cially as he has already been most liberally paid for the first number."

Say anything you like, in short though I really don't believe that the Public will care what you say, or whether you say anything. If you choose, you may publish the first chapter as an insulated fragment, and charge me with $100 of overpayment. I cannot finish it, unless a great change comes over me; and if I make too great an effort to do so, it will be my death; not that I should care much for that, if I could fight the battle through and win it, thus ending a life of much smoulder and scanty fire in a blaze of glory. But I should smother myself in mud of my own making.

I mean to come to Boston soon, not for a week, but for a single day, and then I can talk about my Sanitary prospects more freely than I choose to write.[1] I am not low-spirited, nor fanciful, nor freakish, but look what seem to be realities in the face, and am ready to take whatever may come. If I could but go to England now, I think that the sea-voyage and the "Old Home" might set me all right.

This letter is for your own eye, and I wish especially that no echo of it may come back in your notes to me.

Your friend,
Nathl Hawthorne

P.S. Give my kindest regards to Mrs. Fields, & tell her that one of my choicest ideal places is her drawing-room, and therefore I seldom visit it.[2]

1. Starting in 1863, the Sanitary Commission, which had been established to help better the physical conditions of northern soldiers, sponsored "Sanitary Fairs" to raise money, for which authors often donated books or manuscripts for sale. There is no evidence that NH contributed anything to these fairs.

2. Annie Adams Fields's salon in Boston attracted most of the major literary figures of the day.

TO JAMES T. FIELDS

Philadelphia
Continental House, Saturday evening [9 April 1864]

Dear Fields,

I am sorry to say that our friend Ticknor is suffering under a severe billious attack since yesterday morning. He had previously seemed uncomfortable, but not to an alarming degree. He sent for a physician during the night, and fell into the hands of an allopathist,[1] who of course belabored with pills and powders of various kinds, and then proceeded to cup, and poultice, and blister, according to the ancient rule of that tribe of savages. The consequence is, that poor Ticknor is already very much reduced, while the disease flourishes as luxuriantly as if that were the Doctor's sole object. He calls it a billious colic (or bilious, I know not which) and says it is one of the worst cases he ever knew. I think him a man of skill and intelligence in his way, and doubt not that he will do everything that his views of scientific medicine will permit.

Since I began writing the above, Mr. Burnett of Boston tells me that the Doctor, after this morning's visit, requested the proprietor of the Continental to telegraph to Boston the state of the case. I am glad of it, because it relieves me of the responsibility of either disclosing the intelligence or withholding it. I will only add that Ticknor, under the influence of a blister and some powders, seems more comfortable than at any time since his attack, and that Mr. Burnett (who is an apothecary, and therefore conversant with these accursed matters[)], says that he is in a good state. But I can see that it will not be a very few days that will set him upon his legs again. As regards nursing, he shall have the best that can be obtained; and my own room is next to his; so that I can step in at any moment, but that will be of about as much service as if a hippopotamus were to do him the same kindness. Nevertheless, I have blistered, and powdered, and pilled him, and made my observations on medical science and the sad and comic aspects of human misery.

Excuse this illegible scrawl, for I am writing almost in the dark. Remember me to Mrs. Fields. As regard myself, I almost forgot to say that I am perfectly well. If you could find time to write to Mrs Hawthorne and tell her so, it would be doing me a great favor, for I doubt whether I can find an opportunity just now to do it myself. You would be surprised to see how stalwart I have become in this little time.[2]

Your friend,
N. H.

1. Allopathic medicine treats disease by using remedies which produce effects different from those produced by the specific disease treated; it is the opposite of homeopathy.
2. Ticknor died the next morning.

TO FRANKLIN PIERCE

Concord, Saturday, May 7th. 1864

My Dear Pierce,

I have received yours of Friday last, I believe, but have not it now by me to refer to. I am rejoiced to hear of your well-being, and shall do my best to join you at the Bromfield House on Wednesday next.[1] My own health continues rather poor, but I shall hope to revive rapidly when once we are on the road. Excuse the brevity of my note, for I find some difficulty in writing.

Affectionately yours,
Nathl Hawthorne.

Genl Pierce.[2]

[*In SH's hand*]

My dear General Pierce

I am glad to find Mr Hawthorne could write you even such a short note, for he passed a very wretched night last night.

I am going to Boston also on Wednesday as I have a great many errands to do. It is clouding this morning and therefore I hope there will be a rain soon so as to leave Wednesday fair for your meeting and starting.

Most truly yours
S. Hawthorne.

1. NH was to go on a walking trip through northern New England with Pierce.
2. NH died quietly in his sleep on 17 May in Plymouth, New Hampshire. This is his last known letter.

INDEX

Abbott, Jacob, 111
Alcott, Abba May, 160n
Alcott, Amos Bronson, xxxiii, 86,
  130n, 133, 160, 162–63
Aldrich, Thomas Bailey: letters to,
  249
Alfred, Prince, 232, 233n
Allen, William, 86
Allingham, William, 181, 182n
*American Magazine of Useful and
  Entertaining Knowledge,* 38–40
Arabian Nights Entertainments, 26
Arcturus, 97–98
Arnim, Ludwig Achim, 46n
Audubon, John James, 130n
Auld, Wilson, 174–75
Auld, Mrs. Wilson, 174–75

Bacon, Delia, 203–4; letters to, 201–3
Bacon, Francis, 202n, 203
Bacon, Leonard: letters to, 203–5
Bailey, Gamaliel, 158
Bailey, Mary Otis: letters to, 230–31
Bancroft, Elizabeth, 47n
Bancroft, George, xxxiii, 48, 49; let-
  ters to, 47
Baring Brothers and Company, 219,
  220n
Barker, Elise B., 82
Beekman, James William, 112
Benjamin, Park, 48
Bennoch, Francis, ix, xxxiii, 172n;
  letters to, 238–40, 244–45
Bentley, Richard: letters to, 209
Bodenheimer, Rosemarie, xviiin
Boston Athenaeum, 38, 65

Bowdoin College, xii, 30–36,
  167–168
Boyd, Joseph B.: letters to, 44–45
Boys and Girls Magazine, 111
"The Boys' Wonder-Horn," 46n, 49
Bradford, George Partridge, xxxiii,
  87, 106, 109, 198
Brentano, Clemens, 46n
Bridge, Horatio: ix, xxxiii, 49–50,
  119, 120, 120n, 137; letters to,
  144–146, 165–168, 182–184,
  189–190, 237–238, 241–243; *see
  also* Hawthorne, *Journal of an
  African Cruiser*
Briggs, Charles F., 170n
Bright, Henry Arthur, ix, xxxiii,
  178–179, 181–182, 186, 252; let-
  ters to, 179–180, 223–224, 226–
  227, 231–233
Brook Farm, xxxiii–xxxiv, 81–91,
  94–97, 124, 164
Brown, John, 255n
Browne, Frederick, 121, 121n
Brownson, Orestes A., 47n
Bryan, Mary, 115n
Bryant, William Cullen, 156, 157n
Buchanan, James, 214n; letters to,
  185
Burchmore, Zachariah, 131, 132n,
  170–171
Burley, Susan, 55, 57n
Burns, Robert, 240n
Burton, Warren, 85n, 86, 90

Cade, Jack, 134, 135n
Capen, Nahum, 48n